ETHICS FOR A-LEVEL

Ethics for A-Level

Mark Dimmock and Andrew Fisher

OpenBook Publishers

https://www.openbookpublishers.com

ISBN Paperback: 978-1-78374-388-9
ISBN Hardback: 978-1-78374-389-6
ISBN Digital (PDF): 978-1-78374-390-2
ISBN Digital ebook (epub): 978-1-78374-391-9
ISBN Digital ebook (mobi): 978-1-78374-392-6
DOI: 10.11647/OBP.0125

Cover image: *Malaysia from the Sky*, photo by Ishan @seefromthesky. Unsplash, https://unsplash.com/photos/N2HtDFA-AgM

All paper used by Open Book Publishers is SFI (Sustainable Forestry Initiative), PEFC (Programme for the Endorsement of Forest Certification Schemes) and Forest Stewardship Council(r)(FSC(r) certified.

Printed in the United Kingdom, United States, and Australia
by Lightning Source for Open Book Publishers (Cambridge, UK)

Contents

Preface

1. Exam Specification Details

This book deals with the Ethics components of AQA Philosophy and OCR Religious Studies. It has been written in line with these specifications, covering the material necessary in a way that, we hope, is engaging for students, teachers and anyone interested in understanding ethical study.

Some chapters are, therefore, directly relevant only to one of these two courses. Students studying Ethics as part of OCR Religious Studies do not need to read about the ethics of simulated killing, while students studying AQA Philosophy do not need to consider Natural Law or Situation Ethics. This is not to say that there is not, we hope, some independent value in engaging with these chapters as part of your wider reading.

However, the split is not always so clear. Both OCR and AQA require students to engage with the theory of Utilitarianism, for example. However, the specifications differ slightly and so not all of the content is relevant to all students; relevance will depend on the course being sat. We suggest two options in dealing with this:

- Early on in your course — engage with the content in the chapter regardless of your specification. This should give you a full and informed context in which to evaluate the theory.

- Later in your course and nearer exams — use your specification to focus on the exact content that may figure in your exam. Your teacher is best placed to advise you on this.

2. Book Structure

In writing this book we followed Andrew Fisher's approach of focusing on the judgement of the student in evaluating when they are being taught effectively.[1] We take the student as authoritative on this matter; we want to create an "engaged" student. To this end we include ways that students can check their judgements on whether the material has taught them anything or not. For example, we include sections on "Common Student Mistakes", "Issues to Consider" and "Key Terminology" within every chapter.

---

1   This approach can also be found in: Fisher and Tallant, *How to Get Philosophy Students Talking*.

Following the specification requirements of AQA and OCR, the book deals with *Normative Ethics*, then *Metaethics* and finally *Applied Ethics*. What is the difference?

Consider an analogy put forward by Andrew Fisher (2011).[2] Imagine that ethics is like football.

- The normative ethicist is like *a referee* interested in the rules governing play. What interests him is the general theories that govern our moral behaviour; how do we work out what is right and what is wrong?

- The metaethicist is like a *football commentator*. What interests her is how the very practice of ethics works. For example, the metaethicist might discuss how people use moral language; or comment on the psychology of immoral people; or ask whether moral properties exist.

- The Applied Ethicists are like *the players*. They "get their hands [or feet] dirty". They take the general rules of normative ethics and "play" under them. What interests them is how we should act in specific areas. For example, how should we deal with issues like meat-eating, euthanasia or stealing?

So guided by the AQA and OCR exam specifications, you will find various *normative* theories explained. You will then find those theories *applied* to real life examples. Sandwiched between these is the *Metaethics* chapter which asks: "But what is ethical practice?"

With all three types of ethics covered we hope to provide a good grounding in ethics, both in terms of content and a general philosophical approach. Where possible we give as many examples as possible and avoid technical jargon, although sometimes we need to use specific philosophical terms. With this in mind we have included an extensive Glossary at the end of the volume. Our hope is that you will feel able to pick up this book dip into it, or read it from cover to cover. Whatever you choose we hope you'll gain confidence with the content needed for your exams, that you practice and strengthen your ability to think with clear reasoning and with justification about the topics covered, and get as excited and fascinated by ethics as we are.

References

Fisher, Andrew, *Metaethics: An Introduction* (Oxford: Routledge, 2011), https://doi.org/10.1017/upo9781844652594

—, and Tallant, Jonathan, *How to Get Students Talking: An Instructors Toolkit* (Oxford: Routledge, 2015), https://doi.org/10.4324/9781315670645

---

2   Fisher, *Metaethics*, pp. 1–4.

Introduction

1. Philosophy, Ethics and Thinking

Philosophy is hard. Part of the reason it can feel so annoying is because it seems like it should not be hard. After all, philosophy just involves thinking, and we *all* think — thinking is easy! We do it without…well, thinking. Yet philosophy involves not just *thinking*, but *thinking well*. Of course it is true that we *all* think. But thinking, like football, maths, baking and singing is something we can get better at. Unfortunately, people rarely ask *how*. If you do not believe us, then just open your eyes. Society might be a whole lot better off if we thought well, more often.

Admittedly, doing A-Level Philosophy will not give you the ability to solve the problems of the world; we are not that naive! But if you engage with philosophy, then you will be developing yourself as a thinker who thinks *well*. This is why A-Level Philosophy is useful not merely to would-be philosophers, but also to any would be thinkers, perhaps heading off to make decisions in law, medicine, structural engineering — just about anything that requires you to think effectively and clearly.

However, if Philosophy is hard, then Ethics is *really* hard. This might seem unlikely at first glance. After all, Ethics deals with issues of right and wrong, and we have been discussing "what is right" and "what is wrong" since we were children. Philosophy of Mind, on the other hand, deals with topics like the nature of consciousness, while Metaphysics deals with the nature of existence itself. Indeed, compared to understanding a lecture in the Philosophy of Physics, arguing about the ethics of killing in video games might seem something of a walk in the park. This is misleading, not because other areas of philosophy are easy, but because the complexity of ethics is well camouflaged.

2. Respecting Ethics

When you study A-Level Ethics, and you evaluate what is right and wrong, it can be tempting and comforting to spend time simply defending your initial views; few people would come to a debate about vegetarianism, or abortion, without some pre-existing belief. If you are open-minded in your ethical approach then you need not reject everything you currently believe, but you should see these beliefs as *starting points*, or base camps, from which your enquiry commences.

For example, why do you think that eating animals is OK, or that abortion is wrong? If you think that giving to charity is good, what does "good" mean? For true success, ethics requires intellectual respect. If you might think that a particular position is obviously false, perhaps take this reaction as a red flag, as it may suggest that you have missed some important step of an argument — ask yourself why someone, presumably just as intellectually proficient as yourself, might have once accepted that position.

If you are thinking well as an ethicist, then you are likely to have good reasons for your views, and be prepared to rethink those views where you cannot find such good reasons. In virtue of this, you are providing *justification* for the beliefs you have. It is the philosopher's job, whatever beliefs you have, to ask *why* you hold those beliefs. What *reasons* might you have for those beliefs?

For example, imagine the reason that you believe it is OK to eat meat is that *it tastes nice*. As philosophers we can say that this is not a particularly good reason. Presumably it might taste nice to eat your pet cat, or your neighbour, or your dead aunt; but in these cases the "taste justification" seems totally unimportant! The details of this debate are not relevant here (for more on this topic see Chapter 14). The point is that there *are good and bad reasons* for our beliefs and it is the philosopher's job to reveal and analyse them.[1]

3. The A-Level Student

Philosophy is more than just fact-learning, or a "history of ideas". It is different from chemistry, mathematics, languages, theology etc. It is unique. Sure, it is important to learn some facts, and learn what others believed, but a successful A-Level student needs to do more than simply regurgitate information in order to both maneuverer past the exam hurdles and to become a better ethicist.

One aim of this book is to aid you in engaging with a living discipline. Philosophy, and in particular Ethics, is a live and evolving subject. When you study philosophy you are entering a dialogue with those that have gone before you. Learning about what various philosophers think will enable you to become clearer about what *you* think and add to that evolving dialogue.

You will notice that in this book we have not included "hints and tips boxes", or statements of biography concerning the scholars. Although these things have their place, we did not want the reader to think that they have learnt philosophy if they know what is in the boxes.

---

1   For an excellent introduction to good and bad ways of thinking we recommend John Hospers, 'An Introduction to Philosophical Analysis'.

In reality, university Philosophy departments often work with first year students to lose some of their less academically successful habits. Why? Well, one of the authors has taught ethics at university for many years. Philosophy students often say something like this: "I thought we'd do hard stuff at University! I did Utilitarianism at A-Level, can I have something different to study, please?"

This statement reveals a whole host of things. Most important is the view that to "do" ethics is to remember information. That is why a student can say they have "done Utilitarianism". They have learnt some key facts and arguments. But philosophy is not like this. In order to understand philosophy you need to be authentic with yourself and to ask what *you* think, using this as a guide to critically analyse the ideas learned and lead yourself to your own justifiable conclusion. Philosophy is a living and dynamic subject that we cannot reduce to a few key facts, or a simplistic noting of what other people have said.

Some people distinguish between "ethics" and "morality". We do not. For us, nothing hangs on the difference between them. In this book you will see us switching between the terms, so do not get hung up on this distinction.

4. Doing Ethics Well: Legality versus Morality

Moral questions are distinct from legal questions, although, of course, moral issues might have some implications for the law. That child labour is morally unacceptable might mean that we have a law against it. But it is unhelpful to answer whether something is morally right or wrong by looking to the laws of the land. It is quite easy to see why. Imagine a country which has a set of actions which are *legally* acceptable, but *morally* unacceptable or vice versa — the well-used example of Nazi Germany brings to mind this distinction. Therefore, in discussions about ethics do be wary of talking about legal issues. Much more often than not, such points will be irrelevant.

5. Doing Ethics Well: Prudential Reasons versus Moral Reasons

Something to keep separate are moral reasons and *prudential* reasons. Prudential reasons relate to our personal reasons for doing things.

Consider some examples. When defending slavery, people used to cite the fact that it supported the economy as a reason to keep it. It is true, of course, that this is a reason; it is a prudential reason, particularly for those who benefited from slavery such as traders or plantation owners. Yet, such a reason does not help us with the moral question of slavery. We would say "OK, but so what if it helps the economy! Is it right or wrong?"

6. Doing Ethics Well: Prescriptive versus Descriptive Claims

Another important distinction is between *descriptive* and *prescriptive* claims. This is sometimes referred to as the "is/ought" gap. We return to this in later chapters, especially Chapter 6. But it is such a common mistake made in general ethical chat that we felt the need to underline it.

Consider some examples. Imagine the headline: *"Scientists discover a gene explaining why we want to punch people wearing red trousers"*. The article includes lots of science showing the genes and the statistical proof. Yet, none of this will tells us whether acting violently towards people wearing red trousers is morally acceptable. The *explanation* of why people feel and act in certain ways leaves it open as to how people morally *ought* to act.

Consider a more serious example, relating to the ethics of eating meat. Supporters of meat-eating often point to our incisor teeth. This shows that it is natural for us to eat meat, a fact used as a reason for thinking that it is morally acceptable to do so. But this is a bad argument. Just because we have incisors does not tell us how we morally ought to behave. It might explain why we find it easy to eat meat, and it might even explain why we like eating meat. But this is not relevant to the *moral* question. Don't you believe us? Imagine that dentists discover that our teeth are "designed" to eat other humans alive. What does this tell us about whether it is right or wrong to eat humans alive? Nothing.

7. Doing Ethics Well: Thought-Experiments

You will also be aware, especially in reading this book, of the philosophical device known as a "thought experiment". These are hypothetical, sometimes fanciful, examples that are designed to aid our thinking about an issue.

For example, imagine that you could travel back in time. You are pointing a gun at your grandfather when he was a child. Would it be possible for you to pull the trigger? Or, imagine that there is a tram running down a track. You could stop it, thereby saving five people, by throwing a fat man under the tracks. Is this the morally right thing to do?

The details here are unimportant. What is important, is that it is inadequate to respond: "yes, but that could never happen!" Thought experiments are devices to help us to think about certain issues. Whether they are possible in real life does not stop us doing that thinking. Indeed, it is not just philosophy that uses thought experiments. When Einstein asked what would happen if he looked at his watch near a black hole, this was a thought experiment. In fact, most other subjects use thought experiments. It is just that philosophy uses them more frequently, and they are often a bit more bizarre.

8. Doing Ethics Well: Understanding Disagreement

Finally, we want to draw your attention to a common bad argument as we want you to be aware of the mistake it leads to. Imagine that a group of friends are arguing about which country has won the most Olympic gold medals. Max says China, Alastair says the US, Dinh says the UK. There is general ignorance and disagreement; but does this mean that there is not an answer to the question of "which country has won the most Olympic gold medals?" No! We cannot move from the fact that people disagree to the conclusion that there is no answer. Now consider a parallel argument that we hear far too often.

Imagine that you and your friends are discussing whether euthanasia is morally acceptable. Some say yes, the others say no. Each of you cite how different cultures have different views on euthanasia. Does this fact — that there is disagreement — mean that there is no answer to the question of whether euthanasia is morally acceptable? Again, the answer is no. That answer did not follow in the Olympic case, and it does not follow in the moral one either. So just because different cultures have different moral views, this does not show, by itself, that there is no moral truth and no answer to the question.

If you are interested in the idea that there is a lack of moral truth in ethics, then Moral Error Theorists defend exactly this position in the chapter on Metaethics.

SUMMARY

You will not be assessed, by either AQA or OCR, on the core content of this chapter. If any of the content is specifically relevant to assessment, it is discussed in proper detail in the following chapters.

Still, we hope that we have signposted some errors to avoid when it comes to thinking about ethics, and some strategies to consider instead. It may be worth occasionally revisiting the ideas discussed here during your studies, to test your own lines of argument and evaluate how "thinking well" is progressing for you. This would not be a weakness! Both the authors, and any honest philosopher, can reassure you — philosophy is hard! We hope you find this textbook useful and rewarding in helping you on your own journey through Ethics.

QUESTIONS AND TASKS

1. How would you explain what philosophy is to someone?
2. Do you think philosophy is important? If yes, why? If no, why?
3. List some ethical questions.
4. Can you figure out if your questions are Normative, Applied, or Metaethical?
5. Is there a link be between Applied, Normative and Metaethics? Which type of ethics do you think it would be best to study first, and which last?
6. What is the difference between prudential and moral reasons?
7. What is meant by the "is/ought" gap? Why is it important to remember when discussing ethical questions?
8. What role, if any, does science have in ethical arguments?
9. What are thought experiments? Why might they be useful to philosophers?
10. "Because there are so many different views on moral issues there cannot be any moral truth". What do you think of this line of argument?

References

Hospers, John, *An Introduction to Philosophical Analysis*, 4th ed. (New York and London: Routledge, 1997), https://doi.org/10.4324/9780203714454

PART I
NORMATIVE ETHICS

CHAPTER 1

Utilitarianism

Music snobbery is the worst kind of snobbery. It forces people who like something a bit mainstream, a bit of pop like Girls Aloud or Take That! or ABBA to say "It's my guilty pleasure!" I hate that phrase. It is an insult to top quality pop. It is also an insult to guilt.

Dara Ó Briain (comedian)

1. Utilitarianism: An Introduction

Some things appear to be straightforwardly good for people. Winning the lottery, marrying your true love or securing a desired set of qualifications all seem to be examples of events that improve a person's life. As a normative ethical theory, Utilitarianism suggests that we can decide what is morally right or morally wrong by weighing up which of our future possible actions promotes such goodness in our lives and the lives of people more generally.

2. Hedonism

Hedonism is a theory of well-being — a theory of how well a life is going for the person living that life. What separates Hedonism from other theories of well-being is that the hedonist believes that what defines a successful life is directly related to the amount of pleasure in that life; no other factors are relevant at all. Therefore, the more pleasure that a person experiences in their life then the better their life goes, and vice versa. Whereas other theories might focus on fulfilling desires people have, or an objective list of things such as friendship and health.

The roots of Hedonism can be traced back at least as far as Epicurus (341–270 BC) and Ancient Greece. Epicurus held the hedonistic view that the primary *intrinsic* good for a person is pleasure; meaning that pleasure is always good for a person in and of itself, irrespective of the cause or context of the pleasure. According to this theory pleasure is always intrinsically good for a person and less pleasure is always intrinsically bad.

Hedonism is a relatively simple theory of what makes your life better. If you feel that your life would be better if you won the lottery, married your true love or achieved your desired qualifications, then the hedonistic explanation of these judgments is that these things are good for you only if they provide you with pleasure. Many pleasures may be physical, but Fred Feldman (1941–) is a defender of a theory known as Attitudinal Hedonism. According to this theory, psychological pleasures can themselves count as intrinsically good for a person. So, while reading a book would not seem to produce pleasure in a physical way, a hedonist may value the psychological pleasure associated with that act of reading and thus accept that it can improve a person's well-being. This understanding of hedonistic pleasure may help to explain why, for example, one person can gain so much pleasure from a Lady Gaga album while another gains nothing at all; the psychological responses to the music differ.

3. Nozick's Experience Machine

One important problem for Hedonism is that our well-being seems to be affected by more than just the total pleasure in our lives. It may be the case that you enjoy gaining a new qualification, but there seems to be more to the value of this event than merely the pleasure produced. Many people agree that success in gaining a meaningful qualification improves your life even if no pleasure is obtained from it. Certainly, many believe that the relationship between what improves your life and what gives pleasure is not directly proportional, as the hedonist would claim.

Robert Nozick (1938–2002) attacked the hedonistic idea that pleasure is the only good by testing our intuitions via a now famous thought-experiment. Nozick asks:

> Suppose there was an experience machine that would give you any experience you desired. Super-duper neuropsychologists could stimulate your brain so that you would think and feel you were writing a great novel, or making a friend, or reading an interesting book. All the time you would be floating in a tank, with electrodes attached to your brain. Should you plug into this machine for life, pre-programming your life experiences? [...] Of course, while in the tank you won't know that you're there; you'll think that it's all actually happening [...] would you plug in?[1]

Nozick's challenge to Hedonism is based on the thought that most people who consider this possible situation would opt *not* to plug in. Indeed, if you ask yourself if you would actually choose to leave behind your real friends, family and life in favour of a pre-programmed existence you also might conclude that plugging into the experience machine would not be desirable. However, if Hedonism is correct and our well-being is determined entirely by the amount of pleasure that we experience, then Nozick wonders "what else can matter to us, other than how our lives feel from the inside?"[2] The experience

---

1   R. Nozick, 'The Experience Machine', p. 292.
2   *Ibid.*

machine guarantees us pleasure yet we find it unappealing compared to a real life where pleasure is far from assured. This may suggest that our well-being is determined by other factors in addition to how much pleasure we secure, perhaps knowledge or friendships.

The hedonists need not give way entirely on this point, of course, as they may feel that the experience machine is desirable just because it guarantees experiences of pleasure. Or, you might believe that our suspicions about the machine are misplaced. After all, once inside the machine we would not suspect that things were not real. You may feel that the hedonist could bite-the-bullet (accept the apparently awkward conclusion as a non-fatal implication of the theory) and say that any reticence to enter the machine is *irrational*. Perhaps the lives of those choosing to be plugged in to the machine would go extraordinary well!

4. The Foundations of Bentham's Utilitarianism

Jeremy Bentham (1748–1832) was the first of the "classical utilitarians". Driven by a genuine desire for social reform, Bentham wanted to be as much involved in law, politics and economics as abstract philosophising.

Bentham developed his moral theory of Utilitarianism on the foundation of the type of hedonistic thinking described in section two. For Bentham, the only thing that determines the value of a life, or indeed the value of an event or action, is the amount of pleasure contained in that life, or the amount of pleasure produced as a result of that event or action. Bentham is a *hedonistic utilitarian*. This belief in Hedonism, however, was not something that Bentham took to be unjustified or arbitrary; for him Hedonism could be *empirically justified* by evidence in the world in its favour. According to Bentham:

> Nature has placed mankind under the governance of two sovereign masters, pain and pleasure. It is for them alone to point out what we ought to do, as well as to determine what we shall do.[3]

Bentham moves from this empirical claim about the factors that guide our behaviour to a normative claim about how we *ought* to live. He creates a moral theory based on the bringing about of more pleasure and less pain.

When first understanding Utilitarianism, it is also crucial to understand what is meant by the term "utility". Bentham defined it as "[…] that property in any object, whereby it tends to produce benefit, advantage, pleasure, good, or happiness […] or […] to prevent the happening of mischief, pain, evil, or unhappiness".[4] Utility is thus promoted when pleasure is promoted and when

---

3   J. Bentham, 'An Introduction to the Principles of Morals and Legislation', in *Utilitarianism and Other Essays*, p. 65.
4   *Ibid.*, p. 66.

unhappiness is avoided. Bentham's commitment to Hedonism means for him that goodness is just an increase in pleasure, and evil or unhappiness is just an increase in pain or decrease in pleasure. With this understanding of utility in mind, Bentham commits himself to the *Principle of Utility*:

> *By the principle of utility is meant that principle which approves or disapproves of every action whatsoever, according to the tendency which it appears to have to augment or diminish the happiness of the party whose interest is in question: or, what is the same thing in other words, to promote or to oppose that happiness.*[5]

In effect, this principle simply says that promoting utility, defined in terms of pleasure, is to be approved of and reducing utility is to be disapproved of.

The Principle of Utility, backed by a commitment to Hedonism, underpins the central utilitarian claim made by Bentham. Based on a phrase that he wrongly attributed to Joseph Priestley (1733–1804), Bentham suggests that the measure of right and wrong is the extent to which an action produces the greatest good for the greatest number of people. Of course, what counts as good, for Bentham, is pleasure. We can then rephrase what Bentham himself call his fundamental axiom as a requirement to *promote the greatest pleasure for the greatest number of people, in order to act morally.*

5. The Structure of Bentham's Utilitarianism

In addition to being hedonistic, Bentham's Utilitarianism is also:

1. Consequentialist/Teleological
2. Relativist
3. Maximising
4. Impartial

Bentham's Utilitarianism is *consequentialist* because the moral value of an action or event is determined entirely by the consequences of that event. The theory is also described as *teleological* for the same reason, based on the Greek word *telos* that means "end" or "purpose". If more pleasure follows as a consequence of "Action A" rather than "Action B", then according to the fundamental axiom of Utilitarianism "Action A" should be undertaken and is morally right; choosing "Action B" would be morally wrong.

In addition, Bentham's Utilitarianism is *Relativistic* rather than *Absolutist*. Absolutist moral views hold that certain actions will always be morally wrong irrespective of context or consequences. For example, many campaigning groups suggest that torture is always morally unacceptable whether it is

---

5   *Ibid.*, p. 65.

carried out by vindictive dictators seeking to instil fear in a population or whether it is authorised by democratically elected governments seeking to obtain information in order to stop a terrorist attack. For absolutists then, the act of torture is absolutely wrong in all cases and situations.

Clearly, Bentham cannot hold this type of view because sometimes the pain involved in torture may lead to the promotion of greater pleasure (or less intense pain) overall, such as in the case where torture stops a terrorist atrocity. On this basis, the Benthamite utilitarian must believe that whether a certain action is right or wrong is always relative to the situation in which the action takes place.

Bentham's Utilitarianism is *maximising* because it does not merely require that pleasure is promoted, but that the *greatest* pleasure for the *greatest* number is secured. This means that some actions that lead to pleasure will still not be morally good acts if another action that could have produced even more pleasure in that setting was rejected. Thus, for example, if you gain some pleasure from spending money on a new book, but that money could have produced more pleasure had it been donated to a local charity for the homeless, then buying a new book would be morally wrong even though it led to some pleasure because it did not maximise the total amount of pleasure that was possible in that circumstance.

Finally, Bentham's Utilitarianism is also *impartial* in the sense that what matters is simply securing the maximum amount of pleasure for the maximum number of people; the theory does not give special preference regarding which people are supposed to have access to, or share in, that total pleasure. Bentham's utilitarian theory is associated with the idea of *equal consideration of interests*; as long as total pleasure is maximised then it does not matter if that pleasure is experienced by royalty, presidents, siblings, children, friends or enemies. In the total calculation of pleasure, we are all equal regardless of our status, behaviour or any other social factor.

6. Hedonic Calculus

Hopefully it is now clear that for Bentham the consequences in terms of pleasure production of any action are what determine the morality of that action, and that no other factors are relevant. However, it is not clear how exactly we should go about working out what to do in specific cases. For example:

> You are a military airman flying a fighter jet that is about to intercept a passenger airliner that seems to have been hijacked by an as yet unknown figure. The plane appears to be on a path that could take it either to an airport or, potentially, directly to a major and highly populated city. You are tasked with deciding how to act and must, therefore, choose whether or not to

> fire a missile at the plane. Firing at the plane would kill the passengers but save all lives on the ground, yet not firing may save the passengers, or it may give the passengers only a few more minutes before the plane is flown into a city full of innocents and they are killed in any case. Suggesting that the pilot weigh up the options and choose the action that secures the greatest pleasure for the greatest number is not obviously helpful in making such a difficult decision with so many variables.

Bentham recognised that such *Problems of Calculation* relating to the pleasure associated with future actions needed addressing in order for Utilitarianism to be a workable moral theory. Bentham therefore created the Hedonic Calculus (sometimes known as the Felicific Calculus) in order to help an individual work out how much pleasure would be created by differing possible actions. The Hedonic Calculus, as suggested by Bentham, is based on assessing possible pleasures according to their:

1. Intensity

2. Duration

3. Certainty

4. Remoteness (i.e. how far into the future the pleasure is)

5. Fecundity (i.e. how likely it is that pleasure will generate other related pleasures)

6. Purity (i.e. if any pain will be felt alongside that pleasure)

7. Extent (i.e. how many people might be able to share in that pleasure)[6]

The Hedonic Calculus is therefore supposed to provide a decision-procedure for a utilitarian who is confused as to how to act in a morally tricky situation. Thus, our fighter-pilot might consider the intensity of the pleasure of surviving versus the duration of the pain of death, while also needing to balance these factors against the relative certainty of the possible pains or pleasures. No doubt, the fighter pilot would still face an agonising moral choice but it seems that he would at least have some methodology for working out what Utilitarianism morally requires of him.

7. Problems with Bentham's Utilitarianism

However, whether or not measuring possible actions in terms of "units of pleasure" associated with them is actually plausible is very much an open question and so the problem of calculation is not necessarily solved simply by the existence of the Hedonic Calculus. Consider the most recent highly pleasurable experience that you enjoyed and compare it to a highly pleasurable experience from earlier in your life. It may be that you cannot say confidently

---

6   *Ibid.*, p. 87.

that one provided more pleasure than the other, especially if the experiences were extremely varied; perhaps winning a sporting trophy versus going on your first holiday. Pleasures that are so fundamentally different in nature may simply be incommensurable — they may be incapable of being measured by a common standard such as the Hedonic Calculus.

In addition, the problem of calculation can be extended beyond the issues raised above. Remember that Bentham's Utilitarianism is impartial in the sense that all individuals who gain pleasure as a result of a certain action count towards the total amount of pleasure. However, the following case raises the *Problem of Relevant Beings*:

> You are considering whether or not to approve a new housing development on a piece of unoccupied land outside the current boundary of your town. You are clear that, if approved, the development will create a great deal of pleasure for both new residents and construction workers without any pain being experienced by others. You are aware, however, that the development will require the culling of several badgers and the removal of a habitat currently supporting many birds, stray cats and rodents of various types.

On the surface, this case should be obvious for the utilitarian without any special problem of calculation; the greatest good for the greatest number would be secured if the development were permitted to go ahead. However, this assumes that non-human animals are not relevant to the calculation of pleasures and pains. Yet, if pleasure is all that matters for how well a life goes then it is not clear why animals, that may be able to experience some form of pleasure and can almost certainly experience pain, should be excluded from the calculation process.

Indeed, Bentham, when referring to the moral value of animals, noted that: "The question (for deciding moral relevance) is not 'Can they reason?', nor 'Can they talk?', but 'Can they suffer?'"[7] If the suffering and pain of humans is relevant to moral calculations then surely it is at least plausible that so should the suffering and pain of non-human animals. (There is more on the issue of the moral status of animals in Chapter 14 when the morality of eating animals is investigated.)

Being a maximising ethical theory, Utilitarianism is also open to a *Demandingness Objection*. If it is not the case that pleasure needs to be merely promoted but actually *maximised at all opportunities*, then the standard for acting morally appears to be set extremely high. For example, did you buy a doughnut at some point this year or treat yourself to a magazine? Live the life of a high-roller and treat yourself to a taxi ride rather than walking to your destination? While your actions certainly brought about differing degrees of pleasure to both yourself and to those who gained economic benefit from your

---

7   J. Bentham, *An Introduction to the Principles of Morals and Legislation*, http://www.econlib.org/library/Bentham/bnthPML18.html

decision, it seems that you could have created much more pleasure by saving up your money and ensuring it reached those suffering extreme financial hardships or residing in poverty around the world. As a result of being a maximising moral theory, Utilitarianism seems to make immorality very hard to avoid as it is so utterly demanding on our behaviour.

A further problem for Utilitarianism relates to the *Tyranny of the Majority*. Remember that as a relativistic moral theory, Utilitarianism does not allow for any moral absolutes — such as the absolute right to democracy, or absolute legal or basic human rights. Indeed, Bentham himself dismissed the idea of "natural rights" as a nonsensical concept masqueraded as a meaningful one. However, if we accept that absolute rights are simply "nonsense upon stilts" as Bentham put it, then Utilitarianism seems to be open to cases where the majority are morally required to exploit the minority for the greater good of maximising total pleasure. For example, imagine that total pleasure would be maximised if the resources of a small country were forcibly taken from them to be used freely and exploited by the people of a much larger country (this is hardly unrealistic). However, such forceful theft — only justified by the fact that a greater majority of people would gain pleasure — does not seem to be morally justifiable. Yet, according to Utilitarianism's commitment to maximising pleasure, such an action would not only be morally acceptable but it would be morally required.

As a consequentialist/teleological moral theory Utilitarianism is also open to the *Problem of Wrong Intentions*. This problem can be highlighted by considering the cases of Dominic and Callum.

> Dominic is seating in a coffee shop when a masked intruder bursts in threatening to rob the shop. Dominic, with the intention of saving lives, attempts to stop the intruder but sadly, in the ensuing struggle, the intruder's gun is accidentally fired and an innocent person is killed. Now, consider a second case where an intruder bursts in with a gun but Callum, rather than trying to intervene, immediately ducks for cover with the intention of saving himself and leaving the rest of the customers to fend for themselves. Luckily for Callum, when he ducks for cover he accidentally trips into the would-be thief, knocking him unconscious thus allowing his peaceful detention until police arrive.

According to the utilitarian calculation, Callum acted in a way that maximised pleasure while Dominic acted wrongly because the consequence of his act was tragic pain. However, it seems unfair and wrong to suggest that Callum acted rightly when he had just intended to save himself, although he had a lucky outcome, while Dominic acted wrongly when his intention was to save others but was unlucky in his outcome. Utilitarianism, as a consequentialist theory, ignores intentions and focuses only on consequences.

Utilitarianism also faces the *Problem of Partiality*. This is clear if we consider the familiar moral dilemma of being stuck on a life raft with three other people but with only enough supplies for two people. On the raft with you is a doctor who is confident that he can pass on a cure for cancer if he survives, a world class violinist who brings pleasure to millions each year, and one of your parents or siblings. I am afraid to report that, for the purposes of this example, your parent or sibling is nothing special in comparison to other individuals on the raft. In this circumstance, Utilitarianism would seem to require you not only to give up your own space on the raft but ensure that your parent or sibling joins you in the freezing water with no hope of survival; this is the way of maximising total pleasure in such a scenario. Yet, even if you believe that the morality might call for your own self-sacrifice, it seems extremely unfair not to allow you to give *extra moral weight* to the life of a loved one. Unfortunately for the utilitarian, perhaps, the status as a beloved family member should make no special difference to your judgment regarding how to act. This seems to be not only over-demanding but also overly cold and calculating. Utilitarianism requires *Agent-Neutrality* — you must look at the situation as any neutral observer would and not give special preference to anyone irrespective of your emotional attachments, because each individual must count for one and no more than one.

Finally, Bentham's Utilitarianism also comes under attack from the related *Integrity Objection*, framed most prominently by **Bernard Williams** (1929–2003). As an agent-neutral theory, no person can give up impartiality when it comes to judgements about the impact of a potential action upon their family or loved ones. In addition, no person can give up impartiality when it comes to the impact of an action upon their own feelings, character and general sense of integrity. In order to make clear the potential worry associated with this, Williams describes the fictional case of Jim and the Indians.[8]

> Jim is an explorer who stumbles upon an Indian leader who is about to execute twenty people. Jim knows nothing of their possible crimes or any other factors involved, but he is offered a difficult choice by the Indian chief who is eager to impress his foreign traveller. Jim can either shoot one of the prisoners himself and then the rest will be set free as a mark of celebration, or he can refuse the offer in which case all twenty prisoners will be executed as was planned. It is key to note that Jim does not have control of the situation in the sense that he is powerless to bargain or negotiate with anyone, and nor can he use a weapon to successfully free any prisoners. He has only the two options laid out.

The point of this example is not to establish what the right action is. You may find yourself in agreement with utilitarians who suggest Jim must shoot one prisoner in order to save the lives of the rest. Rather, the purpose of the example is to show that Utilitarianism forces us to reach this conclusion *too quickly*. Given the commitment to Agent-Neutrality, Jim must treat himself as a neutral observer working out which action will produce the greatest good

---

8   B. Williams, 'Jim and the Indians', https://www.unc.edu/courses/2009spring/plcy/240/001/Jim_and_Indians.pdf

for the greatest number. Morally, he is not entitled to give more weight to his own feelings than he would give to the feelings of any other and therefore it does not matter whether Jim is a pacifist and has been a lifelong advocate for prisoner reform and rehabilitation. If the utilitarian calculation suggests that he must shoot one of the prisoners then he must shoot with no regard to any compromising of his integrity and self-identity. You may accept this as an unfortunate consequence of a terrible situation, but it may be a problem for a moral theory if it fails to recognise or respect a person's most sincere and deepest convictions.

8. Mill's Utilitarian Proof

John Stuart Mill (1806–1873) was concerned by many of the problems facing the utilitarian theory put forward by Bentham, but as a hedonist he did not wish to see the theory rejected. Mill sought to refine and improve the Benthamite utilitarian theory in order to create a successful version of Hedonistic Utilitarianism.

Mill was so confident about the prospects for a version of Hedonistic Utilitarianism because he believed that there was an empirically backed proof available to support the principle that the greatest happiness/pleasure should always be secured for the greatest number.[9] Mill's proof, much like Bentham's empirical defence of Hedonism, relies on the evidence from observation that people desire their own happiness. This observation of fact supports Mill's claim that since people desire their own happiness, this is evidence that such happiness is desir*able*. Mill says "…each person's happiness is a good to that person, and the general happiness, therefore, a good to the aggregate of all persons".[10] Since our happiness is good for us, and general happiness is just the total of the happiness of all persons, then general happiness is also good. To put it another way, if individual happiness is a good worth pursuing then happiness in general must be worth pursuing.

In order to justify Hedonism, Mill sought to justify the claim that the good of happiness is the *only* thing that makes our lives go better. Mill defends this claim by suggesting that knowledge, health and freedom etc. (as other plausible goods that might make a life go better) are only valuable *in so far as* they bring about happiness. Knowledge is desired only because it provides happiness when acquired, not because it, by itself and in isolation, makes life go better.

Mill's proof of Utilitarianism in terms of the general desirability of maximising total happiness is, however, open to criticism. For one thing,

---

9   This slippage from talk of "pleasure" to talk of "happiness" is explained in section eight of this chapter.

10   J. S. Mill, 'Utilitarianism', in *Utilitarianism and Other Essays*, p. 308.

the fact that something is desired does not seem to justify the claim that it is desirable. **G. E. Moore** (1873–1958) points out that Mill moves from the factual sense that something is desirable if it is desired to the normative sense that it *should* be desired without any justification. It is possible, for example, to desire to kill another person. This is desirable in the sense people could and do desire it (it is possible to do so — it is an action that is desire-*able*), but not in the sense that we would want them to desire it.

In addition, the idea that other apparent goods, such as knowledge and health, are only valuable in so far as they promote happiness/pleasure is extremely controversial; can you imagine a situation in which you gained value from knowledge without any associated pleasure or happiness? If so, you may have a counter example to Mill's claim.

9. Mill's Qualitative Utilitarianism

In attempting to redraw Bentham's Utilitarianism, Mill's most substantial thought was to move away from Bentham's idea that all that mattered was the *quantity* of total pleasure. Instead, Mill thought that *quality* of pleasure was also crucial to deciding what is moral.

Bentham's Utilitarianism is quantitative in the sense that all Bentham focusses on is the maximisation of hedonically calculated quantities of total pleasure. Thus, he says that "Prejudice apart, the game of push-pin is of equal value with the arts and sciences of music and poetry".[11] All that matters for Bentham is producing pleasure and the way this is achieved is unimportant. If playing on a console affords you more pleasure than reading Shakespeare, then Bentham would view your life as going better if you play the console. However, Mill introduces a quality criterion for pleasure. Mill says that:

> It is better to be a human being dissatisfied than a pig satisfied; better to be Socrates dissatisfied than a fool satisfied. And if the fool, or the pig, is of a different opinion, it is only because they only know their own side of the question.[12]

Bentham could not admit that the unhappy Socrates would be living a life with more value than the happier fool. Mill, on the other hand, believes that *quality*, not merely quantity, of pleasure matters and can therefore defend the claim that Socrates has the better life even by hedonistic standards.

According to Mill, higher pleasures are worth more than lower pleasures. Higher pleasures are those pleasures of the intellect brought about via activities like poetry, reading or attending the theatre. Lower pleasures are animalistic and base; pleasures associated with drinking beer, having sex or

---

11   J. Bentham, *The Rationale of Reward*, p. 206, https://books.google.co.uk/books?id=6igN9srLgg8C
12   J. S. Mill, 'Utilitarianism', p. 281.

lazing on a sun-lounger. What we should seek to maximise are the higher quality pleasures even if the total pleasure (hedonically calculated via Bentham's calculus) turns out to be quantitatively lower as a result. Justifying this distinction between higher and lower quality pleasures as non-arbitrary and not just an expression of his own tastes, Mill says that *competent judges*, those people who have experienced both types of pleasure, are best placed to select which pleasures are higher and lower. Such competent judges, says Mill, would and do favour pleasures of the intellect over the base pleasures of the body. On this basis, Mill is open to the criticism that many people have both read books and drunk beer and that if given the choice would choose the latter. Whether or not Mill's defence of his supposedly non-prejudiced distinction of higher and lower pleasures is successful is an open question for your evaluation and analysis.

10. Mill's Rule Utilitarianism versus Bentham's Act Utilitarianism

In addition to a difference in views regarding the importance of the quality of a pleasure, Mill and Bentham are also separated by reference to Act and Rule Utilitarianism and although such terms emerged only after Mill's death, Mill is typically considered a rule utilitarian and Bentham an act utilitarian.

An act utilitarian, such as Bentham, focuses only on the consequences of individual actions when making moral judgments. However, this focus on the outcome of individual acts can sometimes lead to odd and objection-raising examples. Judith Jarvis Thomson (1929–) raised the problem of the "transplant surgeon".[13]

> Imagine a case where a doctor had five patients requiring new organs to stop their death and one healthy patient undergoing a routine check. In this case, it would seem that total pleasure is best promoted by killing the one healthy patient, harvesting his organs and saving the other five lives; their pleasure outweighs the cost to the formerly healthy patient.

While Bentham does suggest that we should have "rules of thumb" against such actions, for typically they will lead to unforeseen painful consequences, in the case as simply described the act utilitarian appears powerless to deny that such a killing is required in order to maximise total pleasure (just add your own details to secure this conclusion for the act utilitarian).

Rule utilitarians, in whose camp we can place Mill, adopt a different moral decision-procedure. Their view is that we should create a set of rules that, if followed, would produce the greatest amount of total happiness. In the transplant case, killing the healthy man would not seem to be part of the best set

---

13   J. J. Thomson, 'The Trolley Problem', p. 1396.

of utilitarian-justified rules since a rule allowing the killing of healthy patients would not seem to promote total happiness; one outcome, for example, would be that people would very likely stop coming to hospitals for fear for their life! Therefore, if a rule permitting killing was allowed then the maximisation of total happiness would not be promoted overall.

It is through Rule Utilitarianism that we can make sense of Mill's "harm principle". According to Mill, there is:

> ...one very simple principle, as entitled to govern absolutely the dealings of society with the individual in the way of compulsion and control.[14]

That principle is:

> The only purpose for which power can be rightfully exercised over any member of a civilized community, against his will, is to prevent harm to others. His own good, either physical or moral, is not a sufficient warrant.[15]

Even if a particular act of harming another person might bring about an increase in total pleasure on a single occasion, that act may not be condoned by the set of rules that best promotes total pleasure overall. As such, the action would not be morally permitted.

11. Strong versus Weak Rule Utilitarianism

Rule utilitarians may seem to avoid troubling cases like the transplant surgeon and be able to support and uphold individual human and legal rights based on rules that reflect the harm principle. This fact would also help rule utilitarians overcome objections based on the treatment of minorities because exploitation of minority groups would, perhaps, fail to be supported by the best utilitarian-justified set of rules. Yet, rule utilitarians face a troubling dilemma:

1. *Strong Rule Utilitarianism*: Guidance from the set of rules that, if followed, would promote the greatest amount of total happiness must *always* be followed.

2. *Weak Rule Utilitarianism*: Guidance from the set of rules that, if followed, would promote the greatest amount of total happiness can be ignored in circumstances where more happiness would be produced by breaking the rule.

The strong rule utilitarian appears to suffer from what J. J. C. Smart (1920–2012) described as "Rule Worship". No longer focussing on the consequences of the action before them, the strong rule utilitarian appears to ignore the

---

14   J. S. Mill, *On Liberty*, http://www.econlib.org/library/Mill/mlLbty1.html
15   *Ibid.*

option to maximise total happiness in favour of following a general and non-relative rule regarding how to act. The strong rule utilitarian may be able to avoid problems based on treatment of minorities or a lack of absolute legal and human rights, but it is not clear that they survive these problems holding on to a teleological, relativistic utilitarian theory. Utilitarianism seems to be saved from troubling implications only by denying core features.

On the other hand, while Weak Rule Utilitarianism retains a teleological nature it appears to collapse into Act Utilitarianism. The rules provide guidelines that can be broken, and given that the act utilitarian can also offer "rules of thumb" against actions that tend not to produce maximum goodness or utility in general, such as killing healthy patients, it is not clear where this version of Rule Utilitarianism gains a unique identity. In what cases would Act Utilitarianism and Weak Rule Utilitarianism actually provide different moral guidance? This is something you should consider in the light of your own examples or previous examples in this chapter.

12. Comparing the Classical Utilitarians

Bentham

- Hedonist
- All pleasure equally valuable
- Act Utilitarian
- Teleological, impartial, relativistic, maximising

Mill

- Hedonist
- Quality of pleasure matters: intellectual versus animalistic
- Viewed as rule utilitarian
- If strong rule utilitarian, not clear if teleological or relativistic
- Impartial, maximising theory

13. Non-Hedonistic Contemporary Utilitarianism: Peter Singer and Preference Utilitarianism

Utilitarianism is not a dead theory and it did not end with Mill. Henry Sidgwick (1838–1900) is considered to have taken over the baton after Mill, and R. M. Hare (1919–2002) was perhaps chief advocate in the mid twentieth century. However, few contemporary philosophers can claim as much influence in public life outside philosophy as can the preference utilitarian, Peter Singer (1946–).

Singer advocates a non-hedonistic version of Utilitarianism. His utilitarian theory is teleological, maximising, impartial and relativistic but he does not claim that the greatest good for the greatest number can be reduced to pleasure in either raw or higher forms. Instead, Singer believes that what improves a person's life is entirely determined by the satisfaction of their preferences. If you satisfy your preference to achieve a good qualification your life goes better *in virtue of satisfying that preference*. If someone else desires to get a job rather than continue in education, their life goes better for them if they secure their preference and gain employment. Individuals, according to Singer, must be at the core of moral thinking:

> There would be something incoherent about living a life where the conclusions you came to in ethics did not make any difference to your life. It would make it an academic exercise. The whole point about doing ethics is to think about the way to live. My life has a kind of harmony between my ideas and the way I live. It would be highly discordant if that was not the case.[16]

On this basis, when making moral decisions we should consider how best to ensure the maximisation of total preference satisfaction — it does not matter if our preference satisfaction fails to provide pleasure for us. Continuing to follow Bentham's commitment to impartiality, Singer also supports equal weighing of preferences when deciding which action better promotes greater preference satisfaction; all preferences are to weigh equally. This potentially leaves Singer open to the same issues that plagued Bentham. Namely, regarding circumstances where partiality seems desirable, or when the preferences of the majority seem to threaten a minority group, or require us to sacrifice our integrity. Further, the problem of calculation also seems to be relevant, because it is not obvious how you could work out the preferences of others in at least some difficult moral cases (let alone the preferences of animals, if they are also relevant).

In response to a concern regarding the moral relevance of satisfying bloodthirsty or apparently immoral preferences, and counting such satisfaction as a moral achievement (consider the preferences of a nation of paedophiles, for example), we might look to the ideas of Richard Brandt (1910–1997). Brandt, writing about the rationality of certain preferences, suggested that rational preferences were those that might survive cognitive psychotherapy.[17] However, there is a question as to how arbitrary this requirement is and whether or not some unnerving preferences might form the core of certain individual characters therefore being sustained even after such therapy.

---

16   K. Toolis, 'The Most Dangerous Man in the World', https://www.theguardian.com/lifeandstyle/1999/nov/06/weekend.kevintoolis

17   R. Brandt, *Ethical Theory*.

SUMMARY

Utilitarianism remains a living theory and retains hedonistic and non-hedonistic advocates, as well as supporters of both act and rule formulations. The core insight that consequences matter gives the theory some intuitive support even in the light of hypothetical cases that pose serious problems for utilitarians. The extent to which the different versions of Utilitarianism survive their objections is very much up to you as a critically-minded philosopher to decide.

COMMON STUDENT MISTAKES

- Not reflecting the attitudinal aspect of pleasure that Bentham's theory may account for.
- Minimising the long-term impact of actions when it comes to pleasure/pain production.
- Imprecise understanding of the hedonic/non-hedonic split in Utilitarianism.
- Imprecision in use of examples to defend/challenge Utilitarianism.
- Suggesting that "Jim and the Indians" is not a counterexample to Utilitarianism simply because you judge killing the fewer number of people is ultimately the morally right thing to do.

ISSUES TO CONSIDER

1. Is there anything that would improve your life that cannot be reduced to either pleasure or preference satisfaction?
2. Would you enter Nozick's experience machine if you knew you would not come out? Would you put someone you care about into the machine while they were asleep, so that they never had to make the decision?

3. Can pleasure be measured? Does Bentham go about this task correctly?

4. Which is the most serious problem facing Bentham's Act Utilitarianism? Can it be overcome?

5. Does Mill successfully improve Bentham's Act Utilitarianism in any way?

6. Are you ever told to stop watching television and do something else? Is this good for you? Why?

7. Look at the quote at the start of the chapter by Dara Ó Briain — is it possible that some pleasures are inferior in value to others?

8. Do you have convictions or beliefs you would not want to sacrifice for the greater good, should you ever be forced to?

9. Why do utilitarians not give up on the idea of maximising pleasure and just talk in terms of promoting sufficient pleasure? Would this solve or raise problems?

10. Is Weak Rule Utilitarianism merely Act Utilitarianism by another name?

11. Does Strong Rule Utilitarianism deserve to be labelled as a utilitarian theory?

12. If your preferences change after psychotherapy, did the original preferences ever matter?

KEY TERMINOLOGY

Normative	Agent-Neutrality
Relativistic	Hedonic Calculus
Teleological	Utility
Consequentialist	Intrinsic
Principle of Utility	

References

Bentham, Jeremy, *The Rationale of Reward* (London: Robert Heward, 1830), freely available at https://books.google.co.uk/books?id=6igN9srLgg8C

—, 'An Introduction to the Principles of Morals and Legislation', in *Utilitarianism and Other Essays*, ed. by Alan Ryan (London: Penguin Books, 2004).

—, *An Introduction to the Principles of Morals and Legislation*, freely available at http://www.econlib.org/library/Bentham/bnthPML18.html

Brandt, Richard, *Ethical Theory: The Problems of Normative and Critical Ethics* (Englewood Cliffs, NJ: Prentice Hall, 1959).

Mill, John Stuart, *On Liberty* (London: Longman, Roberts, Green & Co., 1869), freely available at http://www.econlib.org/library/Mill/mlLbty1.html

—, 'Utilitarianism', in *Utilitarianism and Other Essays*, ed. by Alan Ryan (London: Penguin Books, 2004).

—, *Utilitarianism*, freely available at https://www.utilitarianism.com/mill1.htm

Nozick, Robert, 'The Experience Machine', in *Ethical Theory*, ed. by Russ Shafer-Landau (Oxford: Blackwell Publishing, 2007).

Thomson, Judith Jarvis, 'The Trolley Problem', *The Yale Law Journal*, 94.6 (1985): 1395–415, https://doi.org/10.2307/796133

Toolis, Kevin, 'The Most Dangerous Man in the World', *the Guardian* (6 November 1999), freely available at https://www.theguardian.com/lifeandstyle/1999/nov/06/weekend.kevintoolis

Williams, Bernard, 'Jim and the Indians', in his *A Critique of Utilitarianism*, freely available at https://www.unc.edu/courses/2009spring/plcy/240/001/Jim_and_Indians.pdf

CHAPTER 2

Kantian Ethics

In spite of its horrifying title Kant's Groundwork of the Metaphysic of Morals *is one of the small books which are truly great; it has exercised on human thought an influence almost ludicrously disproportionate to its size.*[1]

1. An Introduction to Kantian Ethics

Immanuel Kant was born in 1724 in Königsberg in East Prussia, where he died in 1804. Kant is famous for revolutionising how we think about just about every aspect of the world — including science, art, ethics, religion, the self and reality. He is one of the most important thinkers of all time, which is even more remarkable by the fact that Kant is a truly awful writer. His sentences are full of technical language, are very long, and are incredibly dense. You have been warned!

Kant is a rationalist writing during the Enlightenment (1685–1815). He thinks that we can gain knowledge from our senses and through our rational capacities. This means his general philosophical approach starts by asking what we can know *a priori.*

This is key to understanding his work but also makes his writing on ethics seem a bit odd. We think the study of ethics — unlike say maths — ought to direct our eye to what is going on around us in the world. Yet Kant starts by turning his eyes "inward" to thinking about ethical *ideas.*

Kant believes that in doing this people will come to recognise that certain actions are right and wrong irrespective of how we might feel and irrespective of any consequences. For Kant, actions are right if they respect what he calls the Categorical Imperative. For example, because lying fails to respect the Categorical Imperative it is wrong and is wrong irrespective of how we might feel about lying or what might happen if we did lie; it is actions that are right and wrong rather than consequences. This means that Kant's theory is deontological rather than teleological. It focuses on our *duties* rather than our ends/goals/consequences.

---

1   H. J. Paton, 'Preface' in I. Kant, *Moral Law*, p. 7.

There is, however, something intuitive about the idea that morality is based on reason rather than feelings or consequences. Consider my pet cat Spartan. He performs certain actions like scrabbling under bed covers, meowing at birds and chasing his tail. Now consider my daughter Beth, she performs certain actions like caring for her sister and helping the homeless.

Spartan's actions are *not* moral whereas Beth's actions are. Spartan's thinking and actions are driven by his desires and inclination. He eats and plays and sleeps when he desires to do so, there is no reasoning on his part. Beth, in contrast, can reflect on the various reasons she has, reasons to care for her sister and the homeless.

We might think then that humans are moral beings not because we have certain desires but precisely because we are *rational*. We have an ability to "stand back" and consider what we are doing and why. Kant certainly thought so and he takes this insight as his starting point.

2. Some Key Ideas

Duty

Kant's main works in ethics are his *Metaphysics of Morals* (1797) and the *Groundwork of the Metaphysics of Morals* (1785). Neither give practical advice about particular situations but rather through rational reflection, Kant seeks to establish the supreme principle of morality.

He starts from the notion of "duty" and although this is a rather old-fashioned term, the idea behind it should sound familiar. Imagine, your friend has told you that she is pregnant but asks you to promise to keep her secret. Through the coming weeks this juicy bit of gossip is on the tip of your tongue but you do not tell anyone because of your promise. There are things we recognise as being required of us irrespective of what we (really) desire to do. This is what Kant means by duty.

But this raises the question. If it is not desires that move us to do what is right (even really strong desires), what does? In our example, why is it that we keep our promise despite the strong desire to gossip? Kant's answer is "the good will".

Good Will

Kant gives the following characterization of the good will. It is something that is *good irrespective of effects*:

> A good will is good not because of what it effects or accomplishes — because of its fitness for attaining some proposed end: it is good through its willing alone — that is, good in itself.[2]

---

2   I. Kant, *Moral Law*, p. 40.

It is also good without qualification.

It is impossible to conceive anything at all in the world, or even out of it, which can be taken as good without qualification, except a good will.[3]

What does Kant mean? Well, pick anything you like which you think might make an action good — for example, happiness, pleasure, courage, and then ask yourself if there are any situations you can think of where an action having those features makes those actions worse?

It seems there are. Imagine someone who is *happy* when kicking a cat; or someone taking *pleasure* in torture; or a serial killer whose courage allows her to abduct children in broad daylight. In such cases the happiness, pleasure and courage make the actions worse. Kant thinks we can repeat this line of thinking for anything and everything, except one thing — *the good will*.

The good will unlike anything else is good *unconditionally* and what makes a good will good is willing alone; not other attitudes, or consequences, or characteristics of the agent. Even Kant thinks this sounds like a rather strange idea. So how can he (and we) be confident that the good will even exists?

Consider Mahatma Gandhi's (1869–1948) non-violent protest for Indian independence. He stood peacefully whilst the British police beat him. Here is a case where there must have been an overwhelming desire to fight back. But he did not. In this type of action Kant would claim that we "see" the good will — as he says — "shining like a jewel".[4] Seeing such resilience in the face of such awful violence we are humbled and can recognize, what Kant calls, its moral worth. Obviously not all actions are as significant as Gandhi's! However, Kant thinks that any acts like this, which are *performed despite conflicting desires*, are due to the good will. Considering such actions (can you think of any?) means we can recognize that the good will exists.

3. Acting *for the Sake of* Duty and Acting *in Accordance with* Duty

From what we have said above about the nature of duty and good will we can see why Kant says that to act from good will is acting for the sake of duty. We act despite our desires to do otherwise. For Kant this means that acting for the sake of duty is the *only* way that an action can have moral worth. We will see below what we have to do for our actions to be carried out for the sake of duty. However, before we do this, we need to be really clear on this point about moral worth.

---

3   *Ibid.*, p. 39.
4   *Ibid.*, p. 40.

Imagine that you are walking with a friend. You pass someone begging on the street. Your friend starts to weep, fumbles in his wallet and gives the beggar some money and tells you that he *feels* such an empathy with the poor man that he just has to help him.

For Kant, your friend's action has *no* moral worth because what is moving him to give money is empathy rather than duty! He is *acting in accordance with duty*. However, Kant does think your friend should be applauded as such an action is something that is of value although it wouldn't be correct to call it a *moral* action.

To make this point clearer, Kant asks us to consider someone who has no sympathy for the suffering of others and no inclination to help them. But despite this:

> ...*he nevertheless tears himself from his deadly insensibility and performs the action without any inclination at all, but solely from duty then for the first time his action has genuine moral worth.*[5]

In contrast to our friend, this person is acting *for the sake of* duty and hence their action is moral. We must be careful though. *Kant is not telling us to become emotionally barren robots*! He is not saying that before we can act morally we need to get rid of sympathy, empathy, desires, love, and inclinations. This would make Kant's moral philosophy an absurd non-starter.

Let us see why Kant is not saying this. Consider an action such as giving to others. We should ask whether an action of giving to others *would have* been performed *even if* the agent lacked the desire to do so. If the answer is "yes" then the act has moral worth. This though is consistent with the agent *actually having* those desires. *The question for Kant is not whether an agent has desires but what moved the agent to act*. If they acted *because* of those desires they acted in accordance with duty and their action had no moral worth. If they acted for the sake of duty, and just happened to have those desires, then their action has moral worth.

4. Categorical and Hypothetical Imperatives

If we agree with Kant and want to act for the sake of duty what should we do? His answer is that we have to act out of *respect for the moral law*. He has two examples of how this works in practice: lying and suicide. We look at the former in Chapter 13, we will consider Kant's example of suicide at the end of this chapter. However, before doing this we need to get a sense of what Kant has in mind when he talks about acting out of respect for the moral law.

The moral law is what he calls the "Categorical Imperative". He thinks there are three formulations of this.

---

5   *Ibid.*, p. 43.

CI-1: *...act only according to that maxim through which you can at the same time will that it become a universal law.*[6]

CI-2: *So act that you use humanity, in your own person as well as in the person of any other, always at the same time as an end, never merely as a means.*[7]

CI-3: *...every rational being must so act as if he were through his maxim always a lawmaking member in the universal kingdom of ends.*[8]

We will consider these in turn, showing how they are linked. Consider then, CI-1.

Kant's idea is that we use this "test" to see what maxims are morally permissible. If we act in accordance with those then we are acting from duty and our actions have moral worth. Let us look at what this means.

Initially it is worth considering what "categorical" and "imperative" mean. An imperative is just a command. "Clean your room!" is an imperative I give my daughter every Saturday. "Do not park in front of these gates!" is a command on my neighbour's gate. "Love your God with all your heart, mind and soul" is a command from the Bible.

What about the "categorical" part? If a command is categorical then people ought to follow it irrespective of how they feel about following it, irrespective of what consequences might follow, or who may or may not have told them to follow it. For example, the command "do not peel the skin of babies" is categorical. You ought not to do this and the fact that this might be your life's ambition, or that you really want to do it, or that your teacher has told you to do it, is completely irrelevant.

Contrast this with Hypothetical Imperatives. If I tell my daughter to clean her room, this is hypothetical. This is because whether she ought to clean her room is dependent on conditions about her and me. If she does not care about a clean room and about what her dad thinks, then it is not true that she ought to clean her room. Most commands are hypothetical. For example, "study!" You ought to study only *if* certain things are true about you; for example, that you care about doing well, that you want to succeed in the test etc.

Kant thinks that moral "oughts" — for example, "you ought not lie" — are *categorical*. They apply to people irrespective of how they feel about them.

The next thing we need is the idea of a "maxim". This is relatively simple and is best seen through the following examples. Imagine I'm considering whether to make a false promise. Perhaps I think that by falsely promising you that l will pay you back I will be more likely to get a loan from you. In

---

6   *Ibid.*, p. 15.
7   *Ibid.*, p. 66.
8   *Ibid.*, p. 21.

that case my maxim is something like *"whenever I can benefit from making a false promise I should do so"*.

Imagine I decide to exercise because I feel depressed, then I may be said to be acting on the maxim *"Whenever I feel depressed I will exercise"*. A maxim is a general principle or rule upon which we act. We do not decide on a set of maxims, perhaps writing them down, and then try to live by them but rather a *maxim is the principle or rule that can make sense of an action whether or not we have thought about it in these terms*.

5. The First Formulation of the Categorical Imperative

Let's put these bits together in relation to CI-1

> ...*act only according to that maxim through which you can at the same time will that it become a universal law.*[9]

The "test" that CI-1 prescribes is the following. Consider the maxim on which you are thinking about acting, and ask whether you can either (i) conceive that it become a universal law, or (ii) will that it become a universal law. If a maxim fails on either (i) or (ii) then there is no good reason for you to act on that maxim and it is morally impermissible to do so. If it passes the CI test, then it is morally permissible.

Kant is *not* saying that the CI-1 test is a way of working out what is and what is not moral. Presumably we can think of lots of maxims, which are non-moral, which pass the test, for example, "whenever I am bored I will watch TV".

Equally he is not saying that if a maxim cannot be universalized then it is morally impermissible. Some maxims are just mathematically impossible. For example, "whenever I am going to exercise I will do it for an above the average amount of time". This maxim cannot be universalized because we cannot conceive that everyone does something above "average".

Finally, it is worth remembering that the maxim must be able to be *willed* as a universal law. This is important because maxims such as "if your name is Jill and you are 5ft 11, you can lie" will fail to be universalized because you cannot will that your name is Jill or that your height is 5ft11. It has to be possible to will as a universal law and for this to be true it must be at least possible for it actually to come about. This shows that the common concern that we can get any maxim to pass the CI-1 test by simply adding more and more specific details, such as names, heights or locations, *fails*. This is very abstract (what did we tell you about Kant's work!). Let us consider an example.

---

9   *Ibid.*

6. Perfect and Imperfect Duties

Recall the example of making a false promise to secure a loan. The maxim is *"whenever I can benefit from doing so, I should make a false promise"*. The question is whether I could conceive or will that this become a universal law.

I could not. If everyone followed this maxim then we would all believe everyone else could make a false promise if it would benefit them to do so. Kant thinks such a situation is not conceivable because the very idea of making a promise relies on trust. But if "whenever it is of benefit to you, you can make false promises" was to become a universal law then there would be no trust and hence no promising. So by simply thinking about the idea of promising and lying we see the maxim will fail the test and, because we cannot universalize the maxim, then making a false promise becomes morally impermissible. This is true universally for all people in all circumstances for anyone can, in principle, go through the same line of reasoning.

A maxim failing at (i) is what Kant calls a *contradiction in conception,* and failing at (i) means we are dealing with what Kant calls a *perfect duty.* In our example we have shown we have a perfect duty not to make false promises.

Consider another example. Imagine that someone in need asks us for money but we decide not to help them. In this case our maxim is "whenever someone is in need and asks for money do not give them money". Does this pass the CI-1 test?

No it fails the CI-1 test. Although it is true that the maxim passes (i) not giving to the needy does not threaten *the very idea* of giving money away. Kant thinks that anyone thinking about this will see that that maxim will fail at (ii) and hence it is morally impermissible. Here is why.

You cannot know if you will be in need in the future and presumably you would want to be helped if you were in need. In which case you are being inconsistent if you willed that "people should not help those in need" should become a universal law. For you might want people to help those in need in the future, namely, *you.*

So we cannot will the maxim "whenever someone is in need do not help them" to become a universal moral law. Again this is a thought process that *anyone* can go through and it means that this moral claim is true universally for all people in all circumstances. Failing at (ii) is what Kant calls a *contradiction in will,* and failing at (ii) means we are dealing with what Kant calls an *imperfect duty.*

It is absolutely key to recognize that CI-1 is not simply asking "what if everyone did that?" CI-1 is *not a form of Utilitarianism* (see Chapter 1). Kant is not saying that it is wrong to make false promises because if people did then the world would be a horrible place. Rather Kant is asking about whether we can *conceive or will* the maxim to become a universal law.

7. Second Formulation of the Categorical Imperative

The second formulation (CI-2) is the following:

> *So act that you use humanity, in your own person as well as in the person of any other, always at the same time as an end, never merely as a means.*[10]

Kant thinks that CI-1 and CI-2 are two sides of the same coin, though precisely how they are related is a matter of scholarly debate. Put very simply CI-2 says you should not use people, because if you do, you are failing to treat them as a rational agent and this is morally wrong.

For example, if I use your essay without your knowledge then I have not treated you as a rational agent. I would have done had I asked you for your essay and you had freely chosen to let me have it. But given that I did not ask you, I was in a sense *making choices on your behalf* and thus did not treat you as a rational agent. So according to Kant I should always treat you as an end not a means. I should always treat you as a free rational agent.

Kant's theory then has a way of respecting the *dignity* of people. We should treat people with respect and with dignity purely on the basis that they are rational agents, and not because of their race, gender, education, upbringing etc. From this you can also see that Kant's theory allows us to speak about "rights". If someone has a right then they have this right irrespective of gender, education, upbringing etc. For example, Jill has a right to free speech because she is a person, consequently that right will not disappear if she changes her location, personal circumstances, relationship status, political viewpoint etc. After all she does not stop being a person.

Importantly, CI-2 does not say that you *either* treat someone as a means *or* an end. I could treat someone as an end *by* treating them as a means. Suppose that you have freely decided to become a taxi driver. If I use you as a means by asking you to take me to the airport I am also treating you as an end. But Kant does not believe this to be morally wrong because I am respecting you as a rational agent; after all, you *chose* to be a taxi driver. Of course, if I get into your car and point a gun at your head and ask to be taken to the airport then I am not treating you as an end but rather solely as a means, which is wrong.

8. The Third Formulation of the Categorical Imperative and Summary

The final formulation of the Categorical Imperative is a combination of CI-1 and CI-2. It asks us to imagine a kingdom which consists of only those people who act on CI-1. They never act on a maxim which cannot become a universal

---

10   *Ibid.*, p. 66.

law. In such a kingdom people would treat people as ends, because CI-2 passes CI-1. This is why CI-3 is often called the "Kingdom of Ends" formulation:

> ...*every rational being must so act as if he were through his maxim always a lawmaking member in the universal kingdom of ends.*[11]

In summary, we have seen that Kant thinks that acts have moral worth only if they are carried out for the sake of duty. Agents act for the sake of duty if they act out of respect for the moral law, which they do by following the Categorical Imperative in one of its formulations.

Consequently, Kant thinks that acts are wrong and right universally, irrespective of consequences and desires. If lying is wrong then it is wrong in all instances. From all this, it follows that we cannot be taught a set of moral rules for each and every situation and Kant believes that it is up to us to work it out for ourselves by thinking rationally.

There have been, and continue to be, many books and journal articles written about Kant's ethics. He has a profound and deep insight into the nature of morality and he raises some fundamental questions about what it is to be human. Kant's moral theory is radically *Egalitarian* as his theory is blind to individual personal circumstances, race, gender and ethnicity. Everyone is equal before the moral law!

Related to this, his theory respects the rights of individuals and, relatedly, their dignity. Any theory that is to have a hope of capturing our notion of rights needs to be able to respect the thought that a right is not something that disappears if circumstances change. Jill has a right to life, period; we do not say Jill has a right to life "if…" and then have to fill in the blanks. This is precisely something that Kant's theory can give us. CI-1 generates maxims which do not have exceptions and CI-2 tells us that we should *always* treat everyone as an end in themselves and *never* solely as a means to an end. It tells us, for example, that we ought not to kill Jill, and this holds true in all circumstances.

There are, though, a number of tough questions that Kant's work raises. We consider some of these below. However, as with all the philosophical ideas we discuss in this book, Kant's work is still very much alive and has defenders across the world. Before we turn to these worries, we work through an example that Kant gives regarding suicide.

9. Kant on Suicide

Kant is notoriously stingy with examples. One he does mention is suicide (another is lying see Chapter 13). This is an emotive topic and linked to questions about mental health and religion. An attraction of Kant's view is

---

11   *Ibid.*, p. 21.

the ability to apply his Categorical Imperatives in a dispassionate way. His framework should allow us to "plug in" the issue and "get out" an answer. Let's see how this might work.

Kant thinks that suicide is always wrong and has very harsh words for someone who attempts suicide

> He who so behaves, who has no respect for human nature and makes a thing of himself, becomes for everyone an Object of freewill. We are free to treat him as a beast, as a thing, and to use him for our sport as we do a horse or a dog, for he is no longer a human being; he has made a thing of himself, and, having himself discarded his humanity, he cannot expect that others should respect humanity in him.[12]

But why does he think this? How does this fit with Kant's Categorical Imperatives? We will look at the first two formulations.

Fundamental to remember is that for Kant the motive that drives *all* suicide is "avoid evil". By which he means avoiding suffering, pain, and other negative outcomes in one's life. All suicide attempts are due to the fact that we love ourselves and thus want to "avoid evils" that may befall us.

Imagine then that I decide to commit suicide. Given what we have just said about my motives this means I will be acting on this maxim: "From self-love I make as my principle to shorten my life when its continued duration threatens more evil than it promises satisfaction".[13]

Following CI-1 the question then is whether it is possible to universalise this maxim? Kant thinks not. For him it is unclear how we could will it that all rational agents as the result of *self-love* can *destroy themselves* when their continued existence threatens more evil than it promises satisfaction. For Kant self-love leading to the destruction of the self is a *contradiction*. Thus he thinks that we have a *perfect* (rather than an imperfect) duty to ourselves not to commit suicide. To do so is morally wrong. This is how Kant puts it:

> One sees at once a contradiction in a system of nature whose law would destroy life [suicide] by means of the very same feeling that acts so as to stimulate the furtherance of life [self-love], and hence there could be no existence as a system of nature. Therefore, such a maxim cannot possibly hold as a universal law of nature and is, consequently, wholly opposed to the supreme principle of all duty.

Notice a few odd things here in relation to CI-1. The point about universalisation seems irrelevant. Kant could have just said it is a contradiction to will from self-love the destruction of oneself. It seems that there is nothing added by asking us to consider this point universalised. It does not add weight to the claim that it is a contradiction.

---

12   I. Kant, *Lectures on Ethics*, 27; 373.
13   I. Kant, *Grounding for the Metaphysics of Morals*, Ak IV, 422

Second, it is not really a "contradiction" at all! It is different to the lying promise example. In this it seems that the very concept of a promise relies on trust, which lying would destroy. In contrast in the suicide case the "contradiction" seems more like a by-product of Kant's assumption regarding the motivation of suicidal people. So we can avoid the "contradiction" if we allow for the possibility that suicide need not be driven by self-love. If this were true then there would be no "contradiction". Hence, it seems wrong to call the duty not to kill oneself — if such a duty exists — a "perfect" duty. So the first formulation does not give Kant the conclusion that suicide is morally wrong.

Moving to the second formulation. This helps us understand Kant's harsh assessment of people attempting suicide. Remember he calls such people "objects" or "beasts" or "things". So, what is the difference between beasts or objects or things, and humans? The answer is that we are *rational*. Recall, that for Kant our rationality is of fundamental value. If anyone's actions do not recognize someone else's rationality then they have done something morally wrong. This amounts to treating them as merely means to our own end. Given all this you can see what Kant is getting at. For him committing suicide is treating yourself as a mere means to some end — namely the end of avoiding pain and suffering etc. — and not an end in itself. You are treating yourself as a "beast" a "thing" an "object", not as a human being with the gift of reason. This is morally wrong.

Moreover, if you do this, then others treating you with respect *as a rational person* can conclude that you also want others to treat you in this way. Because if you are rational then you must think that it is OK to universalise the maxim that we can treat others as objects, beast and thing. They can thus treat you as a beast, object, and thing and still be treating you with respect as a rationale agent. With regard to attempting suicide your action is wrong because you have ignored your own rationality. You have treated yourself as a mere means to an end.

But, like the first formulation this is very weak. It is unclear why in attempting suicide you are treating yourself as a mere means to an end. You might think you are respecting your rationality *by* considering suicide. Recall, Kant says that it is sometimes fine to treat people as a means to an end, e.g. a taxi driver. It is fine where people have given consent for you to treat them that way. In that case, suicide might be like the taxi driver case. We have freely decided to treat ourselves as a means to an end. We are, then, treating ourselves as a rational agent and not doing something morally wrong by committing suicide.

There are some other things that Kant says about the wrongness of suicide that do not link to the Categorical Imperatives. For example, he talks about humans being the property of God and hence our lives not being something we can choose to extinguish. However, we need not discuss this here.

There is a consensus between Kant scholars that, as it stands, Kant's argument against suicide fails. There are some though who use Kant's ideas as a starting point for a more convincing argument against suicide. For example, see J. David Velleman (1999) and Michael Cholbi (2000).

10. Problems and Responses: Conflicting Duties

If moral duties apply in *all* circumstances, then what happens when we have duties which conflict? Imagine that you have hidden some Jewish people in your basement in Nazi Germany. Imagine then that an SS officer knocks at your door and asks if you are hiding Jews? What might Kant's theory tell us to do? Our duty is to refrain from lying so does this mean we are morally required to tell the SS officer our secret? If this is the conclusion then it makes Kant's theory morally repugnant.

However, *there is no requirement in Kant's theory to tell the truth*, there is just a requirement *not to lie*. Lying is about intentional deceit, so maybe in this example there is a way not to lie. For example, if we simply stayed silent (see Chapter 13).

Even if we respond in this sort of way in this example, presumably we can engineer an example that would not allow for this. For example, perhaps we are in a law court and the SS officer asks us under oath. In that example, silence would not be an option. This certainly would seem to count against Kant's theory for it does seem morally wrong to reveal the location of the Jewish people.

The main point though is that Kant thinks we need to take the features of each individual situation into account. He does not just want us to mindlessly apply generic rules whilst paying no attention to what is before us. So Peter Rickman writes regarding these types of cases:

> ...it should be plain that more than one imperative/moral principle is relevant to the situation. Certainly we should tell the truth; but do we not also have a duty to protect an innocent man from harm? Further, do we not have an obligation to fight evil? We are confronted with a conflict of values here. Unfortunately, as far as I know, there is no explicit discussion of this issue in Kant. One could assume, however, that his general approach of distinguishing the lesser from the greater evil should be applied. I think Kant might say that although lying is never right, it might be the lesser evil in some cases.[14]

So the point is not that these sorts of examples are "knock down" criticisms of Kant's theory but rather that Kant's theory is underspecified and fails to give

---

14   P. Rickman, 'Having Trouble with Kant?', https://philosophynow.org/issues/86/Having_Trouble_With_Kant

guidance with these specific sorts of cases. In fact, we might think that this is an advantage of his theory that has given us the supreme principle of morality and the general way of proceeding but has left it up to us to work out what to do in each situation. We will leave the reader to see if this can be done and in particular, whether it can be done in a way consistent with the other aspects of his moral theory.

11. Problems and Responses: The Role of Intuitions

One of the most common criticisms levelled at Kant's theory is that it is simply counter intuitive. For example, lying, for him, is morally impermissible in all instances irrespective of the consequences. Yet we seem to be able to generate thought experiments that show that this is a morally repugnant position.

However, in Kant's defence we might ask why we should use our intuitions as any form of test for a moral theory. Intuitions are notoriously fickle and unreliable. Even if you pick the oddest view you can think of, you would probably find some people at some point in time that would find this view "intuitive". So how worried should we be if Kant's theory leads to counter intuitive consequences? This then raises a more general methodological question to keep at the forefront of your mind when reading this book. What role, if any, should intuitions have in the formation and the testing of moral theory?

12. Problem and Responses: Categorical Imperatives and Etiquette

Kant argues that what we are morally required to do is a matter of reason. If people reason in the right way then they will recognise, for example, that lying is wrong. However, some philosophers, for example Philippa Foot (1920–2010), have worried about this link to reason. The strength of Foot's challenge is that she agrees that morality is a system of Categorical Imperatives but says that this *need not be due to reason*.

Foot uses the example of *etiquette* to motivate her argument.[15] Rules of etiquette seem to be Categorical Imperatives but are *not* grounded in reason. Consider an example. I had a friend at university who was a sportsman. He was in many teams, his degree was in sports and exercise and if there were ever a spare minute he would be running, on his bike or in the pool. Unsurprisingly he wore a tracksuit and trainers all the time!

---

15   P. Foot, 'Morality as a System of Hypothetical Imperatives'.

During our second year at university a mutual friend died. There was a big formal funeral arranged. My friend decided to go to this funeral in his tracksuit and trainers. I asked him about this and his response was that it was what he liked wearing. However, to my mind at least, this reason, which was based on his desire, did not change the fact that he really ought not have worn a tracksuit. Foot would agree and thinks that rules of etiquette are categorical because they are not dependent on any particular desires someone would have.

However, even if they are categorical, Foot thinks that rules of etiquette are not rules of reason. We do not think that if we reasoned correctly we would recognise that we ought not to wear tracksuits to funerals, or (to think of some other rules of etiquette) we ought not to reply to a letter written in the third person in the first person, or we ought not to put our feet on the dinner table during a meal etc. It is not simply a matter of thinking in the right way but rather to recognise these "oughts" as part of a shared cultural practice.

So although this does not show that Kant is wrong, it does throw down a challenge to him. That is, we need independent reasons to think that the *categorical* nature of moral "oughts" are based on *reason* and not just part of a shared cultural practice. To respond to this challenge, the Kantian would have to put forward the argument that in the particular case of moral "oughts", we have a good argument to ground the categorical nature in reason rather than institutional practices.

13. Problems and Responses: The Domain of Morality

Kant thinks that the domain of morality is merely the domain of reasons and as far as we are agents who can reason then we have duties and rights and people ought to treat us with dignity. The flip side of this is that non-rational agents, such as non-human animals, do not have rights and we can, according to Kant, treat them as we like!

The challenge to Kant's theory is that the scope of morality seems bigger than the scope of reasons. People do think that we have moral obligations toward non-rational agents. Consider someone kicking a cat. We might think that *morally* they ought not to do this. However, Kant's theory does not back this up because, as far as we know, cats are not rational agents. Despite it not being wrong to treat animals in this way, Kant *still thinks that we should not*, because if we did, then we would be more likely to treat humans in this way.

SUMMARY

Kant's moral theory is extremely complicated and badly expressed. However, it is hugely influential and profound. As a system builder Kant's work starts with rational reflection from which he attempts to develop a complete moral system.

He starts from the notion of duty. He shows that what allows us to act for the sake of duty is the good will, and that the good will is unconditionally good. If we want to act for the sake of duty we need to act out of respect for the moral law and this amounts to following the Categorical Imperative. Kant argues that in following the Categorical Imperative, agents will converge on what is morally permissible. Hence Kant can talk about absolute and objective moral truths.

COMMON STUDENT MISTAKES

- Confusing acting in *accordance with* duty and acting *for the sake of* duty.
- Thinking that Kant's theory has no room for emotions.
- Thinking that Kant's Categorical Imperative can be summed up in the question: "how would you like it if everyone did that"?
- Thinking that the Categorical Imperative is a form of Utilitarianism.
- Thinking Kant believes you can never treat someone as a means to an end.

ISSUES TO CONSIDER

1. Think about your life. Do you think there are things you "ought to do"?
2. Do you think that there are things you ought to do irrespective of your desires and inclinations?

3. What are Categorical and Hypothetical Imperatives? Do you think that rules of etiquette are categorical or hypothetical?

4. How might Kant respond to the SS officer example?

5. Can you think of some examples where you might be treating someone solely as means-to-an-end?

6. Would capital punishment pass the CI-2 test?

7. How might CI-2 relate to prostitution? Do you think that Kant would say that it is morally permissible? (See also Chapter 10).

8. Why might Kant's theory be well placed to respect people's rights?

9. Do you think we have any moral obligations towards animals? What would Kant say?

10. What role do you think intuitions should have in assessing moral theories?

KEY TERMINOLOGY

A priori	Good will
Categorical Imperative	Hypothetical Imperative
Deontological	Maxim
Duty	Rationalist
Egalitarian	Rights

References

Cholbi, Michael J., 'Kant and the Irrationality of Suicide', *History of Philosophy Quarterly*, 17.2 (2000): 159–76.

Foot, Philippa, 'Morality as a System of Hypothetical Imperatives', *The Philosophical Review*, 81.3 (1972): 305–16, https://doi.org/10.2307/2184328

Kant, Immanuel, *Moral Law: The Groundwork of the Metaphysics of Morals*, Translated and analysed by H. J. Paton (Oxford: Routledge, 2013).

—, *Lectures on Ethics* (Cambridge: Cambridge University Press, 1997).

Rickman, Peter, 'Having Trouble with Kant?', *Philosophy Now*, freely available at https://philosophynow.org/issues/86/Having_Trouble_With_Kant

Velleman, J. David, 'A Right of Self-termination?', *Ethics*, 109.3 (1999): 606–28, https://doi.org/10.1086/233924

—, *Beyond Price: Essays on Birth and Death* (Cambridge: Open Book Publishers, 2015), https://doi.org/10.11647/OBP.0061; freely available at https://www.openbookpublishers.com/reader/349

CHAPTER 3

Aristotelian Virtue Ethics

To seek virtue for the sake of reward is to dig for iron with a spade of gold.[1]

1. Aristotelian Virtue Ethics Introduction

Aristotle (384–322 BC) was a scholar in disciplines such as ethics, metaphysics, biology and botany, amongst others. It is fitting, therefore, that his moral philosophy is based around assessing the broad characters of human beings rather than assessing singular acts in isolation. Indeed, this is what separates Aristotelian Virtue Ethics from both Utilitarianism and Kantian Ethics.

2. The Function Argument

Aristotle was a *teleologist*, a term related to, but not to be confused with, the label "teleological" as applied to normative ethical theories such as Utilitarianism. Aristotle was a teleologist because he believed that every object has what he referred to as a final cause. The Greek term *telos* refers to what we might call a purpose, goal, end or true final function of an object. Indeed, those of you studying Aristotle in units related to the Philosophy of Religion may recognise the link between Aristotle's general teleological worldview and his study of ethics.

Aristotle claims that "…for all things that have a function or activity, the good and the 'well' is thought to reside in the function".[2] Aristotle's claim is essentially that in achieving its function, goal or end, an object achieves its own good. Every object has this type of a true function and so every object has a way of achieving goodness. The *telos* of a chair, for example, may be to provide a seat and a chair is a good chair when it supports the curvature of the human bottom without collapsing under the strain. Equally, says Aristotle, what makes good sculptors, artists and flautists is the successful and appropriate performance of their functions as sculptors, artists and flautists.

---

1 I. Panin, *Thoughts*, p. 92, https://ia601405.us.archive.org/8/items/thoughts00panigoog/thoughts00panigoog.pdf
2 Aristotle, *The Nicomachean Ethics*, http://sacred-texts.com/cla/ari/nico/index.htm

This teleological (function and purpose) based worldview is the necessary backdrop to understanding Aristotle's ethical reasoning. For, just as a chair has a true function or end, so *Aristotle believes human beings have a telos*. Aristotle identifies what the good for a human being is in virtue of working out what the function of a human being is, as per his Function Argument.

Function Argument

1. All objects have a *telos*.

2. An object is good when it properly secures its *telos*.

Given the above, hopefully these steps of the argument are clear so far. At this point, Aristotle directs his thinking towards human beings specifically.

3. The *telos* of a human being is to *reason*.

4. The good for a human being is, therefore, acting in accordance with reason.

In working out our true function, Aristotle looks to that feature that *separates man from other living animals*. According to Aristotle, what separates mankind from the rest of the world is our ability not only to reason but to *act on reasons*. Thus, just as the function of a chair can be derived from its *uniquely differentiating characteristic*, so the function of a human being is related to our uniquely differentiating characteristic and we achieve the good when we act in accordance with this true function or *telos*.

The notion that man has a true function may sound odd, particularly if you do not have a religious worldview of your own. However, to you especially Aristotle wrote that "…as eye, hand, foot and in general each of the parts evidently has a function, may one lay it down that man similarly has a function apart from all these?"[3]

On the basis that we would ascribe a function to our constituent parts — we know what makes a good kidney for example — so too Aristotle thinks it far from unreasonable that we have a function as a whole. Indeed, this may be plausible if we consider other objects. The component parts of a car, for example, have individual functions but a car itself, as a whole, has its own function that determines whether or not it is a good car.

3. Aristotelian Goodness

On the basis of the previous argument, the good life for a human being is achieved when we act in accordance with our *telos*. However, rather than

---

3   *Ibid.*

---

leaving the concept of goodness as general and abstract we can say more specifically what the good for a human involves. Aristotle uses the Greek term *eudaimonia* to capture the state that we experience if we fully *achieve* a good life. According to Aristotle, *eudaimonia* is the state that all humans should aim for as it is the aim and end of human existence. To reach this state, we must ourselves act in accordance with reason. Properly understanding what Aristotle means by *eudaimonia* is crucial to understanding his Virtue Ethical moral position.

Eudaimonia has been variously translated and no perfect translation has yet been identified. While all translations have their own issues, *eudaimonia understood as flourishing* is perhaps the most helpful translation and improves upon a simple translation of happiness. The following example may make this clearer.

> Naomi is an extremely talented pianist. Some days, she plays music that simply makes her happy, perhaps the tune from the television soap opera "Neighbours" or a rendition of "Twinkle, Twinkle Little Star". On other days, she plays complex music such as the supremely difficult Chopin-Godowsky *Études*. These performances may also make Naomi happy, but she seems to be flourishing as a pianist only with the latter performances rather than the former. If we use the language of function, both performances make Naomi happy but she fulfils her function as a pianist (and *is* a good pianist) only when she flourishes with the works of greater complexity.

Flourishing in life may make us happy but happiness itself is not necessarily well aligned with acting in accordance with our *telos*. Perhaps, if we prefer the term happiness as a translation for *eudaimonia* we mean really or *truly* happy, but it may be easier to stay with the understanding of *eudaimonia* as flourishing when describing the state of acting in accordance with our true function.

Aristotle concludes that a life is *eudaimon* (adjective of *eudaimonia*) when it involves "…the active exercise of the mind in conformity with perfect goodness or virtue".[4] *Eudaimonia* is secured not as the result exercising of our physical or animalistic qualities but as the result of the exercise of our distinctly human rational and cognitive aspects.

4. *Eudaimonia* and Virtue

The quotation provided at the end of section three was the first direct reference to virtue in the explanatory sections of this chapter. With Aristotle's theoretical presuppositions now laid out, we can begin to properly explain and evaluate his conception of the virtues and their link to moral thinking.

---

4   *Ibid.*

According to Aristotle, *virtues are character dispositions or personality traits*. This focus on our dispositions and our character, rather than our actions in isolation, is what earns Aristotelian Virtue Ethics the label of being an *agent-centred* moral theory rather than an *act-centred* moral theory.

Act-Centred Moral Theories

Utilitarianism and Kantian Ethics are two different examples of act-centred moral theories due to their focus on actions when it comes to making moral assessments and judgments. Act-centred moral theories may be teleological or deontological, absolutist or relativist, but they share a common worldview in that particular actions are bearers of moral value — either being right or wrong.

Agent-Centred Moral Theories

Aristotelian Virtue Ethics is an agent-centred theory in virtue of a primary focus on people and their characters rather than singular actions. For Aristotle, morality has more to do with the question "how should I *be*?" rather than "what should I *do*?" If we answer the first question then, as we see later in this chapter, the second question may begin to take care of itself. When explaining and evaluating Aristotelian Virtue Ethics you must keep in mind this focus on character rather than specific comments on the morality of actions.

Aristotle refers to virtues as character traits or psychological dispositions. Virtues are those particular dispositions that are appropriately related to the situation and, to link back to our function, encourage actions that are in accordance with reason. Again, a more concrete example will make clear how Aristotle identifies virtues in practice.

All of us, at one time or another, experience feelings of anger. For example, I may become angry when my step-son thoughtlessly eats through the remaining crisps without saving any for others, or he may feel anger when he has to wait an extra minute or two to be picked up at work because his step-father is juggling twenty-six different tasks and momentarily loses track of time (how totally unfair of him...). Anyway, as I was saying, back to Aristotle, "Anyone can become angry — that is easy. But to be angry with the right person, to the right degree, at the right time, for the right purpose, and in the right way — that is not easy".[5]

For Aristotle, *virtue is not a feeling* itself but an appropriate psychological disposition in response to that feeling; the proper response. The correct

---

5   *Ibid.*

response to a feeling is described as acting on the basis of the *Golden Mean*, a response that is neither excessive nor deficient. The table below makes this more apparent.

Feeling/Emotion	Vice of Deficiency	Virtuous Disposition (Golden Mean)	Vice of Excess
Anger	Lack of spirit	Patience	Irascibility
Shame	Shyness	Modesty	Shamefulness
Fear	Cowardice	Courage	Rashness
Indignation	Spitefulness	Righteousness	Envy

Anger is a feeling and therefore is neither a virtue nor a vice. However, the correct response to anger — the Golden Mean between two extremes — is patience, rather than a lack of spirit or irascibility. Virtues are not feelings, but characteristic dispositional responses that, when viewed holistically, define our characters and who we are.

The Golden Mean ought not to be viewed as suggesting that a virtuous disposition is always one that gives rise to a "middling" action. If someone puts their life on the line, when unarmed, in an attempt to stop a would-be terrorist attack, then their action may be rash rather than courageous. However, if armed with a heavy, blunt instrument their life-risking action may be courageously virtuous rather than rash. The Golden Mean is not to be understood as suggesting that we always act somewhere between complete inaction and breathless exuberance, but as suggesting that we act between the vices of excess and deficiency; such action may well involve *extreme* courage or *exceptional* patience.

In addition to feelings, Aristotle also suggests that we may virtuously respond to situations. He suggests the following examples.

Situation	Vice of Deficiency	Virtuous Disposition (Golden Mean)	Vice of Excess
Social conduct	Cantankerousness	Friendliness	Self-serving flattery
Conversation	Boorishness	Wittiness	Buffoonery
Giving money	Stinginess	Generosity	Profligacy

We must keep in mind the agent-centred nature of Aristotelian Virtue Ethics when considering these examples. A person does not cease to have a witty disposition in virtue of a single joke that might err on the side of buffoonery, or cease to be generous because they fail to donate to charity on one occasion. Our psychological dispositions, virtuous or not, are only to be assessed by judgment of a person's general character and observation over more than single-act situations. If we act in accordance with reason and fulfil our function as human beings, our behaviour will generally reflect our virtuous personality traits and dispositions.

5. Developing the Virtues

In a quote widely attributed to Aristotle, **Will Durrant** (1885–1981) sums up the Aristotelian view by saying that "…we are what we repeatedly do. Excellence, then, is not an act but a habit".[6] It is fairly obvious that we cannot become excellent at something overnight. Making progress in any endeavour is always a journey that requires both effort and practice over time. Aristotle holds that the same is true for human beings attempting to develop their virtuous character traits in attempt to live the good life. You may feel yourself coming to an Aristotelian Virtue Ethical view after reading this chapter and therefore be moved to become wittier, more courageous and more generous but you cannot simply acquire these traits by decision; rather, you must *live* these traits in order to develop them.

Cultivating a virtuous character is something that happens by practice. Aristotle compares the development of the skill of virtue to the development of other skills. He says that "…men become builders by building" and "… we become just by doing just acts".[7] We might know that a brick must go into a particular place but we are good builders only when we know how to place that brick properly. Building requires practical skill and not merely intellectual knowledge and the same applies to developing virtuous character traits. Ethical characters are developed by practical learning and habitual action and not merely by intellectual teaching.

In the end, the virtuous individual will become comfortable in responding to feelings/situations virtuously just as the good builder becomes comfortable responding to the sight of various tools and a set of plans. A skilled builder will not need abstract reflection when it comes to knowing how to build a wall properly, and nor will a skilled cyclist need abstract reflection on how to balance his speed correctly as he goes around a corner.

Analogously, a person skilled in the virtues will not need abstract reflection when faced with a situation in which friendliness and generosity are possibilities; they will simply know on a more intuitive level how to act. This is not to say that builders, cyclists and virtuous people will not sometimes need

---

6   W. Durant, *The Story of Philosophy*, p. 76.
7   Aristotle, *The Nicomachean Ethics*, http://sacred-texts.com/cla/ari/nico/index.htm

to reflect specifically on what to do in abnormal or difficult situations (e.g. moral dilemmas, in the case of ethics) but in normal situations appropriate responses will be natural for those who are properly skilled.

It is the need to become skilled when developing virtuous character traits that leads Aristotle to suggest that becoming virtuous will require a lifetime of work. Putting up a single bookshelf does not make you a skilled builder any more than a single act of courage makes you a courageous and virtuous person. It is the repetition of skill that determines your status and the development of virtuous characters requires a lifetime of work rather than a single week at a Virtue Ethics Bootcamp.

6. Practical Wisdom (*Phronesis*)

Aristotle does offer some specifics regarding how exactly we might, to use a depressingly modern phrase, "upskill" in order to become more virtuous. Aristotle suggests that the aim of an action will be made clear by the relevant virtuous characteristic as revealed by the Golden Mean; for example, our aim in a situation may be to respond courageously or generously. It is by developing our skill of practical wisdom (translation of "*phronesis*") that we become better at ascertaining what exactly courage or generosity amounts to in a specific situation and how exactly we might achieve it.

By developing the skill of practical wisdom, we can properly put our virtuous character traits into practice. For the Aristotelian, practical wisdom may actually be the most important virtuous disposition or character trait to develop as without the skill of practical wisdom it may be difficult to actually practice actions that are witty rather than boorish, or courageous rather than cowardly. Imagine trying to be a philosopher without an acute sense of logical reasoning; you would struggle because this seems to be a foundational good on which other philosophical skills rely. So too it may be with the virtues, practical wisdom supports our instinctive knowledge of how to respond virtuously to various feelings, emotions and situations.

If this still seems to be somewhat opaque, then we may develop our sense of practical wisdom by looking at the actions of others who we do take to be virtuous. A child, for example, will most certainly need to learn how to be virtuous by following examples of others. If we are unsure in our own ability to discern what a courageous response in a given situation is, then we may be guided by the behaviour of Socrates, Jesus, Gandhi, Mandela or King, as examples. If we learn from the wisdom and virtue of others, then just as a building apprentice learns from a master so too virtue apprentices can learn from those more skilled than they in practising virtue. Hopefully, such virtue apprentices will eventually reach a point where they can stand on their own two feet, with their personally developed sense of practical wisdom.

7. Voluntary Actions, Involuntary Actions and Moral Responsibility

Despite the focus on agents and not actions, Aristotle does have something to contribute when it comes to discussions of potential *moral responsibility* as associated with particular actions. We can separate actions into two obvious categories:

1. Voluntary actions
2. Involuntary actions

Very broadly, an action is voluntary when it is freely chosen and involuntary when it is not — these terms are more precisely defined next, in line with Aristotle's ideas. These distinctions matter in ethics because a person might be held to be morally responsible for their voluntary actions but not for their involuntary actions. According to Aristotle, an action is voluntary unless it is affected by *force* or *ignorance*, as understood in the following ways.

Physical Force

Imagine that Reuben is driving his car on his way home from work. Out of the blue, his passenger grabs his hand and forces him to turn the steering wheel, sending the car into oncoming traffic. Without this physical force, Reuben would not have turned the wheel and he very much regrets the damage that is caused. According to Aristotle, Reuben's action is involuntary because of this external physical force and so he is not morally responsible for the crash.

Psychological Force

Think of David, working at a bank when a group of thieves break in armed with guns. David is told that if he does not open the safe then he will be killed. Under this extreme psychological pressure, Aristotle would accept that David's opening of the safe is involuntary, because David would not have opened the safe otherwise and he very much regrets doing so. On this basis, David is not morally responsible in any way for the theft.

In addition to force, ignorance of a certain type can also support an action being labelled as involuntary.

Action from Ignorance

Rhys, a talented musician, wishes to perform a surprise concert for a friend and has been practicing songs from the Barry Manilow back catalogue for weeks. However, in the days before the surprise concert his friend, unbeknown to Rhys, develops an intense and very personal dislike for Manilow. Thus, when Rhys takes to the stage and blasts out his rendition of the classic tune "Copacabana" his friend storms off in much distress. In this situation, Aristotle would accept that Rhys acted involuntarily when causing offence because he was unaware of the changed circumstances; he acted from ignorance when performing the song rather than from malice. Without this epistemic (or knowledge-related) barrier, Rhys would not have acted as he did and he very much regrets the distress caused. For these reasons, Rhys bears no moral responsibility for the upset resulting from his song choice.

Crucially, Aristotle does not allow that all action that involves ignorance can be classed as involuntary, thereby blocking associated claims of moral responsibility.

Action in Ignorance

Laurence has had too much to drink and chooses to climb a traffic light with a traffic cone on his head. Laurence's alcohol consumption has made him ignorant, at least temporarily, of the consequences of this action in terms of social relationships, employment and police action. However, for Aristotle this would not mean that his action was involuntary because Laurence acts in ignorance rather than from ignorance due to an external epistemic (or knowledge-based) barrier. Laurence does not, therefore, escape moral responsibility as a result of his self-created ignorance.

Finally, Aristotle also identifies a third form of action — non-voluntary action — that is also related to ignorant action.

Action from Ignorance with No Regret

Return to the case of Rhys and his Manilow performance but remove any sense of regret on Rhys' part for the distress caused. If, at the moment that the epistemic gap is bridged and Rhys learns of his friend's newly acquired musical views, he feels no regret for his action, then Aristotle would class it as a non-voluntary rather than involuntary action. The action cannot be voluntary as Rhys acted from ignorance, but it is not obviously involuntary as, without a sense of regret, it may have been that Rhys would have performed the action even if he knew what was going to happen.

The detail above is important and your own examples will help your understanding and explanations. The summary, however, is refreshingly simple. *If an action is voluntary, then it is completed free from force and ignorance and we can hold the actor morally responsible. However, if the action is involuntary then the actor is not morally responsible as they act on the basis of force or from ignorance.*

8. Objection: Unclear Guidance

Consider yourself caught in the middle of a moral dilemma. Wanting to know what to do you may consult the guidance offered by Utilitarianism or Kantian Ethics and discover that various specific actions you could undertake are morally right or morally wrong. Moving to seek the advice of Aristotelian Virtue Ethics, you may find cold comfort from suggestions that you act generously, patiently and modestly whilst avoiding self-serving flattery and envy. Rather than knowing how to live in general, you may seek knowledge of what to actually do in this case. Virtue Ethics may therefore be accused of being a theory, not of helpful moral guidance, but of unhelpful and non-specific moral platitudes.

In response, the virtue ethicist may remind us that we can learn how to act from considering how truly virtuous people might respond in this situation, but this response raises its own worry — how can we identify who is virtuous, or apply their actions to a potentially novel situation? Although a defender of Virtue Ethics, **Rosalind Hursthouse** (1943–) gives a voice to this common objection, putting forward the worry directly by saying that "'Virtue Ethics does not, because it cannot, tell us what we should do... It gives us no guidance whatsoever. Who are the virtuous agents [that we should look to for guidance]?"[8] If all the virtue ethicist can offer to a person wondering how to act — perhaps wondering whether or not to report a friend to the police, or whether or not to change careers to work in the charity sector — is "look to the moral exemplars of Socrates and Gandhi and how they would act in this situation", then we might well sympathise with the objector since very often our moral dilemmas are new situations, not merely old ones repeated. Asking "what would Jesus do", if we deem Jesus to be a morally virtuous role model, might not seem very helpful for an MP trying to determine whether or not to vote for an increase in subsidies for renewable energy technologies at huge

---

8   R. Hursthouse, 'Normative Virtue Ethics', pp. 701–03.

expense, and potential financial risk, to the tax-payer (to take a deliberately specific example).

Despite her statement of the objection, Hursthouse thinks that this is an unfair characterisation of Virtue Ethics. Hursthouse suggests that Virtue Ethics provides guidance in the form of "v-rules". These are guiding rules of the form "do what is honest" or "avoid what is envious".[9] These rules may not be specific, but they do stand as guidance across lots of different moral situations. Whether or not you believe that this level of guidance is suitable for a normative moral theory is a judgment that you should make yourself and then defend.

9. Objection: Clashing Virtues

Related to the general objection from lack of guidance, a developed objection may question how we are supposed to cope with situations in which virtues seem to clash. Courageous behaviour may, in certain cases, mean a lack of friendliness; generosity may threaten modesty. In these situations, the suggestion to "be virtuous" may again seem to be unhelpfully vague.

To this particular objection, the Aristotelian virtue ethicist can invoke the concept of practical wisdom and suggest that the skilled and virtuous person will appropriately respond to complex moral situations. A Formula One car, for example, will be good when it has both raw speed and delicate handling and it is up to the skilled engineer to steer a path between these two virtues. So too a person with practical wisdom can steer a path between apparently clashing virtues in any given situation. Virtue ethicists have no interest in the creation of a codified moral rule book covering all situations and instead put the onus on the skill of the virtuous person when deciding how to act. Again, whether this is a strength or weakness is for you to decide and defend.

10. Objection: Circularity

An entirely different objection to Aristotelian Virtue Ethics is based on a concern regarding logical circularity. According to Aristotle, the following statements seem to be correct:

1. An act is virtuous if it is an act that a virtuous person would commit in that circumstance.

2. A person is virtuous when they act in virtuous ways.

---

9   *Ibid.*

This, however, looks to be circular reasoning. If virtuous actions are understood in terms of virtuous people, but virtuous people are understood in terms of virtuous actions, then we have unhelpfully circular reasoning.

Julia Annas (1946–) responds to this apparent problem by arguing that there is nothing dangerously circular in this reasoning because it is simply a reflection of how we learn to develop our virtuous dispositions.[10] Annas suggests the analogy of piano-playing:

1. Great piano playing is what great pianists do.

2. A pianist is great when he "does" great piano playing.

In this case, there does not seem to be any troubling circularity in reasoning. It is not the case that whatever a great pianist plays will be great, but rather that great pianists have the skills to make great music. So too it is with virtues, for virtuous people are not virtuous just because of their actual actions but because of who they are and how their actions are motivated. It is their skills and character traits that mean that, in practice, they provide a clear guide as to which actions are properly aligned with virtues. Thus, if we wish to decide whether or not an act is virtuous we can assess what a virtuous person would do in that circumstance, but this does not mean that what is virtuous is determined by the actions of a specifically virtuous individual. The issue is whether or not a person, with virtuous characteristics in the abstract, would actually carry that action out. Virtuous people are living and breathing concrete guides, helping us to understand the actions associated with abstract virtuous character dispositions.

11. Objection: Contribution to *Eudaimonia*

The final distinct objection to Aristotelian Virtue Ethics considered in this chapter stems from the Aristotelian claim that living virtuously will contribute to our ability to secure a *eudaimon* life. A challenge to this view may be based on the fact that certain dispositions may seem to be virtuous but may not actually seem to contribute to our flourishing or securing the good life.

As an example of this possible objection in practice, consider the following. Shelley is often described as generous to a fault and regularly dedicates large amounts of her time to helping others to solve problems at considerable cost, in terms of both time and effort, to herself. Working beyond the limits that can reasonably be expected of her, we may wish to describe Shelley as virtuous given her generous personality. However, by working herself so hard for others, we may wonder if Shelley is unduly limiting *her own* ability to flourish.

---

10   J. Annas, *Intelligent Virtue.*

Responses to this initial statement of the objection are not hard to imagine. We may say that Shelley has either succumbed to a vice of excess and is profligate with her time rather than generous, or we may accept that she is generous rather than profligate and accept the uncomfortable conclusion and say that this virtuous character trait is helping her to flourish. This second claim may seem more plausible if we ruled out a description of Shelley wasting her time.

Still, this objection may stand up if you can envisage a situation in which someone could be properly described as rash rather than courageous or wasteful rather than generous and, because of these traits, actually be contributing to their own flourishing. You should consider your own possible cases if you seek to support this general objection.

12. Moral Good and Individual Good

For Aristotle, moral goodness and individual goodness may seem to be intimately linked. After all, a virtuous person will be charitable and friendly etc. and as a result of these characteristics and dispositions will both advance their own journey towards *eudaimonia* and make life better for others. Hedonism (which claims that pleasure is the only source of well-being — see Chapter 1), as a rival theory attempting to outline what is required for well-being, might be thought to fail because it downplays the importance of acting in accordance with reason, so hedonists do not therefore live according to their *telos* or true function.

Aristotle says of his ideally virtuous person that they will have a unified psychology — that their rational and non-rational psychologies will speak with one voice. On the contrary, the non-virtuous person will have a psychology in conflict between their rational and non-rational elements. In considering who has the better life from their own individual perspectives — the happy Hedonist or the Aristotelian virtuous person — you should again form your own reasoned judgment.

It is important to note, as we conclude this chapter, that Aristotle does not suggest that living a virtuous life is sufficient to guarantee a state of *eudaimonia* for a person. External factors such as poverty, disease or untimely death may scupper a person's advance towards *eudaimonia*. However, for Aristotle, being virtuous is necessary for the achievement of *eudaimonia*; without the development of virtues it is impossible for a person to flourish even if they avoid poverty, disease, loneliness etc.

SUMMARY

Aristotelian Virtue Ethics is very different in nature to the other act-centred normative moral theories considered in this book. Whether this, in itself, is a virtue or a vice is an issue for your own judgment. The lack of a codified and fixed moral rule book is something many view as a flaw, while others perceive it as the key strength of the theory. Some, meanwhile, will feel uncomfortable with Aristotle's teleological claims, differing from those who are happy to accept that there is an objectively good life that is possible for human beings. Regardless, there is little doubt that Aristotelian Virtue Ethics offers a distinct normative moral picture and that it is a theory worthy of your reflections.

COMMON STUDENT MISTAKES

- Understanding virtues as feelings.
- Misunderstanding the function of a human being (*eudaimonia*).
- Thinking that the Golden Mean always suggests "neutral" or "middling" actions.
- Incorrect differentiation between voluntary, involuntary and non-voluntary actions.
- Claiming that Virtue Ethics offers no guidance whatsoever in moral situations.
- Claiming that Virtue Ethics is uninterested in actions.

ISSUES TO CONSIDER

1. Who has the better life — the happy hedonist or the virtuous individual?

2. Are the virtues fixed and absolute? Or can virtues be relative to culture and time?

3. Is becoming moral a skill? Is morality based on "knowing that" or "knowing how"?

4. Can Virtue Ethics offer useful guidance?

5. Is the Golden Mean a useful way of working out virtuous characteristics?

6. Are some virtues more important than others? Why?

7. Can you think of a virtue that does not contribute to *eudaimonia*?

8. Can you think of something that contributes to *eudaimonia* that is not a virtue?

9. If there is no purpose to life, is there any point in subscribing to Aristotelian Virtue Ethics?

10. What should you do if virtues seem to clash when faced with different possible actions?

11. Who might count as virtuous role models and why?

12. Do human beings have a *telos* or proper function?

KEY TERMINOLOGY

Act-centred	Phronesis
Agent-centred	Virtue
Dispositions	*Telos*
Eudaimonia	Golden mean

References

Annas, Julia, *Intelligent Virtue* (Oxford: Oxford University Press, 2011).

Aristotle, *The Nicomachean Ethics*, translated by William David Ross (Oxford: Clarendon Press, 1908), freely available at http://sacred-texts.com/cla/ari/nico/index.htm

Hursthouse, Rosalind, 'Normative Virtue Ethics', in *Ethical Theory*, ed. by Russ Shafer-Landau (Oxford: Blackwell Publishing, 2007), pp. 701–09.

Panin, Ivan, *Thoughts* (Grafton: Ivan Panin, 1887), freely available at https://ia601405.us.archive.org/8/items/thoughts00panigoog/thoughts00panigoog.pdf

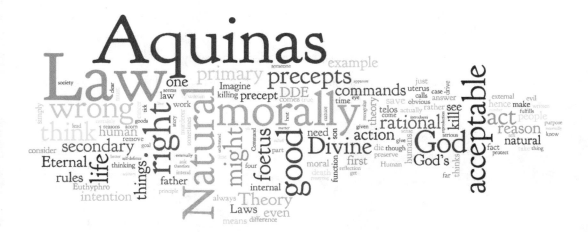

CHAPTER 4

Aquinas's Natural Law Theory

Grace does not destroy nature but perfects it.[1]

They show that the requirements of the law are written on their hearts, their consciences also bearing witness, and their thoughts sometimes accusing them and at other times even defending them.[2]

1. Introduction to Aquinas

Thomas Aquinas (1225–1274) was an intellectual and religious revolutionary, living at a time of great philosophical, theological and scientific development. He was a member of the Dominican Friars, which at that time was considered to be a cult, and was taught by one of the greatest intellects of the age, **Albert the Great** (1208–1280). In a nutshell Aquinas wanted to move away from Plato's thinking, which was hugely influential at the time, and instead introduce Aristotelian ideas to science, nature and theology.

Aquinas wrote an *incredible* amount — in fact one of the miracles accredited to him was the amount he wrote! His most famous work is *Summa Theologica* and this runs to some three and half thousand pages and contains many fascinating and profound insights, such as proofs for God's existence. The book remained a fundamental basis for Catholic thinking right up to the 1960s! But do not worry we will only be focusing on a few key ideas! Specifically *books I–II, questions 93–95.*

2. Motivating Natural Law Theory: The Euthyphro Dilemma and Divine Command Theory

The likely answer from a religious person as to *why* we should not steal, or commit adultery is: "because God *forbids* us"; or if we ask *why* we should love our neighbour or give money to charity then the answer is likely to be "because God *commands* it". Drawing this link between what is right and wrong and

1   T. Aquinas, *Summa Theologica*, I, I:8, http://www.summatheologica.info/summa/parts/?p=1
2   T. Aquinas, *Romans*, 2:15.

what God commands and forbids is what is called the *Divine Command Theory* (DCT).

There is a powerful and influential challenge to such an account called the *Euthyphro dilemma* after the challenge was first raised in Plato's *Euthyphro*. The dilemma runs as follows:

Either God commands something is right because it is, *or* it is right because God commands it. If God commands something because it is right, then God's commands do not make it right, His commands only tell us what is right. This means God simply drops out of the picture in terms of *explaining why* something is right.

If on the other hand something is right *because* God commands it then *anything* at all could be right; killing children or setting fire to churches could be morally acceptable. But if a moral theory says this then that looks as if the theory is wrong.

Most theists reject the first option and opt for this second option — that God's commands *make* something right. But they then have to face the problem that it make morality haphazard. This *"arbitrariness problem"* as it is sometimes called, is the reason that many, including Aquinas, give up on the Divine Command Theory.

So for Aquinas what role, if any at all, does God have when it comes to morality? For him, God's commands are there to help us to *come to see* what, as a matter of fact, is right and wrong rather than determine what is right and wrong. That is, Aquinas opts for the first option in the Euthyphro dilemma as stated above. But then this raises the obvious question: if it is not God's commands that make something right and wrong, then what does? Does not God just fall out of the picture? This is where his Natural Law Theory comes in.

3. Natural Law Theory

Aquinas's Natural Law Theory contains four different types of law: *Eternal Law, Natural Law, Human Law and Divine Law*. The way to understand these four laws and how they relate to one another is via the Eternal Law, so we'd better start there…

By "Eternal Law'" Aquinas means God's rational purpose and plan for *all* things. And because the Eternal Law is part of God's mind then it has always, and will always, exist. The Eternal Law is not simply something that God decided at some point to write.

Aquinas thinks that *everything* has a purpose and follows a plan. He, like Aristotle, is a teleologist (the Greek term *"telos"* refers to what we might call a purpose, goal, end/or the true final function of an object) (see Chapter 3;

not to be confused with a telelogical ethical *theory* such as Utilitarianism) and believes that *every* object has a *telos*; the acorn has the *telos* of growing into an oak; the eye a *telos* of seeing; a rat of eating and reproducing etc. (notice this links to his view on sex, see Chapter 10). If something fulfils its purpose/plan then it is following the Eternal Law.

Aquinas thinks that something is *good* in as far as it fulfils its purpose/plan. This fits with common sense. A *"good"* eye is one which sees well, an acorn is a good if it grows into a strong oak tree.

But what about humans? Just as a good eye is to see, and a good acorn is to grow then a good human is to…? Is to what? How are we going to finish this sentence? What do you think?

Aquinas thinks that the answer is *reason* and that it is this that makes us distinct from rats and rocks. What is right for me and you as humans is to act according to reason. If we act according to reason then we are partaking in the *Natural Law*.

If we all act according to reason, then we will all agree to some overarching general rules (what Aquinas calls *primary precepts*). These are *absolute* and binding on all rational agents and because of this Aquinas rejects *relativism*.

The first primary precept is that *good is to be pursued and done and evil avoided.* He thinks that this is the guiding principle for all our decision making.

Before unpacking this, it is worth clarifying something about what "law" means. Imagine that we are playing Cluedo and we are trying to work out the identity of the murderer. There are certain rules about how to move around the board, how to deal out cards, how to reveal the murderer etc. These rules are all written down and can be consulted.

However, in playing the game there are other rules that operate which are so obvious that they are neither written down nor spoken. One such rule is that a claim made in the game cannot both be true and false; if it *is* Professor Plum who is the murderer then it cannot be true that it *is not* Professor Plum who is the murderer. These are *internal rules* which *any* rational person can come to recognize by simply thinking and are not external like the other rules — such as you can only have one guess as to the identity of the murderer. When Aquinas talks of Natural Laws, he means internal rules and not external ones.

Natural Law does not generate an external set of rules that are written down for us to consult but rather it generates general rules that any rational agent can come to recognize simply in virtue of being rational. For example, for Aquinas it is not as if we need to check whether we should pursue good and avoid evil, as it is just part of how we already think about things. Aquinas gives some more examples of primary precepts:

1. *Protect and preserve human life.*

2. *Reproduce and educate one's offspring.*

3. *Know and worship God.*

4. *Live in a society.*

These precepts are *primary* because they are true for *all people in all instances* and are consistent with Natural Law.

Aquinas also introduces what he calls the *Human Law* which gives rise to what he calls *"Secondary Precepts"*. These might include such things as do not drive above 70mph on a motorway, do not kidnap people, always wear a helmet when riding a bike, do not hack into someone's bank account. Secondary precepts are *not generated by our reason* but rather they are imposed by governments, groups, clubs, societies etc.

It is *not* always morally acceptable to follow secondary precepts. It is only morally acceptable *if* they are consistent with the Natural Law. If they are, then we ought to follow them, if they are not, then we ought not. To see why think through an example.

Consider the secondary precept that *"if you are a woman and you live in Saudi Arabia then you are not allowed to drive"*. Aquinas would argue that this secondary precept is practically *irrational* because it treats people differently based on an arbitrary difference (gender). He would reason that if the men in power in Saudi actually really thought hard then they too would recognize that this law is morally wrong. This in turn means that Aquinas would think that *this* human law *does not* fit with the Natural Law. Hence, it is morally wrong to follow a law that says that men can, and women cannot, drive. So although it is presented as a secondary precept, because it *is not* in accordance with Natural Law, it is what Aquinas calls an *apparent good*. This is in contrast with those secondary precepts which *are* in accordance with the Natural Law and which he calls the *real goods*.

Unlike primary precepts, Aquinas is *not* committed to there being only one set of secondary precepts for all people in all situations. It is consistent with Aquinas's thinking to have a law to drive on the right in the US and on the left in the UK as there is no practical reason to think that there is one correct side of the road on which to drive.

It is clear that on our own we are not very good at discovering primary precepts and consequently Aquinas thinks that what we ought to do is talk and interact with people. To discover our real goods — our secondary precepts which accord with Natural Law — we need to be part of a society. For example, we might think that "treat Christians as secondary citizens" is a good secondary precept until we talk and live with Christians. The more we can think and talk with others in society the better and it is for this reason that "live in society" is itself a primary precept.

But looking at what we have said already about Natural Laws and primary and secondary precepts, we might think that there is no need for God. If we can learn these primary precepts by rational reflection then God simply drops out of the story (recall the Euthyphro dilemma above).

Just to recap as there a lots of moving parts to the story. We now have Eternal Law (God's plans/purpose for all things), Natural Laws (our partaking in the Eternal Law which leads to primary precepts), Human Laws (humans making specific laws to capture the truths of the Natural Laws which lead to secondary precepts) and now finally Aquinas introduces the *Divine Law*.

The Divine Law, which is discovered through *revelation*, should be thought of as the Divine equivalent of the Human Law (those discovered through rational reflection and created by people). Divine laws are those that God has, in His grace, seen fit to give us and are those "mysteries", those rules given by God which we find in scripture; for example, the ten commandments. But why introduce the Divine Law at all? It certainly feels we have enough Laws. Here is a story to illustrate Aquinas's answer.

A number of years ago I was talking to a minister of a church. He told me about an instance where a married man came to ask his advice about whether to finish an affair he was having. The man's reasoning went as follows — "I am having an affair which just feels so right, we are both very much in love and surely God would want what is best for me! How could it be wrong if we are so happy?"

In response, the minister opened the Bible to the Ten Commandments and pointed out the commandment that it says that it is wrong to commit adultery. Case closed. The point of this story is simple. We can be confused and mistaken about what we think we have most reason to do and because of this we need someone who actually knows the mind of God to guide us, and who better to know this than God Himself. This then is precisely what is revealed in the Divine Law.

Or consider another example. We recognize that we find it hard to forgive our friends and nearly always impossible to forgive our enemies. We tell ourselves we have the right to be angry, to bear grudges, etc. Isn't this just human? However, these human reasons are *distortions* of the Eternal Law. We need some guidance when it comes to forgiveness and it is where the Divine Law which tells us that we should forgive others — including our enemies. Following the Human Laws *and* the Divine Laws will help us to fulfil our purposes and plans and be truly happy.

4. Summary of Aquinas's Natural Law Theory

For Aquinas everything has a function (a *telos*) and the good thing(s) to do are those acts that fulfil that function. Some things such as acorns, and eyes, just do that naturally. However, humans are free and hence need guidance to find the right path. That right path is found through *reasoning* and generates the "internal" Natural Law. By following the Natural Law we participate in God's purpose for us in the Eternal Law.

However, the primary precepts that derive from the Natural Law are quite general, such as, *pursue good and shun evil*. So we need to create secondary precepts which can actually guide our day-to-day behaviour. But we are fallible so sometimes we get these secondary precepts wrong, sometimes we get them right. When they are wrong they only reflect our apparent goods. When they are right they reflect our real goods.

Finally, however good we are because we are finite and sinful, we can only get so far with rational reflection. We need some *revealed guidance* and this comes in the form of Divine Law. So to return to the Euthyphro dilemma. God's commands through the Divine Law are ways of *illuminating* what is in fact morally acceptable and *not what determines* what is morally acceptable. Aquinas rejects the Divine Command Theory.

5. Putting this into Practice: The Doctrine of Double Effect (DDE)

Let's consider some examples to show that what we have said so far might actually work. Imagine someone considering suicide. Is this morally acceptable or not? Recall, it is part of the Natural Law to preserve and protect human life. Clearly suicide is not preserving and protecting human life. It is therefore irrational to kill oneself and cannot be part of God's plan for our life; hence it is morally unacceptable.

Imagine that someone is considering having an abortion after becoming pregnant due to rape. The same reasoning is going to apply. We ought to preserve and protect human life and hence an abortion in this case is morally wrong.

However, as we will see, Aquinas thinks that there are *some* instances where it *is* morally acceptable to kill an innocent person and therefore there may be occasions when it is morally acceptable to kill a foetus. But how can this be correct? Will this not violate the primary precept about preserving life? The answer is to understand that for Aquinas, *an action is not just about what we do externally but is also about what we do internally* (i.e. our motivations). With this distinction he can show that, for example, killing an innocent *can be* morally acceptable.

To make this clear, Aquinas introduces one of his most famous ideas: the *"Doctrine of Double Effect"*. Let's see how this works.

> Imagine a child brought up in a physically, sexually and emotionally abusive family. He is frequently scared for his life and is locked in the house for days at a time. One day when his father is drunk and ready to abuse him again he quickly grabs a kitchen knife and slashes his father's artery. His father bleeds out and dies in a matter of minutes. Do you think the son did anything wrong?

Many people would say that he did nothing morally wrong and in fact, some might even go as far as to say that he should get a pat on the back for his actions. What about Aquinas? What would he say?

We might think that given the Natural Law to "preserve and protect life" he would say that this action is morally wrong. But, in fact, he would say the son's action was not morally wrong (Aquinas discusses self-defence in the *Summa Theologica* (II–II, Qu. 64)).

So why is the son killing the father not in direct contradiction with the primary precept? Aquinas asks us to consider the difference between the external act — the fact that the father was killed, and the internal act — the motive.

In our example, the action is one of *self-defence* because of the son's internal action and because of this, Aquinas would think the killing is morally acceptable. This distinction and conclusion is possible because of Aquinas's Doctrine of Double Effect which states that if an act fulfils four conditions then it is morally acceptable. If not, then it is not.

1. The first principle is that the act must be a *good* one.

2. The second principle is that the act must come about before the consequences.

3. The third is that the intention must be good.

4. The fourth, it must be for serious reasons.

This is abstract so let's go back to our example. The act of the son was performed to *save his own life* so that is good — we can tick (1). Moreover, the act to save his life came about first — we can tick (2). The son did not first act to kill his father in order to save his own life. That would be doing evil to bring about good and that is never morally acceptable. The intention of the son was to preserve and protect his life, so the intention was good — tick (3). Finally, the reasons were serious as it was his life or his father's life — tick (4).

So given that the act meets all four principles, it is in line with the DDE and hence the action is *morally acceptable*, even though it caused someone to die and hence seems contrary to the primary precept of preserving life.

We can draw a contrasting case. Imagine that instead of slashing his father in self-defence, the son *plans* the killing. He works out the best time, the best day and then sets up a trip wire causing his father to fall from his flat window to his death. Does this action meet the four criteria of the DDE? Well, no, because the son's *intention is to kill the father rather than save his own life* — we must put a cross at (3).

We have already seen that suicide is morally impermissible for Aquinas, so does that mean that *any* action you take that leads knowingly to your own death is morally wrong? No. Because even though the external act of your own death is the same, the internal act — the intention — might be different. *An action is judged via the Natural Law both externally and internally.*

Imagine a case where a soldier sees a grenade thrown into her barracks. Knowing that she does not have time to defuse it or throw it away, she throws herself on the grenade. It blows up, killing her but saving other soldiers in her barracks. Is this wrong or right? Aquinas says this is morally acceptable given DDE. If we judge this act *both* internally and externally we'll see why.

The intention — the internal act — was *not* to kill herself even though she could *foresee* that this was certainly what was going to happen. The act itself is good, to save her fellow soldiers (1). The order is right, she is not doing evil so good will happen (2). The intention is good, it is to save her fellow soldiers (3). The reason is serious, it concerns people's lives (4).

Contrast this with a soldier who decides to kill herself by blowing herself up. The intention is not good and hence the DDE does *not* permit this suicidal action.

Finally, imagine that a woman is pregnant and also has inoperable uterine cancer. The doctors have two choices; to take out the uterus and save the mother, but the foetus will die; or leave the foetus to develop and be born healthy, but the woman will die. What would Aquinas say in this instance? Well using the DDE he would say that it is morally *acceptable* to remove the cancer.

The action is to remove the cancer; it has the foreseeable consequences of the foetus dying but that is not what is intended. The action — to remove the cancer — is good (1). The act of removing the cancer comes before the death of the foetus (2). The intention to save the woman's life is also good (3). Finally, the reasons are serious as they are about the life and death of the woman and the foetus (4).

So even though this is a case where the doctor's actions bring about the death of the foetus it would be acceptable for Aquinas through his Natural Law Theory, as is shown via the DDE.

6. Some Thoughts about Natural Law Theory

There are many things we might consider when thinking through Aquinas's Natural Law Theory. There are some obvious problems we could raise, such as the problem about whether or not God exists. If God does not exist then the Eternal Law does not exist and therefore the whole theory comes tumbling down. However, as good philosophers we ought always to operate with a *principle of charity* and grant our opponent is rational and give the strongest possible interpretation of their argument. So, let's assume *for the sake of argument* that God exists. How plausible is Aquinas's theory? There are a number of things that we can pick up on.

Aquinas's theory works on the idea that if something is "natural", that is, if it fulfils its function, then it is morally acceptable, but there are a number of unanswered questions relating to *natural*.

We might ask, why does "natural" matter? We can think of things that are not "natural" but which are perfectly acceptable, and things which *are* natural which are not. For example, wearing clothes, taking medication and body piercing certainly are not natural, but we would not want to say such things are morally wrong.

On the other hand we might consider that violence *is* a natural response to an unfaithful partner, but also think that such violence is morally unacceptable. So it is not true that we can discover what is morally acceptable or not simply by discovering what is natural and what is not.

Put this worry aside. Recall, Aquinas thinks that reproduction is natural and hence reproduction is morally acceptable. This means that sex that *does not* lead to reproduction is morally unacceptable. Notice that Aquinas is not saying that if sex does not lead to pregnancy it is wrong. After all, sometimes the timing is not right. His claim is rather that if there is *no potential* for sex to lead to pregnancy then it is wrong. However, even with this qualification this would mean a whole host of things such as homosexuality and contraception are morally wrong. We might take this as a reason to rethink Aquinas's moral framework (we discuss these apparent problems in more detail in Chapter 10).

There is, though, a more fundamental worry at the heart of this approach (and Aristotle's) to ethics. Namely, they think that *everything* has a goal (*telos*). Now, with some things this might be plausible. Things such as the eye or an acorn have a clear function — to grow, to see — but what about humans? This seems a bit less obvious! Do humans (rather than our individual parts) really have a *telos*? There are certainly some philosophers — such as the existentialists, for example **Simone de Beauvoir** (1908–1986) — who think that there is no such thing as human nature and no such thing as a human function or goal. But if we are unconvinced that humans have a goal, then this whole approach to ethics seems flawed.

Next we might raise questions about DDE. Go back to our example about abortion. For Aquinas it *is* morally acceptable to remove the uterus even if we know that in doing so the foetus will die. What is not morally acceptable is to intend to kill the foetus by removing the uterus. On first reading this seems to makes sense; we have an intuitive feel for what DDE is getting at. However, when we consider it in more detail it is far from clear.

Imagine two doctors who (apparently) do exactly the same thing, they both remove the uterus and the foetus dies. The one intends to take out the uterus — in full knowledge that the foetus will die — the other intends to kill the foetus. For the DDE to work in the way that Aquinas understands it, this difference in intention makes the moral difference between the two doctors. However, is there really a moral difference? To put pressure on the answer that there is, ask yourself what you think it means to intend to do something. If the first doctor says "I did not intend to kill the foetus" can we make sense of this? After all, if you asked her "did you know that in taking out the uterus the foetus would die?" she would say "yes, of course". But if she did this and the foetus died, did not she intend (in some sense) to kill the foetus? So this issue raises some complex question about the nature of the mind, and how we might understand intentions.

Finally, we might wonder how easy it is to work out what actually to do using the Natural Law. We would hope our moral theory gives us direction in living our lives. That, we might think, is precisely the role of a moral theory. But how might it work in this case?

For Aquinas, if we rationally reflect then we arrive at the right way of proceeding. If this is in line with the Natural Law and the Divine Law then it is morally acceptable. If it is out of line, then it is not. The assumption is that the more we think, the more rational we become, the more convergence there will be. We'll all start to have similar views on what is right and wrong. But is this too optimistic? Very often, even after extensive reflection and cool deliberation with friends and colleagues, it is not obvious to us what we as rational agents should do. We all know people we take to be rational, but we disagree with them on moral issues. And even in obviously rational areas such as mathematics, the best mathematicians are not able to agree. We might then be sceptical that as rational agents we will come to be in line with the Natural and Divine Laws.

SUMMARY

Aquinas is an intellectual giant. He wrote an incredible amount covering a vast array of topics. His influence has been immense. His central idea is that humans are created by God to reason — that is our function. Humans do the morally right thing if we act in accordance with reason, and the morally wrong thing if we don't.

Aquinas is an incredibly subtle and complex thinker. For example, his Doctrine of Double Effect makes us to reflect on what we actually mean by "actions", "intentions" and "consequences". His work remains much discussed and researched and typically still plays a central role in a Christian Ethics that rejects Divine Command Theory.

COMMON STUDENT MISTAKES

- Thinking that Aquinas is a Divine Command Theorist.
- Thinking that Eternal Law is something that God decided to write.
- Thinking that Natural Laws are laws of science — e.g. law of thermodynamics.
- Thinking that all the "laws" are absolute.
- Thinking that it is always morally required of us to follow secondary precepts.
- Thinking that Aquinas is committed to there being only one set of secondary precepts for all people in all situations.

ISSUES TO CONSIDER

1. If God exists then what — if anything — do you think that has to do with what is right and wrong?

2. We might answer the "arbitrariness" dilemma by citing God's nature. Why might this answer be problematic?

3. What is the Eternal Law?

4. What are Natural Laws and primary precepts?

5. What are Human Laws and secondary precepts?

6. What are Divine Laws?

7. Just as a good eye is to see, and a good acorn is to grow then a good human is to…? Is to what? How are we going to finish this sentence?

8. People often talk about what is "natural"? What do you think they mean by this? How useful is the notion of "natural" in a moral theory?

9. Think of a descriptive claim. Think of a prescriptive claim. Why might it be problematic moving from one to the other?

10. If people thought long enough, do you think there would be convergence on what is morally right and wrong?

11. What is the Doctrine of Double Effect?

12. What is the difference — if anything — between intending to bring about some end and acting where you know your action will bring about that end?

KEY TERMINOLOGY

Apparent goods	Primary precepts
A priori	Real goods
A posteriori	Secondary precepts
Eternal Law	Internal acts
External acts	Doctrine of Double Effect
Natural Law	

References

Aquinas, Thomas, *Summa Theologica*, freely available at http://www. summatheologica.info/summa/parts/?p=1

—, *Romans (Commentary on the Letter of Saint Paul to the Romans)*

Plato, *Euthyphro*, translated by Benjamin Jowett, freely available at http:// classics.mit.edu/Plato/euthyfro.html

CHAPTER 5

Fletcher's Situation Ethics

Every man must decide for himself according to his own estimate of conditions and consequences...[1]

People like to wallow or cower in the security of the law.[2]

1. Situation Ethics Introduction

In the introduction to *The Situation Ethics: The New Morality* Joseph Fletcher (1905–1991) develops what he calls an ethical non-system. His book caused a "fire storm" amongst the public because it legitimised the general post-war dissatisfaction with authority. At the time it was written it seemed to make some radical claims such as that it is not wrong to have extramarital sex, to be homosexual, or to have an abortion. All that said, Fletcher's work is not widely discussed nor respected in philosophical circles. It is badly argued, idiosyncratic and rehashes old ideas.

Although there is the clothing of religion in the book — Fletcher uses religious terms such as *"agápe"* and cites famous theologians such as Rudolf Bultmann (1884–1976) — the central ideas do not rely on the truth of any particular religion. As he says his argument has "...nothing special to do with theological...faith"[3]

Fletcher calls this ethical "non-system" *Situationism* and a Bible story will illustrate the general point of the book. In Mark 3:1–6 we are told that Jesus healed a man with a withered hand in the Jewish Temple; an act which we would consider to demonstrate Jesus's *love* for all. However, the Pharisees tell him off because he has performed this healing on the Sabbath day and the Jewish law says that no one can work on the Sabbath.

Fletcher's work is an attempt to show how acts can be morally acceptable even if they go against so-called moral laws (if you've read Chapter 3 on Aristotle you might already have an answer to this). Fletcher says that Jesus' act is morally acceptable — despite going against the Jewish law — because he acted to bring about the most love.

1   K. E. Kirk, *Conscience and its Problems*, p. 331.
2   J. F. Fletcher, *Situation Ethics*.
3   *Ibid.*, p. 15.

2. Fletcher's Overall Framework

Fletcher says there are two unattractive views in ethics: *"Legalism"* and *"Antinomianism"*, and one attractive view which sits in between them: *"Situationism"*.

Legalism

Someone who is following the system of Legalism is someone who "blindly" observes moral rules without being sensitive to the situation. Fletcher has in mind a simple minded deontologist who holds that actions are right and wrong irrespective of the consequences. For example, we ought to tell the truth in all situations, even if this means that, say, millions of people die.

Various Christian sects are legalistic; for instance, some might refuse medical help — such as blood transfusions — when someone in their community is ill because they think it is against God's commands. Or consider an example of Islamic Legalism (obviously, just as in the Christian sect, these are not wholly representative of either religion). In 2002 the religious police of Saudi Arabia refused to let a group of girls escape from a burning building because they were wearing "inappropriate" clothing, which was against the will of Allah. One witness said he saw three policemen "beating young girls to prevent them from leaving the school because they were not wearing the *abaya*".[4] Fifteen girls died.

Antinomianism

The other extreme is Antinomianism ("anti" meaning against; "nominalism" meaning law). This is the view that says that an agent can do whatever he or she wants in a situation. Fletcher calls this an *"existential"* view because it is one that says that people are *always free* to choose what they want. Any supposed laws and rules limiting the actions of people are simply a way of trying to comfort them because they are scared of absolute freedom. If Antinomianism is right and if an agent believes that something is right, then it is. Antinomianism means the moral agent is erratic and random, is unpredictable, and any decisions taken are *ad hoc*. There are no laws nor guiding principles, just agents and their conscience and the institutions in which they find themselves.

A Middle Ethics: Situationism

We might think that Legalism and Antinomianism exhaust the possibilities. If we reject moral laws then are not we forced into lawless moral anarchy? Fletcher thinks not.

---

4   'Saudi Police "Stopped" Fire Rescue', BBC News, http://news.bbc.co.uk/1/hi/world/middle_east/1874471.stm

Fletcher says that there *is* a moral law, and hence he rejects Antinomianism. But there is only *one* moral law, so he rejects Legalism. Fletcher's one moral law is that we ought to always act so as to bring about the most love for the most people ("*Agápē* Calculus"). Fletcher's Situationism is then a *teleological* theory. It is directed at the consequences that will determine whether an action is right or wrong.

Of course, *any* teleological theory will ask us to look at the details of the situation; consider Chapter 1 where we talk about Bentham and Mill's Utilitarianism. So, Fletcher's view is not unique. What makes his view different is the centrality of "love", or as he calls it *agápē*.

Fletcher thinks that there *can* be moral *principles* but that these differ from *laws*. Principles are generalizations which are context-sensitive and which derive from the one law regarding maximizing love. For example, we might have a moral principle that we ought not to murder. This is a *principle* because we might think in that *in general* murder is wrong because it does not bring about the most love. However, it is not a *law* because for Fletcher, murder is not wrong in *all* situations. This then is similar to the discussion of Rule-Utilitarianism in Chapter 1.

For example, a situation might arise where the child of a terrorist would have to be murdered in order to get information to stop a nuclear attack. Fletcher would say that here is a situation where we ought not to follow the principle do not murder but rather do the most loving thing, which in this case turns out to be murder. From the universal law we can only derive principles, not other universal laws. As Fletcher puts it: "we cannot milk a universal from a universal".[5]

This mean that for Fletcher it might, on occasions, be morally acceptable to break the Ten Commandments. In fact, he says something stronger, that in some situations it is our *duty* to break these commandments. He thinks that there are four working principles of Situationism.

3. The Four Working Principles of Situationism

Principle 1. Pragmatism

The situationalist follows a strategy which is *pragmatic*. What does that mean? Well it does *not* mean that Fletcher is a pragmatist. "Pragmatism" is a very specific and well worked-out philosophical position adopted by the likes of John Dewey (1859–1952), Charles Peirce (1839–1914) and William James (1842–1910). Fletcher does not want his theory associated with these views and rejects all the implications of this type of "Pragmatism".

---

5   J. F. Fletcher, *Situation Ethics*, p. 27.

What makes his view pragmatic is very simple. It is just his attraction to moral views which do not try to work out what to do in the abstract (e.g. Kant's Categorical Imperative (see Chapter 2)), but rather explores how moral views might play out in each *real life situations*.

Principle 2: Relativism

Even with his rejection of Antinomianism and his acceptance of one supreme principle of morality, Fletcher, surprisingly, still calls himself a relativist. This does not mean he is a relativist in the sense that we can simply choose what is right and wrong rather it is just an appeal for people to stop trying to "lay down the law" for all people in all contexts. If situations vary then consequences vary and what we ought to do will change accordingly. This is a very simple, unsophisticated idea, like his ideas on pragmatism, and Fletcher just means that what is right or wrong is related to the situation we are in.

Principle 3: Positivism

His use of "positivism" is not the philosophical idea with the same name but rather is where:

> Any moral or value judgment in ethics, like a theologian's faith propositions, is a decision — not a conclusion. It is a choice, not a result reached by force of logic...[6]

So when challenged as to *how* he can justify that the only law is to maximize love, Fletcher will say that he cannot. It is not a result of logic or reasoning, rather it is a decision we take, it is like the "theologian's faith".

Principle 4: Personalism

Love is something that is experienced by *people*. So Personalism is the view that if we are to maximize love we need to consider the person in a situation — the "who" of a situation. Summing up this Fletcher says:

> Love is of people, by people, and for people. Things are to be used; people are to be loved... Loving actions are the only conduct permissible.[7]

These then are his "four working principles": pragmatism, relativism, positivism and personalism.

---

6   *Ibid.*, p. 47.
7   *Ibid.*, p. 51.

4. How to Work out What to Do: Conscience as a Verb not a Noun

For Fletcher "conscience" plays a role in working out what to do. He says "conscience" is a verb and not a noun. This sounds complicated but it really is not (for complex and sophisticated discussions of conscience see Chapter 9).

First consider what he means when he says conscience "is not a noun". Conscience is not the name of an internal faculty nor is it a sort of internal "moral compass". This is how people typically think of conscience and it is often portrayed in cartoons with a devil and angel sitting on someone's shoulder whispering into her ears.

Rather for Fletcher conscience is a verb. Imagine we have heard some bullies laughing because they have sent our friend some offensive texts and we are trying to decide whether or not to check his phone to delete the texts before he does. The old "noun" view of conscience would get us to think about this in the abstract, perhaps reason about it, or ask for guidance from the Holy Spirit, a guardian angel etc.

According to Fletcher this is wrong. Instead, we need to be in the situation, and experience the situation, we need to be doing (hence "verb") the experiencing. Maybe, we might conclude that it is right to go into our friend's phone, maybe we will not but whatever happens the outcome *could not have been known beforehand*. What our conscience would have us do is revealed when we live in the world and not through armchair reflection.

5. The Six Propositions of Situation Ethics

Fletcher gives six propositions (features) of his theory.

1: Only one 'thing' is intrinsically good; namely, love, nothing else at all

There is one thing which is intrinsically good, that is good irrespective of context, namely love. If love is what is good, then an action is right or wrong in as far as it brings about the most amount of love. Echoing Bentham's Hedonic Calculus (see Chapter 1) Fletcher defends what he calls the:

> agapeic calculus, *the greatest amount of neighbor welfare for the largest number of neighbors possible.*[8]

Notice that here he talks about *"welfare"* rather than "love". Fletcher does this because of how he understands love which, importantly, is not about having feelings and desires. We discuss this below.

---

8   *Ibid.*, p. 95.

2: *The ruling norm of Christian decision is love, nothing else*

As we have seen in the first proposition, the *only* way to decide what we ought to do (the ruling norm) is to bring about love. We need to be careful though because for Fletcher "love" has a technical meaning.

By love Fletcher means *"agápē"* — from ancient Greek. *Agápē* has a very particular meaning. Initially it is easier to see what it *is not*. It is not the feeling we might have towards friends or family member which is better described as brotherly love (*philēo*). Nor is it the erotic desire we might feel towards others (*érōs*).

Rather *agápē* is an *attitude* and not a feeling at all, one which does not expect anything in return and does not give any special considerations to anyone. *Agápē* regards the enemy in the same way as the friend, brother, spouse, lover. Given our modern context and how people typically talk of "love" it is probably unhelpful to even call it "love".

Typically people write and think about love as experiencing an intense feeling. In cartoons when a character is in love their hearts jump out of their chest, or people "in love" are portrayed as not being able to concentrate on things because they "cannot stop thinking" about someone.

This is not what love means for Fletcher. In the Christian context *agápē* is the type of love which is manifest in how God relates to us. Consider Christ's love in saying that he forgave those carrying out his execution or consider a more modern example. In February 1993, Mrs Johnson's son, Laramiun Byrd, 20, was shot in the head by 16-year-old Oshea Israel after an argument at a party in Minneapolis, Minnesota. Mrs Johnson subsequently forgave her son's killer and after he had served a 17 year sentence for the crime, asked him to move in next door to her. She was not condoning his actions, nor will she ever forget the horror of those actions, but she does love her son's killer. That love is *agápē.*

3: *Love and justice are the same, for justice is love distributed, nothing else*

For Fletcher, practically all moral problems we encounter can be boiled down to an apparent tension between "justice" on the one hand and "love" on the other. Consider a recent story:

> Trevell Coleman, better known as the rapper G Dep, was a rising star on the New York hip-hop scene and had been signed to P Diddy's Bad Boy record label. He also had a wife, Crystal, and twin boys.
>
> Yet Trevell, who was brought up a Catholic and always retained his faith, had a terrible secret, as an 18-year-old, he had mugged and shot a man. He never knew what happened to his victim, yet 17 years later, in 2010, he could no longer bear the guilt and went to the police — a step almost unimaginable for someone from the Hip Hop world.
>
> A police search of their cold case files revealed the case of John Henkel — shot and killed in 1993 at exactly the same street corner in Harlem where Trevell says he committed his

> crime. He is now serving a jail sentence of 15 years to life for Henkel's murder. Yet he has no regrets; "I wanted to get right with God", he says.
> Trevell's choice was perhaps hardest to bear for his wife Crystal, who now has to bring up their teenage boys on her own.

This could be expressed as a supposed tension between "love" of family and doing the right thing — "justice". Fletcher thinks that most other moral problems can be thought of in this way. Imagine we are trying to decide what is the best way to distribute food given to a charity, or how a triage nurse might work in a war zone. In these cases we might put the problem like this. We want to distribute fairly, but how should we do this?

Fletcher says the answer is simple. To act justly or fairly is precisely to act in love. "Love is justice, justice is love".[9]

4: *Love wills the neighbor's good when we like him or not*

This is self-explanatory. As we noted above, *agápē* is in the business of loving the unlovable. So related to our enemies:

> Christian love does not ask us to lose or abandon our sense of good and evil, or even of superior and inferior; it simply insists that however we rate them, and whether we like them nor not, they are our neighbors and are to be loved.[10]

5: *Only the ends justify the means, nothing else*

In direct rejection of the deontological approaches Fletcher says that any action we take, as considered as an action independent of its consequences is literally, "meaningless and pointless". An action, such as telling the truth, only acquires its status as a means by virtue of an end beyond itself.

6: *Love's decisions are made situationally, not prescriptively*

Ethical decisions are not cut and dried most of the time and they exist in a grey area. No decision can be taken before considering the situation. Fletcher gives the example of a women in Arizona who learned that she might "bear a defective baby because she had taken thalidomide". What should she do? The loving decision was not one given by the law which stated that all abortions are wrong. However, she travelled to Sweden where she had an abortion. Even if the embryo had not been defective according to Fletcher her actions were "brave and responsible and right" because she was acting in light of the particulars of the situation so as to bring about the most love.

---

9 *Ibid.*, p. 89.
10 *Ibid.*, p. 107.

6. Problems with Fletcher's Situationism

Fletcher's Situationism is a hopelessly confused and confusing moral theory. Fletcher's work has the annoying tendency to present trivially true claims as if they are profound philosophical insights.

At the most general level, Fletcher commits the *fallacy of appealing to authority*. This is simply the mistake of thinking that an argument is strengthened by saying that someone else — normally someone in "authority", holds it.

Fletcher uses many quotations from famous theologians and mentions famous philosophers, such as Aristotle, as a substitute for argument. Unfortunately simply appealing to others is not an argument. To see how useless this approach is consider the following: "Walker's crisps are healthy because Gary Lineker says so".

The other concern throughout Fletcher's work is that he is simply unclear and inaccurate, especially when dealing with the two central ideas: "love" and "situation".

In some places he talks about love being an "attitude". In other places he says it is what we ought to *bring about* as an *end point*. Which is it? Is it a loving "attitude" in virtue of which we act? Or is it about bringing about certain consequences?

To see why this might be problematic, consider a case where we act out of the attitude of *agápē* but the consequence is one of great death and destruction. Suppose we act in good "conscience" as Fletcher calls it but our act brings about horrendously dire consequences. According to Fletcher have we done right or wrong? It is not clear.

If he does say that what we did is "wrong" then fine, *agápē* should not be thought of as an attitude, but rather some feature of consequences. This reading is of course in line with his *agápē* calculus. Ok, so then imagine the devil acting out of hatred and malice but — due to his lack of knowledge — happens to bring about a vast amount of love in the world. Has the devil acted in the morally right way? If the "*agápē* calculus" is used then "yes". So, according to Fletcher has the devil done the right thing? It is not clear.

Notice it is no good saying "well we cannot decide because it depends on the situation!" Because we have just given you the details of the situation. If you need more information, just make some up and then reframe the question. So what Fletcher means by "love" is not clear. Nor is what he means by "situation".

If you were writing a book on Situationism you would expect a clear and extended discussion of these concepts. However, there is no discussion of it in his key text and this is an important omission. To see how thorny the issue actually is consider the following. A politician stands up and says "given the current situation we need to raise taxes". Our first response is probably going to be "what situation?" The point, simply put, is that there is no obvious way of knowing what is meant by "situation". What we will choose to consider in any situation will depend on what is motivating us, what our dispositions are, what agendas we have.

Consider a moral example. A terminally ill patient wants to die; given the situation what ought we to do? The point is what does, and does not, get considered in "the situation", will be dependent on what we *already think* is important. Do we consider his religious views, the fact that he has three cats which depend on him? What about the type of illness, the type of death, who he leaves behind, the effect it might have on the judicial system, the effect on the medical profession etc.

So then, as a way of actually working out what we ought to do, Fletcher's prescription that we should "ask what will bring about the most love in the situation" is singularly unhelpful. It seems perfectly plausible that one person might see the situation in one way and someone else see it in another, and hence we get two different claims about what we ought to do. You might think this is OK, on Fletcher's account. But recall he rejects Antinomianism (Relativism).

It is in fact quite easy to generate lots and lots of worries about Fletcher's account. This is because his theory is based on a very crude form of Utilitarianism. Have a look at Chapter 1 where we suggest some problems and simply replace "happiness" with *agápē*. Here is one example.

Utilitarianism is accused of being counter intuitive. If we could only save our dad or five strangers from drowning, the utilitarian would argue we should save the strangers because five lots of happiness is better than one. But is not it admirable and understandable to save a loved one over strangers?

The situationalist will have exactly the same problem. We might imagine that saving five strangers would bring about more "love" than saving your dad. In which case we ought to save the strangers over your dad. But is not it admirable and understandable to save a loved one over strangers?

You can simply repeat this substitution for most of the problems we cited regarding Utilitarianism, e.g. it being "too demanding" and hence generate a whole host of problems for Fletcher.

We leave you with the following quotation from Graham Dunstan writing in the Guardian, regarding Fletcher's book:

> It is possible, though not easy, to forgive Professor Fletcher for writing his book, for he is a generous and lovable man. It is harder to forgive the SCM Press for publishing it.

SUMMARY

Fletcher's Situational Ethics gained a popular following as it allowed the religious believer to fit their views into the rapidly changing and nuanced moral and political landscape of the 1960s. Fletcher's position has a central commitment to God's love — *agápē*. It is this central focus on *agápē* as the moral guide for behaviour that allows Fletcher to claim that an action might be right in one context, but wrong in a different context — depending on the level of *agápē* brought about. In fact, Fletcher thinks that sometimes what might be morally required of us is to break the Ten Commandments.

Despite how popular the theory was it is not philosophically sophisticated, and we soon run into problems in trying to understand it. His position is worth studying though (not just because it is on the curriculum!) because it opens up the conceptual possibility that a committed Christian/Jew/Muslim etc. may consider the answers to moral questions to depend on the diverse situations we find ourselves in.

COMMON STUDENT MISTAKES

- Mixing up Fletcher's use of "Positivism" with Ayer's use of "positivism".
- Thinking that Fletcher's is a "pragmatist".
- Think that situation ethics allows you do to anything you want.
- Think that love is about feelings.
- Think that by "conscience" Fletcher means a "moral compass".

ISSUES TO CONSIDER

1. Why do you think Fletcher's book was so popular at the time of publication?
2. If an alien visited earth and asked "What is love?" how would you answer them?

3. How does Situationism differ from "Utilitarianism" if at all?

4. If we act from love, does that mean we can do anything?

5. What does it mean to say that conscience is a verb rather than a noun? Do you think we have a conscience? If you do, should we think of it as a verb or a noun?

6. Why does Fletcher say that his theory is: "fact-based, empirical-based, data-conscious and inquiring"?

7. What do you think a Christian would make of Fletcher's theory?

8. What do you think "situation" means?

9. What does Fletcher mean by "positivism"?

10. What is the "fallacy of appealing to authority"? Can you give your own example?

11. Pick one challenge to Utilitarianism, and reform the challenge as one towards Situationism.

KEY TERMINOLOGY

Agápē

Agápē calculus

Eros

Legalism

Pragmatic

Conscience

Consequentialism

References

Fletcher, Joseph F., *Situation Ethics: The New Morality* (Louisville and London: Westminster John Knox Press, 1966).

Kirk, Kenneth E., *Conscience and Its Problems: An Introduction to Casuistry* (Louisville: Westminster John Knox Press, 1999).

'Saudi Police "Stopped" Fire Rescue', *BBC News* (15 March 2002), freely available at http://news.bbc.co.uk/1/hi/world/middle_east/1874471.stm

PART II
METAETHICS

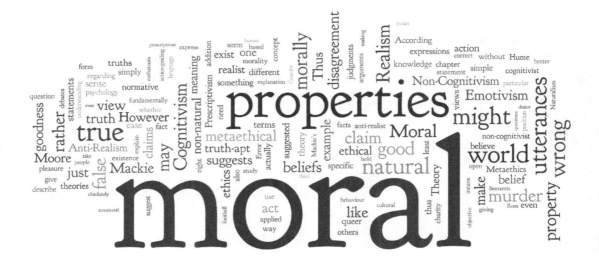

Metaethical Theories

But in every case in which one would commonly be said to be making an ethical judgment, the function of the relevant ethical word is purely 'emotive'. It is used to express feeling about certain objects, but not to make any assertion about them.[1]

WARNING

In purely length terms, this is a longer chapter than any other in this textbook. In addition, it contains lots of key terminology that will be unique to this chapter. Thus, we don't advise that this chapter should be read/considered/ crammed in merely one sitting.

Rather, we suggest that you choose specific sections of the chapter, perhaps informed by your course specifications or our suggested tasks at the end of the chapter, and engage with those sections in any one sitting. In addition, the first "Issue to Consider" at the conclusion of this chapter should be especially useful in guiding your journey through Metaethics. The ideas herein are no more complex, fundamentally, than elsewhere in the book; the breadth should not be daunting if properly managed.

1. Metaethics: Introduction

The prefix "meta" is derived from the Greek for "beyond". Metaethics is therefore a form of study that is beyond the topics considered in normative or applied ethics. Recall as we stated in the introduction, the differences between these forms of ethical study are helpfully captured in an analogy put forward by Fisher (2011) involving different participants in a game of football.

- *Applied Ethics* is the study of how we should act in specific areas of our lives; how we should deal with issues like meat-eating, euthanasia or stealing (to use examples familiar to this textbook). To use the football analogy, the applied ethicist kicks the philosophical football around just as a footballer kicks the ball on the field. A good applied ethicist

---

1 A. J. Ayer, 'A Critique of Ethics', p. 21.

might score goals and be successful by offering specific arguments that convince us to change our moral views in a particular corner of our lives.

- *Normative Ethics* is focussed on the creation of theories that provide general moral rules governing our behaviour, such as Utilitarianism or Kantian Ethics. The normative ethicist, rather than being a football player, is more like a referee who sets up the rules governing how the game is played. Peter Singer, for example, focuses on advancing applied ethical arguments within the normative framework of his Preference Utilitarianism (discussed in Chapter 1).

- *Metaethics* is the study of how we engage in ethics. Thus, the metaethicist has a role more similar to a football commentator rather than to a referee or player. The metaethicist judges and comments on how the ethical game is being played rather than advancing practical arguments, or kicking the football, themselves. For example, the metaethicist might comment on the meaning and appropriateness of ethical language, just as the football commentator might remark on the appropriateness of particular tactics or set-piece routines.

Nobody is perfect, and it is therefore possible that some of you are not avid football fans. To respect this possibility, here is a non-football based explanation of what Metaethics amounts to. Metaethical conclusions do not tell us how we should morally act or which type of decision is morally correct in any one particular circumstance. Instead, Metaethics is focussed on questions regarding how ethical study — at both normative and applied levels — works. Some typical metaethical questions are:

- When we say something is "morally good", what do we *mean*?

- If the claim that "euthanasia is morally wrong" is true, what makes it *true*?

- If moral claims are sometimes true, what methods do we use to access these moral truths?

You should not expect a metaethical argument to provide specific guidance regarding how to act, but you should expect a metaethical argument to critique the foundations of normative or applied action-guiding moral theories.

2. The Value of Metaethics

A former colleague once suggested that Metaethics was entirely and frustratingly pointless — academia for academia's sake, she thought. There are, however, good reasons for thinking that metaethical arguments can be just as worthy and valuable as their normative and applied counterparts.

One such factor in favour of Metaethics is as follows. If ethics is fundamentally concerned with good behaviour or, as per Aristotle (his theory is detailed in Chapter 3), good characters, then it would seem to be desirable to properly understand what exactly "good" amounts to.

Analogously, we would not consider attempting applied mathematics without first understanding what was meant by fundamental concepts like addition or subtraction. Nor would we consider attempting surgery on a person without being sure of the meanings of terms like blood, heart or liver. Understanding goodness — what it is and how we might access it — seems like a fundamental presupposition of successful ethical study, rather than a merely abstract topic of philosophical debate.

3. Cognitivism versus Non-Cognitivism

Key to the successful study of Metaethics is understanding the various key terminological distinctions that make up the "metaethical map". Metaethical theories can be categorised, at least for our purposes, in respect of where they fall in the debates between Cognitivism and Non-Cognitivism, and Realism and Anti-Realism. Thus, it is a prerequisite for understanding and evaluating metaethical theories that you understand these two debates. In this section, we deal with the debate between cognitivists and non-cognitivists.

If you are a Moral Cognitivist (the "moral" prefix is assumed from hereon) then you have a particular view about the *meaning* of moral terms and a particular view about the *psychology* behind moral utterances. The former version of Cognitivism, concerned with meaning, is captured in the discussion of *Semantic Cognitivism* while the latter version of Cognitivism, concerned with psychology, is captured in the discussion of *Psychological Cognitivism*. Cognitivism, as discussed in the remainder of this chapter, is a combination of these two positions.

Semantic Cognitivism

Semantic Cognitivism (*not to be confused with Realism*) suggests that when we make moral claims of the form "murder is wrong" or "helping others is right" our claims can be true or false (what philosophers call *truth-apt*). According to the semantic cognitivist, what makes our moral statements true or false is whether or not they accurately pick out, or refer to, specifically moral aspects of the world. Thus, the semantic cognitivist views our *moral language as essentially descriptive* in nature; we try to describe genuinely moral features of the world and our moral claims are true when our descriptions are accurate and false when they are inaccurate.

This position really is as simple as it sounds, even though it is by no means uncontroversial. Consider a semantic cognitivist about the meaning of statements in a news report. When the reporter says that "the defendant stepped into the courthouse and gave his name and his date of birth", then this statement will be *truth-apt* — it will be the kind of statement that can be described as true or false. Whether it is true or false will be determined by the accuracy of this statement as a description of features of the world; if the statement correctly refers to the features of the world identified then it will be true, if it does not then it will be false. The situation is the same for the semantic moral cognitivist, if the utterance "murder is wrong" really does pick out a moral property of wrongness associated with murder then it will be true, and false otherwise.

Crucially, keep in mind that Semantic Cognitivism only goes as far as suggesting that moral claims are truth-apt — capable of being true or false. Semantic Cognitivism, by itself, does not suggest anything about moral claims ever actually being true. To put it in another way *Cognitivism has nothing to do with what actually exists in the world* (that is Realism versus Anti-Realism — see below). Instead, it is purely a theory explaining the meaning of moral statements.

Psychological Cognitivism

Psychological Cognitivism (not to be confused with Realism) is the view that when we utter a moral statement we give voice to a belief, rather than any other type of non-belief attitude. So, when I utter the statement "Leicester City won the Premier League in 2015–2016", I express my belief that this happened. According to the psychological cognitivist, I also express a belief when I make claims such as "murder is wrong" or "helping others is right".

From here, Semantic and Psychological Cognitivism will be assumed to go together to form the cognitivist position. This is reasonable because it is most natural to think of a truth-apt utterance as being the expression of a belief, for we assume that a belief is the kind of thing that can be true or false and refers to the world. In ethics then, cognitivists claim that moral statements express truth-apt beliefs that are made true or false according to how accurately they describe the world. Moral language and moral psychology, according to the cognitivist, are not especially different to the language and psychology common to many other disciplines such as science, news journalism or non-fiction history books.

You might be wondering what all the fuss is about so far; it is probably fair to say that Cognitivism is the common sense position when it comes to moral language and our associated psychology. Of course, you might think, ethical claims are truth-apt and that we express ethical beliefs, for what else could we be doing when we engage in normative or applied ethics? Richard Joyce (1966–) is of this view when it comes to Cognitivism and our moral utterances, suggesting that "…if something walks and talks like a bunch of [truth-apt, belief-state] assertions it's highly likely that it is a bunch of [truth-apt, belief-state] assertions".[2]

Semantic Non-Cognitivism

Semantic Non-Cognitivism might, given the plausibility of its cognitivist rival, seem to be an undesirable position. According to the semantic non-cognitivist when we utter sentences such as "murder is wrong" we are not attempting to describe any moral features of the world but we are simply expressing an attitude or feeling — perhaps disgust, or anger, in this case. Attitudes are not the types of things that can be true or false because they are not truth-apt; they do not aim at truth and do not attempt to describe or refer to any feature of the world. Consider what happens when you get frustrated with your work, for example, and exclaim "Ahhhhh!" This is an expression of an attitude, it is not something which describes the world and it is not truth apt. The semantic non-cognitivist thus argues that our moral utterances are more like "Ahhhhh!" than they are like "the defendant entered the courthouse"; they are non-descriptive, non-truth-apt expressions.

Psychological Non-Cognitivism

Psychological Non-Cognitivism is a view that is described by (though not defended by) Ralph Wedgwood (1964–). According to Wedgwood, psychological non-cognitivists hold that the psychology behind our non-truth-apt moral expressions is not to be understood as based on "belief", but rather based on "…desires, preferences, emotions, intentions or the like".[3]

Your cry of "Ahhhhh!" in frustration does not express a belief that your work is annoying — even though people might take you to be annoyed — but, most likely, a desire or preference for your work to be over. Such mental states are fairly common and unremarkable; it is just that they are different to belief states.

---

2   R. Joyce, *The Myth of Morality*, p. 14.
3   R. Wedgwood, *The Nature of Normativity*, p. 37.

When discussing Non-Cognitivism from this point, it should be understood as a position combining both the semantic and psychological elements. According to the non-cognitivist our moral utterances are not capable of being true or false and are expressions of attitudes/preferences/desires/emotions etc. rather than expressions of belief. Responding to a moral utterance by saying "true" or "false" would be to fail to properly comprehend the meaning of that moral statement just as it would be a mistake to respond to a cry of "Ahhhhh!" by saying "false". The non-cognitivist thus suggests a fairly radical understanding of our common views regarding what moral utterances mean and how moral discourse works. Later, specific non-cognitivist views will be explained and evaluated and you can judge the desirability of this revision of our normal understanding for yourself.

4. Realism versus Anti-Realism

The second key fork in the road that separates metaethical theories is the choice between Moral Realism and Moral Anti-Realism (as with Cognitivism, the "Moral" prefix is assumed from hereon). As before, understanding these broad positions is crucial to understanding and critiquing the specific metaethical theories outlined later in this chapter.

Realism

Realism is a view about what *exists*. It is the view that moral properties exists independently of human beings and can be located in the world. Just as an action can possess properties such as being "Salika's action", "a violent action", or a "depressing action" so too it might possess the property of being a "morally wrong action". Peter Railton (1950–) describes himself as in favour of a position that might be called "stark, raving Moral Realism" in virtue of believing that mind-independent moral truth exists in the world.[4]

Realism in ethics is somewhat controversial, but Realism in geography is far less controversial and might be a helpful guide to the realist view in ethics. When a geographer speaks of the water in Lake Ontario, the "Geography realist" believes that such water exists and has various properties and qualities (temperature, depth etc.) that exist independently and objectively; the water would have a particular temperature irrespective of any human belief about that temperature. Analogously, *in ethics, realists hold that certain moral properties or facts exist and that they exist objectively and independently of the minds or beliefs of individual people* (or at least, realists relevant for our discussion, such as Railton, believe this). Importantly, realists thus believe in the possibility of

---

4   P. Railton, 'Moral Realism', p. 165.

error — believing that "murder is wrong" does not *make* murder wrong. What would make murder wrong would be the presence of an actual moral property of wrongness (objective and mind-independent) associated with the act of murder.

Anti-Realism

Anti-Realism is simply the denial of Realism. Anti-realists deny the existence of any mind-independent, objective, moral properties. The moral anti-realist is thus akin to the anti-realist about dragons or leprechauns in that they simply deny their existence.

Anti-realists tend to be (though need not be) non-cognitivists, a fact that should not be surprising given that non-cognitivists do not believe that our moral utterances aim of truth. However, the next section paints the metaethical map more specifically in respect of how Cognitivism, Non-Cognitivism, Realism and Anti-Realism might be combined to form specific metaethical theories.

5. The Metaethical Map

The broad explanations of Cognitivism, Non-Cognitivism, Realism and Anti-Realism have been crucial because they allow the following categorisation of specific metaethical views to make sense. You really need to learn what these terms mean if any of the following is going to make sense. Drawing out the metaethical map might be very helpful, to this end.

Example theories which are both cognitivist and realist
>   *Moral Naturalism*
>   *Moral Non-Naturalism (e.g. intuitionist realist accounts)*

Theories both cognitivist and anti-realist
>   *Moral Error Theory*

Theories both non-cognitivist and realist
>   We only know of one person holding this view: Kahane.[5]

Theories both non-cognitivist and anti-realist
>   *Emotivism*
>   *Prescriptivism*

The natural bedfellows between the broad positions outlined are thus Cognitivism and Realism, and Non-Cognitivism and Anti-Realism. If we

---

5   G. Kahane, 'Must Metaethical Realism Make a Semantic Claim?'

aim for truth in our moral utterances, it makes sense to think that there are properties existing that we are trying to refer to and accurately describe.

However, if our moral utterances do not aim for truth then this may neatly sit with the view that no such moral properties exist (otherwise, why would we not try to describe them?).

The outlying theory is Moral Error Theory, which combines the cognitivist view that our moral utterances are expressions of truth-apt beliefs with the view that there are *no* realist objective moral properties in the world. Thus, moral error theorists believe that our moral utterances are always, in every circumstance, false. This is a controversial view and is explored in more depth in sections ten and eleven.

6. Cognitivist and Realist Theory One: Naturalism

Naturalists hold that there are moral properties in the world that make true at least some of our ordinary moral beliefs. Unsurprisingly, naturalists also hold that these moral properties are perfectly natural properties rather than being non-natural. To understand this claim, we need a better grip of what the philosophical and ethical naturalist actually means by the term "natural".

Naturalists in ethics hold that moral properties are as natural as those properties discussed and examined in the sciences, for example. So, the property of being "wet" is a perfectly natural property as is the more complex property of "being magnetic". These properties can be investigated by scientists and are not supernatural or beyond the study of natural sciences.

Gilbert Harman (1938–) suggests that "…we must concentrate on finding the place of value and obligation [morality] in the world of facts as revealed by science".[6] If murder has the property of being morally wrong, then this property is natural if it fits into the world of facts as revealed by science.

Simon Blackburn (1944–) (though not a realist himself) outlines the desirability and purpose of this commitment to Naturalism when he says that: "The problem is one of finding room for ethics, or placing ethics within the *disenchanted*, non-ethical order which we inhabit, and of which we are a part".[7]

Moral Naturalism thus speaks to those who wish to defend Realism and truth in ethics, without resorting to non-natural justifications based on Gods, Platonic Forms and the like. The naturalist seeks to fit moral properties into the non-mystical world of ordinary science.

Utilitarianism is a normative ethical theory that is underpinned by a metaethical Naturalism. Jeremy Bentham and John Stuart Mill, if you recall

---

6   G. Harman, *Explaining Value and Other Essays in Moral Philosophy*, p. 79.
7   S. Blackburn, *Ruling Passions*, p. 49.

from Chapter 1, defined moral goodness in terms of the act (or set of rules) that promoted the greatest amount of pleasure/happiness for the greatest number of people. Utilitarians thus view good as an entirely natural properties for there is nothing mystical, enchanted or supernatural about pleasure; scientists can perfectly well understand pleasure in terms of neural firings or psychological explanations.

In addition, both Philippa Foot and Rosalind Hursthouse have sought to place Virtue Ethics (as discussed in its Aristotelian form in Chapter 3) within a naturalist metaethical framework.

According to Hursthouse, human beings function well if they meet four particular ends — survival, reproduction, enjoyment/freedom from pain, and possession of an appropriate functional role within a group. As rational beings, we can determine the character traits and dispositions that can help us to meet these aims and such character traits and dispositions will then be virtuous. Virtue Ethics, thus defined, would therefore be a normative theory based on Naturalism because what makes something good or virtuous is entirely determined by natural factors to do with our psychology, behaviour, biology and social dynamics. As with Utilitarianism, no mystical or supernatural stuff is required to explain the virtues and associated moral goodness.

Does Naturalism lead to Relativism? Harman claimed that, if correct, Naturalism *would* naturally lead us to Moral Relativism and away from Moral Absolutism (these theories are more specifically discussed in Chapter 1). Harman suggests that if ethical guidelines and rules were absolute in nature then they would need to apply irrespective of contingent situations or contingent lifestyles; murder, for example, would be wrong irrespective of any specific situational factors if the claim that "murder is wrong" were *absolutely* true. However, if moral properties are natural properties, then Relativism may make more sense in virtue of the fact that natural properties can vary in presence from case to case.

For example, it is not *absolutely* true that "London is north of Paris" because at some point continental plates will shift and these cities could move in relative location to each other. Nor is it absolutely true that "sections of the Australian coast have coral reefs", since human activity and climate change might change this natural fact. Equally then, if a natural property is what makes true the claim that "murder is wrong" then this natural property might seem to depend upon the amount of pleasure produced, or else on some other *changeable* natural factor. If moral properties are natural properties, then actions might not be absolutely wrong but might instead be wrong relative to the changeable presence of those natural properties.

Michael Smith (1954–) rejects Harman's claim and suggests that Naturalism is, in and of itself, irrelevant to the debate between moral relativists and moral absolutists. Smith argues that absolutists and relativists will differ on questions regarding the rationality or reasonableness of human behaviour and that these questions cannot be settled by taking a stance on Naturalism or Non-Naturalism in ethics.

For Smith, important questions relevant to the absolutist and relativist debate are *a priori* rather than *a posteriori* — meaning that these debates must be analysed and investigated by methods that do not involve testing the world. Thus, testing the world in order to determine the natural or non-natural status of moral properties cannot settle the *a priori* differences between relativists and absolutists.

7. Objections to Naturalism

G. E. Moore was a supporter of Cognitivism and Realism. However, Moore was not a naturalist — he was a non-naturalist — and objected to the idea that moral properties were natural properties. Moore's objection to identifying moral properties as natural properties was two-fold. Firstly, he thought that moral properties were fundamentally simple and secondly he thought the identification of the moral with the natural failed what he termed the *Open Question Argument*.

Moore's first objection to Naturalism, *from simplicity*, is based on an analogy between moral properties and colour properties. According to Moore, the concept of the colour yellow is a fundamentally simple concept in so far as it cannot be explained in terms of any other concept or property. Consider, as an example of a complex property, the idea of a horse. A horse can be explained to someone who has never come into contact with the animal because the concept of a horse can be reduced to simpler part. As a mammal of a typically brown colour, with certain organs and certain dimensions. In an obvious way, the concept of a horse can be broken down to simpler components.

Moore denies that the same is true for the concept of yellow. Yellow cannot be explained to someone who has not come into visual contact with it, because yellow is a simple concept that cannot be broken down into simpler component parts. Yellow is just yellow, and we can say nothing else about it that will explain it in simpler terms. The same, says Moore, is true for moral properties. According to Moore:

> If I am asked, 'What is good?' my answer is that good is good, and that is the end of the matter. Or if I am asked 'How is good to be defined?' my answer is that it cannot be defined, and that is all I have to say about it.[8]

---

8   G. E. Moore, 'The Open-Question Argument: The Subject Matter of Ethics', p. 35.

On this basis, Moore cannot accept that moral properties can be reduced to natural properties as this would imply that moral properties are not fundamentally simple. The utilitarian, for example, defines goodness in terms of pleasure and so reduces goodness to pleasure. Moore suggests that moral naturalists make a mistake in trying to ground simple moral properties in terms of other natural properties.

As it stands, Moore's analogy between goodness and yellow has some argumentative pull but lacks sufficient robustness. However, Moore's Open Question Argument more formally drives home his point.

Moore suggests that we take some putative moral claim such as "giving to charity is good". For goodness, Moore suggests we follow the naturalist's lead and insert some natural property such as "pleasure". Now, we have the claim that "giving to charity is pleasurable". This identification between goodness and pleasure is the type of identification a naturalist about goodness might have in mind.

However, according to Moore it remains an *open question* as to whether or not something creating pleasure is actually good. The question remains meaningful in a way that it should not remain meaningful if goodness is actually reducible to pleasure. After all, it is not possible to meaningfully ask whether or not a bachelor is an unmarried man as the concept of a bachelor can be reduced to the concept of an unmarried man. Thus, if this utilitarian-style naturalist is correct about the identification of goodness and pleasure, it should not be a meaningful question — an open question — to ask whether a pleasurable act is a morally good act. Yet, it seems to remain open as to whether Action A is good, even if I am told that Action A is pleasurable.

Moore suggests that any attempted reduction of a moral property to a natural property will leave a meaningful open question of the form "this act possesses the natural property suggested" but "is it a good act"? Julia Tanner provides a modern example of the Open Question Argument in action:

> Some people talk as if they think that that which has evolved is the same thing as being good. Thus, for instance, capitalism may be justified on the basis that it is merely an expression of 'the survival of the fittest' and 'the survival of the [fittest]' is good. To make such an argument is, according to Moore, to commit the naturalistic fallacy because good has been defined as something other than itself, as 'the survival of the fittest'.[9]

Tanner refers to the *Naturalistic Fallacy*, which is Moore's own terminology for the mistake of attempting to reduce the moral property to the natural property. All such attempted reductions will fail because it will always be possible to meaningful ask whether the suggested natural property is actually good; if this question is open then goodness does not equal the suggested natural

---

9   J. Tanner, 'The Naturalistic Fallacy', http://www.richmond-philosophy.net/rjp/rjp13_tanner.php

property. Think of the Open Question Argument as the searchlight seeking out those who commit the naturalistic fallacy.

It is worth noting that Moore's arguments, although directed against naturalistic reductions of goodness, are just as powerful against *non-natural* reductions of goodness. Any attempt to reduce the concept of goodness to, for example, "what God wills'" will also fail because the question of "this is what God wills, but is it good?" appears to remain open. Self-evidently, this non-natural reduction is not an example of a naturalistic fallacy, but it can be no more acceptable if, like Moore, you believe that good is a fundamentally simple concept.

8. Cognitivist and Realist Theory Two: Non-Naturalism

Moore's critique of Naturalism sets the scene for his own metaethical view. According to Moore, moral properties do exist but they are fundamentally simple *non-natural* properties. The best way to understand what non-natural means is as follows. If Goodness is non-natural then it is not the kind of property that is discoverable through the kind of *empirical* means that help us to identify natural properties, such as in the sciences. How we might come to know non-natural properties depend on the particular theory under consideration. However, typically non-naturalists think that we *intuit* the presence of these simple non-natural properties via a *moral sense*. So although intuitions are about *how* we discover moral properties rather than what moral properties are like, typically non-naturalists are also intuitionists.

Richard Price (1723–1791) suggested that truths are intuited when they are acquired "without making any use of any process of reasoning".[10] More contemporarily, W. D. Ross (1877–1971) suggested that we intuit self-evident moral truths "without any need of proof, or of evidence beyond itself".[11] An example should make this method of intuiting non-natural moral properties much clearer.

Becky is watching a BBC news report on a woman who has been helped to hear for the first time in her life via the use of new medical technology. Having been so helped, the news report points out that this person has made a documentary which involves her passing on this technology to poor children who are living with deafness in Bangladesh. While watching the report and the associated interview, Becky intuits the fact that the doctors have acted in a morally good way in researching and implementing the cure for this woman's deafness and that she too is acting morally well in helping others to hear. The

---

10 R. Price, 'A Review of the Principle Questions in Morals', p. 159.
11 W. D. Ross, *The Right and the Good*, p. 29.

moral goodness is self-evident in the situation and does not require Becky to use her faculties of reason to identify it; the property of goodness is picked up via her moral sense.

W. D. Ross specifically suggests that there are various self-evident *prima facie* duties that we can intuit (*prima facie* meaning, in this sense, apparent on first glance); duties that should guide our behaviour but that sometimes can be overridden by other competing duties. Ross outlines duties such as not harming others, not lying, and keeping promises. Ross suggests that no formal empirical or logical defence of these duties is appropriate because they are self-evident. We cannot argue *to* the claim we should not lie, only *from* it in terms of how to act in specific situations.

If you are an intuitionist and a realist this might offer a route to surviving both the Open Question Argument and the Naturalistic Fallacy. Intuitionists claim that moral properties are fundamentally simple and non-natural, open to apprehension via our moral sense. When we utter moral sentences we seek to describe the presence of such properties accurately and, sometimes, we will correctly and appropriately refer to the presence of these non-natural properties in the world. When we so appropriately refer, we make true moral statements.

9. Objections to Intuitionism

Intuitionism offers a way around the Open Question Argument and the Naturalistic Fallacy, consequently it has a number of modern proponents (e.g. Ralph Wedgewood). However, objections to a basic Intuitionism are not particularly difficult to conceive of.

Firstly, Intuitionism might be thought to struggle when explaining moral *disagreement*. If moral truths are self-evident and can be intuited, then why do even self-professed intuitionists such as Moore and Ross have radically different ethical views (Moore is a teleologist, whereas Ross intuits proto-Kantian moral truths).

In response, Ross has suggested that we need a certain moral maturity to our intuitive sense, just as our other faculties require maturity and tuning to properly pick up on features of the world. Indeed, Samuel Clarke (1675–1729) suggested that, amongst other things, stupidity may lead to our intuitions going astray and this may explain continuing moral disagreement. If only we were less daft, our intuitive moral sense might be more reliable!

In addition, on a related note, we may wonder how such intuitive moral judgments might be properly verified. If you support the *Verification Principle* — which you may be lucky enough to come across in a unit on Religious Language — then you believe that statements that cannot be empirically verified (tested against the world to determine their truth or falsity) or are true by definition are meaningless.

If moral judgments are intuitively supported judgments about non-natural properties, then it is not clear *how* we could verify whether it is Moore or Ross, to use two examples, who intuits goodness correctly. Certainly, we could not use empirical means to test for the presence of non-natural properties in the world. Thus, verificationists may suggest that moral statements — if Intuitionism is correct — would be meaningless in virtue of our inability to verify such statements.

Finally, returning to the theme of disagreement, we might posit evidence that our intuitions are so unreliable that they are better understood as irrational moral judgments expressing our own feelings or personal beliefs, rather than judgments giving voice to the existence of mind-independent, objective, non-natural moral properties.

Consider responses to the standard ethical dilemma of a trolley case. In one version, you can redirect a train to save five people tied to the track, but doing so will kill one person tied in the path of the redirected train. In a second case, you can save five people tied to the track by pushing one rather portly gentleman to his death in front of the train to stop its progress. Most responders favour saving five over one in the first case, but favour saving one over five in the second case. If our intuitions point so divergently when we make moral judgments, might we be better to assume our pre-rational intuitive responses are expressions of feelings or initial beliefs, rather than a reflection of objective truths?

Perhaps responses based on moral maturity or stupidity will apply here also, but this may be harder to hold when explaining one person's own personal divergent intuitions about such cases rather than disagreement across a group of different people.

J. L. Mackie (1917–1981) also offers criticisms of Intuitionism, but these are explored in the next section as they feed into explanation of Mackie's own Moral Error Theory. It is, as ever, for you to judge whether the intuitionist has any plausible defence of their theory against the criticisms suggested thus far.

10. Cognitivist and Anti-Realist Theory One: Moral Error Theory

Thus far, we have seen that Cognitivism tends to be associated with Realism. Mackie breaks with this trend with his Moral Error Theory. Mackie accepts that our moral utterances are expressions of truth-apt beliefs, but denies Realism. In so doing, Mackie denies that possibility that our truth-apt beliefs are ever true, because a moral description of the world can never accurately describe a world without any moral properties in it.

In Mackie's own words, "Although most people in making moral judgments implicitly claim, among other things, to be pointing to something objectively prescriptive, these claims are all false".[12] By prescriptive, Mackie means action-guiding and Mackie denies that any objective guides to action (moral properties, in our terms) actually exist.

Mackie's view is startling and raises loads of questions about how we should live if morality is entirely false. Although interesting, these discussions are not for this chapter. Instead, we must explain and evaluate Mackie's theory as it stands rather than consider its implications if true. A theory having depressing or liberating implications does not make that theory any more or less likely to be accurate (though it is surprising how often even the best philosophers are prone to such mistaken thinking).

Mackie's Anti-Realism is supported by the following two arguments. It should be made clear that Mackie's arguments are directed against *both Naturalistic and Non-Naturalistic Realism*.

Argument from Relativity

Mackie's first objection to Realism is built out of his appreciation of the depth of moral disagreement, and so shares something with one of the objections to Intuitionism offered in the previous section. Mackie suggests that in other plausible realist disciplines, such as the sciences or history views begin to coalesce around the truth over time and disagreement is, at least in part, conquered.

Disagreement occurs in these disciplines because there is a barrier to true knowledge and scientists and historians will sometimes, through no fault of their own, be blind to the facts. However, sometimes the facts become clear and disagreement thereby reduces.

Yet, in ethics, philosophers still disagree over the same issues that they were arguing over 2000+ years ago, questions such as "when is war acceptable" and "when can promises be broken". If moral truths really did exist and Realism was correct, should we not have expected to find some of these truths by now? Thus, Mackie views disagreement in ethics — deep disagreement that seems impervious to solution through rational means — as evidence that Realism is incorrect; there are no moral facts to settle the debates or at least some of those debates would have been settled by now! Of course, if you think that some moral debates have been settled, then you could use this to criticise this Mackian argument.

---

12   J. L. Mackie, *Ethics: Inventing Right and Wrong*, p. 35.

Argument Queerness

Mackie's second anti-realist argument is his most famous. Moral properties — be they natural or non-natural — are supposed to be *action-guiding*. If it is true that murder is wrong, then we should not murder, *even if we might want* to. Equally, if it is true that giving to charity is right, then we should give to charity, *even if we might not want to* At its core, morality is supposed to offer reasons for action that we cannot simply ignore even if we like murdering or hate charitable giving. This aspect of morality, however, raises issues at the metaethical level.

David Hume (1711–1776) recognised the potential problem with the action-guiding quality of morality when he spoke of the "is-ought" gap. According to Hume:

> *In every system of morality, which I have hitherto met, I have always* [remarked], *that the author proceeds for some time in the ordinary ways of reasoning, and establishes the being of a God, or makes observations concerning human affairs; when all of a sudden I am* [surprised] *to find, that instead of the usual copulations of propositions, is, and is not, I meet with no proposition that is not connected with an* ought, *or an* ought not. *This change is imperceptible, but is however, of the last consequence.*[13]

Hume wonders why and how we move from statements about what *is* the case, to statements about how we *ought* to act. We do not make such a link between "is" and "ought" in areas other than morality — the fact that a horse is running at Goodwood does not, of itself, give you an "ought" regarding how to act in response. The fact that a moral property *is*, on the other hand, does seem to give rise to such an "ought" regarding behaviour. How can this be explained?

Hume has his own suggestion for explanation, and this is outlined in section twelve. Mackie, however, takes this Humean worry in his own direction. Mackie suggests that *properties themselves* that carry such an action-guiding quality, that offer an "ought" just because they are, would be extremely *queer* properties. He says that "[if] there were objective values [moral properties], then they would be entities or qualities or relations of a very strange sort, utterly different from anything else in the universe".[14]

Mackie suggests that if we can explain moral thinking without resorting to positing the existence of such queer and utterly unique entities then we would be better off. The simpler explanation is not to grant existence to weird properties, but just to suggest that there are no properties and that our moral beliefs reflect cultural and personal beliefs. Just as we do not tend to suggest that aliens or ghosts exist on the basis of first-hand testimony (competing explanations based on drunkenness or tiredness, for example, seem more

---

13   D. Hume, *A Treatise on Human Nature*, http://www.davidhume.org/texts/thn.html
14   J. L. Mackie, *Ethics*, p. 38.

plausible) so we perhaps ought not to grant that moral properties exist just because we happen to talk about them.

Indeed, support for Anti-Realism through a complaint about the queerness of moral properties is further supported via consideration of *Hume's fork*.

Hume divided knowledge into two camps — knowledge gained from *relations of ideas* and knowledge gained from *matters of fact*. Knowledge claims like "2+2=4", or various geometric claims like "triangles have three sides", are established in the former way whereas knowledge claims like "Alastair is wearing a blue shirt today" are established in the latter way.

This split of types of knowledge is referred to as Hume's fork, yet claims to moral knowledge do not seem to fit either side of the fork. Moral knowledge is not derivable simply from relations of ideas (it is not supposed to be like geometric or mathematical truth and cannot be deduced *a priori* without any testing the world through our senses).

Nor, however, is it derivable simply from matters of fact, given the "is-ought" gap referred to above (*a posteriori*, sense-based, worldly and scientific empirical observations reveal what is, not what ought to be). If moral knowledge does not fit into either side of Hume's fork, then it will be the case that either moral knowledge is a completely unique type of knowledge accessed in a completely unique way or, more plausibly perhaps, moral knowledge does not actually exist. But if we cannot know that moral properties exist then we should not be realists.

Hume, certainly, would have rejected the idea that moral properties existed based on the application of his famous fork. Remember, however, that Hume favoured *Non-Cognitivism* and Anti-Realism rather than (like Mackie) Cognitivism and Anti-Realism.

On a similar theme, Mackie strengthens the argument from queerness by referring to the queer method of understanding that we would need in order to come into contact with queer moral properties. Mackie suggests that we would need a special moral faculty in order to access queer moral properties. Although Mackie admires the honesty of the intuitionist in admitting the existence of such a queer moral sense, he does not think that it is credible to believe in the existence of such a radically different faculty for accessing realist moral properties in the world.

As before, if we can explain our moral beliefs without needing to admit the existence of queer properties, then why admit to the existence of a queer method for grasping queer properties? Moral Realism, according to Mackie, thus requires an unnecessarily queer metaphysics (what exists) and an unnecessarily queer epistemology (how we know what exists). For these reasons, Mackie is an anti-realist.

11. Objections to Moral Error Theory

Realists have various responses to Mackie. Firstly, realists might just agree and accept the conclusion that moral properties would be queer in virtue of bridging the "is-ought" gap; they may simply deny that such queerness is a problem. Indeed, intuitionists may be very happy to accept the uniqueness of moral properties in virtue of their fundamental simplicity and their irreducibility to other properties. Naturalists, meanwhile, may simply wonder why something being different to other things should be seen as a problem; is it not the case that everything is different to everything else, in at least some sense? In addition, Mackie's views regarding the importance and depth of moral disagreement can be criticised.

A. J. Ayer (1910–1989), for example, felt that moral disagreements existed only where there were disagreements over the non-moral facts. On this view, Max and Ethan disagree over the morality of meat-eating only because they disagree over the *non-moral fact* of how much pain is endured by animals sent for slaughter. If all the non-moral facts were clear, then their disagreement would no longer persist. Thus, Ayer would have felt that moral disagreement is not as deep and pervasive as Mackie suggests.

A different response to moral disagreement is to defend the idea of moral progress. It may be tempting to argue that moral disagreement has actually reduced over time because we have come into contact with truths regarding the badness of slavery, sexism and racism etc. Moral Error Theory denies the possibility of moral progress in virtue of denying any moral truth; progress requires correct answers. If you believe that progress has been made in ethics, perhaps in the form of human rights being identified, then you have a reason to disagree with Moral Error Theory.

Moral Error Theory is also highly counterintuitive. It says that all of your moral beliefs are false and that they could *never* be true because no moral truth making properties exist in the world. It suggests that murder is not morally wrong (but it is not morally right either!) and that giving to charity is not morally right (but it is not morally wrong either!). Given there is no truth to be found in ethics, it might be thought that we should abandon our faulty moral language entirely — a rather extreme metaethical conclusion!

However, if you *do* accept Cognitivism as an accurate explanation of moral language and psychology, but find it hard to grant that objective, mind-independent moral facts or properties actually exist in the world, then Moral may be worth these seeming costs.

12. Non-Cognitivism

Prior to an explanation and evaluation of the specific theoretical options for the non-cognitivist, it is worthwhile just providing a few words in favour of Non-Cognitivism more generally.

If you are impressed by anti-realist arguments but do not wish to end up an error theorist, then it may be worth denying Cognitivism rather than following Mackie. Indeed, this is what the majority of anti-realists tend to do. Thus, non-cognitivists will be unconcerned by the lack of moral properties in the world because they deny that our moral utterances are attempts to pick such properties out.

As well as supporting Anti-Realism, Hume's identification of the "is-ought" gap might be taken as helpful evidence for Non-Cognitivism. If moral utterances carry with them an action-guiding force, this may be because moral utterances are not descriptive beliefs but are instead expressions of attitudes, feelings or emotions. This picture is certainly what Hume had in mind given his *Humean Theory of Motivation*. Hume claimed that beliefs alone cannot motivate behaviour because beliefs are motivationally inert. The function of a belief as a psychological state is to offer a motivationally neutral description of the world; beliefs say what we believe "is" and do not *by themselves* lead to us to action. To be motivated to actually act, according to Hume, a belief must be *coupled with a desire* in our heads. The following case should make Hume's claim clearer.

Liz *believes* that her friends will soon be arriving for a barbecue. However, Liz lacks any desire to cater for her friends and so does not act. Liz's belief, by itself, does not and cannot motivate action on her part. Now, if we change the situation and add to Liz's psychology a *desire* to feed and cater for her friends, then Liz would come to be motivated to act and prepare a delightfully sumptuous feast. Thus, Hume argues, desires are required in the explanation of our actions.

So why is this relevant to a defence of Non-Cognitivism? Well, when a person utters a moral phrase, if the phrase is sincerely uttered, then they'll be motivated. For example, if I utter the words "giving to charity, for those who can afford to do so, is morally required", then you would expect me to be motivated to give charity if I were able to do so; if I chose not to give to charity in that circumstance you might question the sincerity of my moral utterance.

Moral utterances, and relevant moral motivations, seem to be remarkably well tied to each other. Now, if moral utterances were expressions of moral *beliefs* we would need to, in addition to the moral belief, grant the existence of a continuous desire to do what we believe is moral. However, if moral utterances were themselves moral desires then we need not add the extra belief into our psychology. If the phrase "giving to charity is morally right" is simply an expression of my desire that everyone should give to charity, then it is exceedingly simple to explain why our moral utterances and our motivations tend to track each other so well — our moral utterances are just expressions of our moral desires! But the claim that our moral judgements are simply an expression of our desires just is Non-Cognitivism.

13. Non-Cognitivist and Anti-Realist Theory One: Emotivism

A. J. Ayer and C. L. Stevenson (1908–1979) were defenders of Emotivism, a metaethical view that held considerable sway for a time in the early parts of the twentieth century. According to Emotivism, the moral statement that murder is wrong is simply an expression of emotion against the act of murdering. It gives formal linguistic voice to what is essentially a negative "boo" to murder. Indeed, Emotivism is referred to as the "boo/hurrah" metaethical theory; when we claim that something is morally wrong we boo that action and when we claim that something is morally right we hurrah that action. This explains the connection between morality and motivation; we express motivationally-relevant emotional distaste or emotional approval when we use moral words rather than expressing motivationally inert moral beliefs.

Although a verificationist about language himself, Ayer *did not* wish to deny that moral utterances had a meaning even though, as a non-cognitivist and anti-realist, he plainly could not suggest that moral utterances were empirically verifiable or open to real-world testing in order to determine their truth value (moral utterances, on this view, are not truth-apt beliefs attempting to describe the world). Thus, Ayer suggested that moral utterances had an *emotive meaning*. Ayer, speaking of the claim that "stealing money is wrong" says this is simply an act of "…evincing my moral disapproval of it. It is as if I had said, 'You stole that money' in a peculiar tone of horror, or written it with the addition of some special exclamation marks".[15] Thus, the moral judgment meaningfully reveals an emotion, even if not a description of the world. Emotivism does *not*, therefore, straightforwardly lead to *nihilism* as some meaning for moral values and moral judgments is preserved. On this basis, there is no pull to the idea that we should stop using moral language.

Stevenson, in addition, suggested of moral terms like "right", "wrong", "good" and "bad" that they have only emotive meanings in the sense of approval and disapproval. Therefore, just as we cannot say that a "boo" is false, for it is not truth-apt so too we cannot say that a linguistic boo of the

---

15   A. J. Ayer, 'The Emotive Theory of Ethics', p. 106.

form "stealing is wrong" is either true or false. Stevenson thus argued that Emotivism captured the "magnetism" of morality — our moral utterances track our motivations because our moral utterances are expressions of the emotions that underpin our motivations.

14. Objections to Emotivism

Despite early popularity, Emotivism is not a popular position today and it is widely considered to be an unduly and unhelpfully simplistic form of Non-Cognitivism. We consider three objections here.

Firstly, on a psychological level, Emotivism is unlikely to feel correct. When I suggest that a certain action is right or wrong, I take myself to be making a claim that is true and making a claim that reflects how I take the world to be (reflecting a moral belief in my head). I do not consider myself to be booing an action in a rather academic and indirect way. We might question whether abstract philosophising about the meaning of words should ever trump our own psychological reflections when it comes to what we mean when we utter moral sentences. Can it be the case that Ayer or Stevenson knew better than I what I meant when I said that "terrorism is morally wrong"? Can they know better than you, if you take yourself to be making truth-apt and descriptive moral judgments?

Secondly, some of our moral utterances do not seem to be in the least part emotional. For example, Charlotte may feel that "it is wrong to avoid paying tax" but be quite depressed about this judgment. If we were cognitivists, this emotional divorce could be easily explained; Charlotte believes there to be a moral fact that is independent of her mind and her desires and this fact depresses her. However, it is not immediately obvious how Emotivism might explain Charlotte's "boo to avoiding tax" when she harbours a desire to avoid tax herself. Perhaps we can have second-order emotions *about our emotions* (Charlotte is sad that she feels negatively towards tax avoiding), or perhaps Charlotte feels that others should not avoid tax — boo them — while she is happy act in this way — hurrah for her own tax avoidance. However, both of these responses require careful statement and defence if you seek to pursue them.

Finally, we can return to moral disagreement. Consider a sincere moral disagreement between William and Wendy over the issue of euthanasia. Wendy says that euthanasia is morally right in at least some cases, whilst William says that euthanasia is morally wrong in all circumstances. William and Wendy may seem to be disagreeing via utilising logic and reason just as scientists, or economists, or computer technicians, disagree over a substantively correct answer that is independent of their own minds.

However, once the facts of matter are agreed upon the emotivist must reduce this disagreement to a series of emotional boo's and hurrah's regarding euthanasia, where truth is never the aim of the moral utterances. Suggesting that moral debates are always emotive rather than factual, and so are swayed only by emotional rather than rational means, is a controversial claim given that moral reasons seem to be deployed very carefully in just such debates. Indeed, the emotivist explanation of moral debate seems to suggest moral arguments have more in common with arguments over which ice-cream flavour is best (boo for chocolate, hurrah for vanilla) than with truth-based disagreements in other academic disciplines. If this is not how we believe moral debates should be described, then Emotivism has a problem. As Richard Brandt suggests "Ethical statements do not look like the kind of thing the emotive theory says they are".[16] Brandt, as per the above discussion, feels that moral utterances are things we take to be truth-apt, contra the emotivist interpretation of those moral utterances.

The previous objection to Emotivism may *seem to* highlight possible links between Emotivism and moral relativism. But do not be deceived. Recall from Chapter 1 that relativists, as opposed to absolutists, hold that no moral claim is ever absolutely true in all circumstances. As a specific type of relativist, the cultural relativist may suggest that the claim "murder is wrong" can be true in some cultural settings and false in others depending on the different cultural standards for behaviour. Thus, there may be some suggestion that Cultural Relativism and Emotivism have the same set of grounding beliefs — no absolute moral truths exist and moral expressions reflect the culturally backed emotions of particular speakers, rather than anything more absolutely and mind-independently true.

However, this is a mistake. Contra Emotivism, cultural relativists do tend to believe in a form of realist moral truth, even if such relativists do not hold that absolute moral truths exist. Whilst the cultural relativist may admit that ethical judgments often reflect personal and culturally supported emotions, they define goodness as a genuine property that is determined or fixed in nature by the cultural standards of a given society.

Thus, if "murder is wrong" is a true relative to my culture, *then it is still true*. I am, therefore, mistaken if I claim that "murder is acceptable", at least within the boundaries of my society even if not in the societies of others. This truth is non-absolute and relative to culture, but the cultural relativist accepts that it exists and that our moral statements attempt to describe such truths. On the other hand, the emotivist, obviously, does not accept that our moral statements are such attempted descriptions of realist, albeit relativistic, moral truths.

---

16   R. Brandt, *Ethical Theory: The Problems of Normative and Critical Ethics*, p. 226.

15. Non-Cognitivist and Anti-Realist Theory Two: Prescriptivism

R. M. Hare was a committed non-cognitivist and anti-realist but he was not a defender of a simple emotivist position. Instead, Hare was a metaethical *prescriptivist.*

As a prescriptivist, Hare felt that our moral utterances express more than just emotional approval and disapproval. Instead, our moral utterances express a subjective prescription for others to act in accordance with our moral judgments. So, for example, if William claimed that "euthanasia is morally wrong" then this utterance means that William wants others to cease supporting or deciding in favour of euthanasia. Prescriptivism thus attempts to capture the action-guiding nature of moral utterances without resorting to claims of moral truth.

Prescriptivism also seems to better account for moral disagreement than does Emotivism, because Prescriptivism suggests that the action-guiding normative edge of moral utterances is fundamentally built into the meaning of a moral statement. In addition, perhaps crucially, Prescriptivism also allows us to legitimately criticise another person for their moral views without needing to invoke claims of realist moral truth or realist moral falsehood. Consider the following example.

Cristina claims that "murder is universally and absolutely morally wrong". According to the prescriptivist, this is not a descriptive belief but is a reflection of Cristina's non-cognitive attitude that no one should ever murder. However, if Cristina later utters the words "murdering this terrible dictator is morally acceptable", then we can criticise Cristina's inconsistency. On the one hand, she wants no one to ever murder whilst on the other hand also wanting the murder of a terrible dictator. It is not that Cristina had made a false moral claim that justifies criticism of her, according to the prescriptivist, but it is her *inconsistency* in the actions she prescribes for others that justifies criticism. Thus, we cannot cry "false!" against Cristina, but we can cry "inconsistent". This, at least, may give some genuine meaning back to moral disagreement and provide a method for legitimately and rationally criticising the moral claims of others. Prescriptivism is, on this basis, often viewed as a step-up on Emotivism when it comes to non-cognitivist and anti-realist metaethical theories.

16. Objections to Prescriptivism

Many of the challenges to Prescriptivism carry over from the challenges suggested regarding Emotivism. The prescriptivist must also explain why they know better the meaning of our moral statements than we do, at least if we take ourselves to be making truth-apt and descriptive claims about moral properties in the world.

In addition, we might accept that Prescriptivism captures the qualities of moral disagreement better than Emotivism, but deny that the picture of moral disagreement offered by the prescriptivist is good enough. After all, is inconsistency the most serious objection we can make to someone with whom we disagree morally? Prescriptivism does not allow us to suggest that a racist who believes "it is morally acceptable to kill those of a different racial background" utters something false. Indeed, so long as the racist holds morally consistent views then we have no grounds to criticise his position at all. If we feel that retaining the ability to cry "false!" — with proper, rational and realist justification — is important when confronting the moral views of racists, sexists and other morally deplorable individuals, then Prescriptivism does not offer the tools that we need. Of course, the prescriptivist may reply that we cannot claim that Realism is correct just because we wish it to be so and that Prescriptivism, like it or not, is actually the proper understanding of the meaning of our moral judgments. Again, this is a judgment you should make for yourself.

SUMMARY

There is much more that could be said in this chapter. Metaethical theories are as varied and nuanced as their normative rivals, and it is impossible to give a fair hearing to all of them in a single chapter. Catherine Wilson has authored an enquiry into Metaethics that reflects the challenge of coming to your own, first-person, view on these issues.[17] However, we have tried as far as possible on this whistle-stop tour to outline these theories clearly and to give them such a fair hearing. It is for you to decide where you sit in the debate between Cognitivism and Non-Cognitivism, Realism and Anti-Realism, and, more generally, to decide how much importance Metaethics has relative to the normative and applied camps of ethical study.

17   C. Wilson, *Metaethics from a First Person Standpoint*, https://www.openbookpublishers.com/reader/417

COMMON STUDENT MISTAKES

- Not breaking down the chapter so as to be firmly in grasp of the meanings of key terms, and then the nature of the theories, before trying to engage in evaluation.

- Confusing Cognitivism, Non-Cognitivism, Realism and Anti-Realism.

- Misunderstanding the queerness complaint.

- Forgetting the importance of asking a meaningful question when explaining the mechanism of the Open Question Argument.

- Not using analogies appropriately — think of other realist/naturalist/cognitivist/non-cognitivist disciplines and examples, then compare these to ethics.

- Ignoring the explanations of disagreement offered by intuitionists.

- Not linking criticisms of one position to support for another position; e.g. Moore's attack on Naturalism explains his intuitionist views and Mackie's attack on Realism justifies his anti-realist position.

- Not using examples to aid explanation because not directly dealing with obviously normative or applied issues.

ISSUES TO CONSIDER

1. Can you create your own Metaethical Map? Try drawing out a flow-chart style diagram that separates Cognitivism and Non-Cognitivism, followed by the associated theories. If feeling confident, then try to add weaknesses and strengths to your map. *We recommend this as an excellent study aide!*[18]

2. Does Emotivism lend support to Relativism?

3. Does Naturalism lend support to Absolutism?

4. Does something being queer (in Mackie's sense of the term) make it less likely that it exists?

5. Does moral disagreement lend support to Anti-Realism?

6. Can a philosopher ever know what you mean better than you know?

---

18 For an *excellent* Metaethical map see A. Miller, *An Introduction to Contemporary Metaethics*, p. 8.

7. Is Metaethics as important as normative or applied ethics?

8. Are moral judgments meaningless if they are about non-natural properties? If they are non-cognitive?

9. Do we just know what is right or wrong based on common sense? Does this support Intuitionism?

10. Can you give another example of an Open Question Argument, with a different candidate natural moral property?

11. Is there such a thing as moral progress? What does this suggest in terms of Metaethics?

12. Can a non-cognitivist properly explain moral disagreement?

13. What is the Humean account of motivation? Why does it support Non-Cognitivism?

KEY TERMINOLOGY

A priori	Prescriptivism
A posteriori	*Prima facie*
Anti-Realism	Queer
Cognitivism	Realism
Empirical	Relativism
Naturalistic Fallacy	Semantic
Non-Cognitivism	Truth-apt
Normative	Verificationism

References

Ayer, A. J., 'A Critique of Ethics', in *Ethical Theory*, ed. by Russ Shafer-Landau (Oxford: Blackwell, 2007).

—, 'The Emotive Theory of Ethics', in *Ethics: Essential Readings in Moral Theory*, ed. by George Sher (London: Routledge, 2012), pp. 103–10.

Blackburn, Simon, *Ruling Passions* (Oxford: Oxford University Press, 1998).

Brandt, Richard, *Ethical Theory: The Problems of Normative and Critical Ethics* (Englewood Cliffs: Prentice Hall, 1959).

Fisher, Andrew, *Metaethics: An Introduction* (Oxford: Routledge, 2011), https://doi.org/10.1017/upo9781844652594

Harman, Gilbert, *Explaining Value and Other Essays in Moral Philosophy* (Oxford: Clarendon Press, 2000).

Hume, David, *A Treatise on Human Nature* (London: John Noon, 1739), freely available at http://www.davidhume.org/texts/thn.html

Joyce, Richard, *The Myth of Morality* (Cambridge: Cambridge University Press, 2001), https://doi.org/10.1017/cbo9780511487101

Kahane, G., 'Must Metaethical Realism Make a Semantic Claim?', *Journal of Moral Philosophy*, 10.2 (2013): 148–78, https://doi.org/10.1163/174552412x628869

Mackie, J. L., *Ethics: Inventing Right and Wrong* (New York: Penguin, 1977).

Miller, A., *An Introduction to Contemporary Metaethics* (Cambridge: Polity, 2003).

Moore, G. E., 'The Open-Question Argument: The Subject Matter of Ethics', in *Arguing About Metaethics*, ed. by Andrew Fisher and Simon Kirchin (London: Routledge, 2006), pp. 31–47.

Price, Richard, 'A Review of the Principle Questions in Morals', in *The British Moralists 1650–1800*, ed. by D. D. Raphael (Oxford: Clarendon Press, 1969), pp. 131–98.

Railton, Peter, 'Moral Realism', *The Philosophical Review*, 95.2 (1986): 163–207, https://doi.org/10.2307/2185589

Ross, W. D., *The Right and the Good* (Oxford: Oxford University Press, 1930), https://doi.org/10.1093/0199252653.001.0001

Tanner, Julia, 'The Naturalistic Fallacy', *The Richmond Journal of Philosophy*, 13 (2006), freely available at http://www.richmond-philosophy.net/rjp/rjp13_tanner.php

Wedgwood, Ralph, *The Nature of Normativity* (Oxford: Oxford University Press, 2007), https://doi.org/10.1093/acprof:oso/9780199251315.001.0001

Wilson, Catherine, *Metaethics from a First Person Standpoint* (Cambridge: Open Book Publishers, 2016), https://doi.org/10.11647/OBP.0087; freely available at https://www.openbookpublishers.com/reader/417

PART III
APPLIED ETHICS

CHAPTER 7

Euthanasia

His enemies put it bluntly. Singer says it's OK to kill disabled babies. Singer says seriously damaged human beings are on a par with apes. Singer says it would have been OK to kill his own mother. These charges are spat out of the sides of their mouths. One theologian I spoke to said contemptuously, 'Peter Singer takes the most basic human instincts and tries to reason them out of existence. What does he expect us to do, hug him?'[1]

1. Euthanasia Introduction

There is an old adage that only two things in life are certain — death and taxes. While the morality of the latter would be an interesting topic itself (and you may look to issues discussed in Chapter 8 for some inspiration), it is the morality of an issue connected to the former that draws the focus of this chapter. Specifically, we consider the ethical issues surrounding euthanasia (sometimes labelled as "mercy killing").

2. Key Terms

The etymology of euthanasia helps to reveal the meaning of the term. Like most upstanding and respectable philosophical terms, euthanasia has its roots in Ancient Greek language; it is based on a combination of the terms *eu* meaning "well" and *thanatos* meaning "death". Euthanasia is thus the act of seeking to provide a good death for a person who otherwise might be faced with a much more unpleasant death — hence the term "mercy killing".

There are different ways to categorise the various types of euthanasia and it is critical to be confident and familiar with these categorisations.

Voluntary Euthanasia

Voluntary euthanasia occurs when a person makes their own choice to have their life terminated in order to avoid future suffering.

1   J. Hari, 'Peter Singer: Some People are More Equal than Others', http://www.independent.co.uk/news/people/profiles/peter-singer-some-people-are-more-equal-than-others-551696.html

124

APPLIED ETHICS

Non-Voluntary Euthanasia

Non-voluntary euthanasia occurs when a decision regarding premature and merciful death is made by another person, because the individual to be euthanised is unable to make a decision for themselves. This form of euthanasia is most commonly associated with young infants or patients in a coma who cannot, due to the nature of their age or condition, make any decision for themselves.

The above offers a differentiation of types of euthanasia in terms of the person making the decision. In addition, we can differentiate between types of euthanasia based on the *method* involved in ending a life.

Active Euthanasia

If a person is actively euthanised it means that their death was caused by external intervention rather than natural causes, most likely through a lethal injection or the voluntary swallowing of a deadly cocktail of drugs.

Passive Euthanasia

Passive euthanasia occurs when a person is allowed to die due to the deliberate withdrawal of treatment that might keep them alive. Thus, a person who is passively euthanised is allowed to die via natural causes even though methods to keep them alive might be available. A person who has a life-support machine switched off, for example, dies via natural causes but only as a result of a decision to allow natural causes to take effect.

Although euthanasia that is both voluntary and passive is not particularly common, euthanasia could come in any combination of methods and decision-makers as laid out. Legality of the forms of euthanasia varies from nation to nation; Belgium allows for voluntary and active euthanasia, the UK does not.

In the next two sections, we outline two different forms of medical afflictions that will ground discussion of arguments in favour and against the varying forms of euthanasia. As an applied ethical issue, it is important to make ethical claims in the light of practical and real-world factors.

3. Case One: Persistent Vegetative State

A person is in a Persistent Vegetative State (hereafter PVS) when they are biologically able to support their own continued existence, but they have no meaningful psychological interaction with the world around them. A patient in a PVS, according to the National Health Service in the United Kingdom, can neither follow an object with their eyes nor respond to the sounds of voices and will show no discernible sign of emotion. The vegetative state is defined as persistent when the condition is in place for up to a year and doctors view no prospect of recovery as plausible. The PVS label may seem crude or upsetting, but the message about the difference between the physical and the psychological state of the patient is stark.

In the US, Terri Schiavo fell into a PVS when she suffered oxygen deprivation to her brain as a result of a heart attack. Although she survived the heart-attack, her husband ultimately came to the view that her continued existence was not desirable and that she would be better off being allowed to die.

In the United Kingdom, the parents of Tony Bland — a victim of the Hillsborough football disaster in 1989 — made a similar decision regarding the life of their son after he fell into a PVS. Tony Bland's parents campaigned for their son to be allowed to "die with dignity" rather than continue existing in his emaciated state. One can only attempt to imagine the emotional turmoil for the relatives in such cases and it is worth mentioning that Terri Schiavo's parents ultimately fought a legal battle against their son-in-law in attempt to ensure that Terri was not allowed to die.

When considering the morality of euthanasia for patients in a PVS, it is clear that we should be considering only non-voluntary euthanasia, due to the fact that such patients are clearly unable to make any kind of voluntary decision regarding their future interests. For the sake of simplicity, we will assume there are no relevant letter of intent from such patients, written in case they should lose their faculties, describing their desires should they fall into such a condition. However, you may find it rewarding to consider the moral implications of such a letter. Would the letter provide a voluntary decision that morally ought to be respected even when the patient is in a PVS?

4. Case Two: Incurable and Terminal Illness

Imagine a patient who has been diagnosed with an incurable disease that will ultimately bring about their death. As the condition progresses over time, the patient knows that their ability to live a normal life will decrease and that their physical suffering will increase. You can imagine for yourselves the range of diseases and conditions that may have such unfortunate effects upon a person.

Unlike the patient in a PVS, the patient in this example retains the ability to ask for euthanasia themselves and so these cases can highlight moral issues surrounding voluntary euthanasia. Again, for simplicity in our discussion, we do not consider where the line can be drawn regarding patients in fit or unfit psychological states when it comes to an ability to make a voluntary decision to be euthanised, although this is also an issue that would reward further moral thought.

5. Pro-Euthanasia: Argument One

In this section, we consider the first of the arguments in favour of the moral acceptability of euthanasia. This argument is a general argument and would apply to both non-voluntary and voluntary forms of euthanasia. However, the argument, if sound, would also seem to suggest that active euthanasia is more morally acceptable than passive euthanasia for reasons discussed at the end of this section.

This initial argument can be labelled as the *argument from quality of life*. According to this relatively simple idea, sometimes life is actually less preferable than death. On such occasions, when quality of life is so dreadful that a person would be "better off" dead, then euthanasia would be morally justifiable. Evidently, much turns on what counts as a worthwhile life. Recalling the section on well-being from Chapter 1, there are various philosophical positions that might seek to provide a criterion to measure the quality of a person's life. A hedonist, for example, would suggest that the quality of a life depends on how much happiness/pleasure a person experiences; a supporter of a desire-satisfaction theory would suggest the quality of a life depends on how many of a person's desires are satisfied; an objective-list theorist would suggest that the quality of a life depends on how many objectively valuable goods a person possesses — goods including, but not limited to, knowledge and love, for example.

Whichever one of these views a person supports, or even if they understand other factors as being determinants of the quality of a life, there can little doubt that a person in a PVS has, at best, a non-existent quality of life in virtue of their extreme psychological limitations. Suggesting that some form of consciousness is necessary to having any kind of quality of life, **Jonathan Glover** (1941–) says:

> I have no way of refuting someone who holds that being alive, even though unconscious, is intrinsically valuable [valuable irrespective of the form of being alive]. But it is a view that will seem unattractive to those of us who, in our own case, see a life of permanent coma as in no way preferable to death. From the subjective point of view, there is nothing to choose between the two.[2]

Deprived of happiness and other capabilities, the life of a patient in a PVS seems to be at best utterly neutral and at worst negative in respect of quality of life, perhaps depending on any experience of physical pain. Patients in a PVS are not merely bed-ridden like some who might have suffered severe strokes or other such afflictions; they are biological entities lacking the distinguishing psychological qualities of typical human beings. This may go some way to

---

2   J. Glover, *Causing Death and Saving Lives*, p. 45.

explain why some (but by no means all) partners and parents of people in PVS's are willing to favour an end to the patient's life.

The case of Diane Pretty is informative when considering the quality of life of a person with a terminal illness who is nearing the end of their life. Diane Pretty suffered from motor-neurone disease and although she remained mentally proficient, the worsening of her condition over time led her to request to be allowed to die quickly and without undue suffering. Although the point in time cannot be sharply labelled, it seems extremely plausible that many of those with worsening terminal illnesses will reach a point in time where their quality of life is non-existent or negative in virtue of their physical suffering and their inability to enjoy life, satisfy desires or acquire objectively valuable goods. I recall, as a young teenager, listening to Diane Pretty express her desire to be allowed to die and wondering how anyone could reach a point where they would not want to see one more sunrise or live one more day — these questions, I suggest, reflected more of my inability to empathise with her daily existence than they did with undue depression on her part.

Thus, if we focus on the quality of life for patients in a PVS, or for those nearing the final stages of a terminal illness, we may well grant that there is a time when quality of life either becomes negative or ceases to be relevant. If we suggest that a life with no discernible quality of life is not worthwhile, then euthanasia may appear morally justifiable.

If you find the argument from quality of life convincing, then you may judge that active euthanasia is far more morally defensible than passive euthanasia; after all the judgment that euthanasia is morally acceptable may seem to be the load-bearing judgment, with the choice of method more of a practical than a moral issue. Indeed, in this context, passive euthanasia might seem to be the *worst* of all worlds.

According to Peter Singer, "Having chosen death [as a morally acceptable course of action] we should ensure that it comes in the best possible way".[3] The best possible way, if we remain interested in quality of life, might seem to be a lethal injection designed to send a patient painlessly to sleep before shutting down their organs, or a selection of drinkable liquids that have the same effect. The best possible way might not seem to involve turning off a life support machine or withdrawing proactive treatment in order to allow nature to take its course, when the course of nature may be directed by starvation, dehydration or secondary infections. Although these passively viewed death-causing effects may be managed with pain killers, Singer's relatively simple thought is that if death is deemed morally desirable, then why not simply provide death actively rather than passively?

---

3   P. Singer, *Practical Ethics*, p. 186.

In addition, if we recall the ideas of Situation Ethicist Joseph Fletcher (as outlined in Chapter 5) then we may wonder whether or not (assuming death is morally desirable) passively allowing death to occur is actually less loving than actively bringing death about. As a relativistic normative ethical theory, Situation Ethics provides no absolute guidance regarding the moral acceptability of euthanasia in any of its forms; situation-specific, practical and pragmatic judgments will need to form the basis of moral judgments in individual cases. However, it is important to consider how *loving* active euthanasia might actually be in the circumstance where the death of the patient is actually our ambition.

6. Pro-Euthanasia: Argument Two

The second argument we can offer in support of euthanasia — both in voluntary and non-voluntary forms — can be labelled the *argument from resource use*. Whereas the former argument attempted to defend the moral acceptability of euthanasia by utilising the perspective of the patient and their associated quality of life, this argument may seem a little more detached and you may or may not view this as a strength or weakness.

According to Peter Singer, the non-voluntary euthanising of a severely disabled and suffering young infant child (who cannot express any wishes regarding their future) may be justifiable on the following grounds:

> When the death of a disabled infant will lead to the birth of another infant with better prospects of a happy life, the total amount of happiness will be greater if the disabled infant is killed.[4]

Singer's suggestion may sound callous, and if you view killing an innocent life as an absolute moral wrong then you may view his claim as immediately morally out of bounds (this kind of objection to euthanasia is considered in a later section). For now, however, let us take Singer's claim at face value. Being a preference utilitarian (further detail on this theory is available in Chapter 1), Singer makes his judgment regarding how to act in such a case based on the quality of life of the individuals involved. So, on his view, the disabled infant may have a lower quality of life than a healthy child who might be born in their stead because the latter, and not the former, can secure greater preference satisfaction. Thus, we morally ought to bring about the situation in which the healthy child is born.

If we assume that those who are in a PVS, or those suffering near the end of a terminal condition, have a low quality of life then we might think that spending our limited medical resources on maintaining their existence, rather

---

4   *Ibid.*, p. 163.

than spending those resources elsewhere, is not morally desirable. This kind of argument will appeal to a teleologist rather than a deontologist, for it ascribes moral values to actions based on *consequences rather than duties*. In this setting, the consequences of spending resources on PVS patients may be less positive than spending those same resources on effectively treating other diseases or funding medical research to benefit future generations.

Some financial figures may put this possible argument into context. According to the Madison County Record, Christina McCray (a patient in a PVS) had medical bills that average out to $250,000 per year.[5] If we consider the years of life that a patient in a PVS may have, along with the number of PVS patients that exist, then the cost of keeping such individuals alive becomes clearer. If medicine is sometimes about making difficult decisions, then it may become clear why non-voluntary euthanasia of such patients might be considered desirable (at least with the support of the family). In addition, if a patient with a poor quality of life, who is facing future suffering with associated expensive care, voluntarily requests euthanasia then it may be that their death will allow resources to be better directed to other patients who might have their suffering reduced more significantly.

It is worth noting, for those uncomfortable with this kind of resource allocation planning when it comes to treating ill, suffering and frail patients that decisions in the National Health Service are already being made in the light of teleological and quality-of-life based reasoning. The NHS utilises QALYs when making financial planning and treatment costing decisions. QALY is shorthand for Quality Adjusted Life Year, a measurement designed to consider the benefits of different treatment costs in respect of their pay-offs to the patients involved. If a potential treatment will lead to a patient being free from pain and able to perform daily activities (this is a somewhat rough definition, but enough for our purposes) then the year in which this outcome is expected can be given a value of 1. Each following year can then be given a value between 0 and 1 according to the expected lasting impacts of the treatment. Thus, allocating spending to different forms of treatment for different patients can be objectively calculated against a common standard in order to inform those spending decisions in terms of where the better consequences might be secured.

The argument from resource use is, therefore, an extension of the use of a QALY to inform medical decision-making. If the positive consequences of spending money on treating patients who might be cured or helped to have a higher quality of life are greater than spending money to keep people alive

---

5   *Madison-St. Clair Record*, http://madisonrecord.com/stories/510564252-nursing-expert-testifies-that-plaintiff-s-bills-could-be-8-4-million

who either wish to die and have a diminishing quality of life or who are in a PVS, then spending on the former is morally defensible rather than spending on the latter. Again, you might consider how loving it is to spend money keeping a patient in a PVS alive versus investing in research for cures and treatments that could improve the quality of life for other patients in a world where resources are finite.

7. Pro-Euthanasia: Argument Three

The final argument we will offer in favour of euthanasia is an argument often viewed as the most powerful in this applied ethical area, the *argument from personal autonomy*. This argument proceeds from the fairly plausible assumption that people should have the right to make their own decisions and should be able to decide the paths of their own lives. If the right to choose our own path applies in life, then why would this not apply in respect of our choice of how and when to die?

Perhaps the most famous philosophical proponent of a right to personal autonomy and decision-making was John Stuart Mill. As discussed in Chapter 1, Mill elucidated the harm principle, which suggested that the only legitimate government interference in a person's life is to stop that person from harming others; all other interference is not to be justified. If you subscribe to this principle, then you seemingly must believe that a person voluntarily requesting euthanasia should not be denied the right to die, unless their dying would cause harm to another person. If we discount emotional harm (because many normal things that we do seem to cause emotional harm to other people — getting a job over another candidate, for example) then it is not easy to envisage a circumstance in which a terminally ill patient, requesting a merciful death before their suffering becomes too extreme, would have a death that causes physical harm to another person. Therefore, if we believe in the power and moral right of the individual to act in the way that they deem correct, unless physically harming another, then we must seemingly allow that voluntary euthanasia is morally justifiable. Singer sums up the position:

> ...the principle of respect for autonomy tells us to allow rational agents to live their own lives according to their own autonomous decisions, free from coercion or interference; but if rational agents should autonomously choose to die, then respect for autonomy will lead us to assist them to do as they choose.[6]

---

6   P. Singer, *Practical Ethics*, p. 195.

We have spoken above of voluntary euthanasia specifically, for the patient in a PVS obviously cannot choose how to die. If we return to the earlier mentioned possibility of a *letter of intent*, written prior to the condition taking hold, then in certain instances non-voluntary euthanasia may also be justified on this basis — though of course, such cases seem to a species of voluntary euthanasia.

However, if we would trust loved ones to make other important medical decisions for us if we were incapacitated, then perhaps the same should apply in this context and non-voluntary euthanasia might be justifiable in virtue of properly respecting the choices made by one relative on behalf of another. It is for you to consider if a theory of personal autonomy can be extended to familial autonomy in such a way.

8. Anti-Euthanasia: Argument One

Thus far we have only outlined pro-euthanasia arguments. In fact, we have really only provided pro-*active* euthanasia arguments in virtue of Singer's suggestions regarding the undesirability of passive euthanasia. It is now time to give anti-euthanasia, and anti-active euthanasia, arguments their fair hearing.

The first objection to euthanasia may be termed the *objection from Sanctity of Life*. The Sanctity of Life ethic is usually founded on religious, and specifically Christian, thinking. Essentially, a belief that life is sacred suggests an absolute value to life, of a type that means it is worthwhile in all circumstances; in Glover's earlier words it is the view that life has an intrinsic value that supersedes any qualitative aspect. For Sanctity of Life theorists and supporters as described in this section, problems with the quality of a life *never* undermine the ultimate value and worth of a life.

It is not necessary to be religious to hold the view that all lives are worth preserving, irrespective of quality. A non-religious person may prefer to speak of an absolute right to life that cannot be taken away through non-voluntary euthanasia, and cannot be revoked by personal decree in the context of voluntary euthanasia. However, more often, the view is supported by Biblical reference. In the Bible, we are told that God said: "Let us make mankind in our image, in our likeness".[7]

In addition, our bodies are described as sacred and as containing God's Holy Spirit: "Don't you know that you yourselves are God's temple and that God's Spirit dwells in your midst? If anyone destroys God's temple, God will destroy that person; for God's temple is sacred, and you together are that

---

7   Genesis 1:26, https://www.biblegateway.com/passage/?search=Genesis+1%3A26-28&version=NIV

temple".[8] These quotes not only reveal the sanctity of our bodies and the cause of that sanctity — our creation in the image of God and the presence of God's spirit within us — they also reveal the punishment for those who might take life; might this relate to doctors who administer euthanasia?

Whilst the arguments from *quality of* life and use of resources were avowedly teleological in nature, considering the painful and potentially costly consequences of continued life, the argument from Sanctity of Life is *deontological* in nature since it relates to a duty to avoid killing. Linking the Sanctity of Life view to both abortion and euthanasia, Mother Teresa gave a statement of the appeal of this ethical stance:

> For me, life is the most beautiful gift of God to mankind, therefore people and nations who destroy life by abortion and euthanasia are the poorest. I do not say legal or illegal, but I think that no human hand should be raised to kill life, since life is God's life us in us.[9]

All human life, whether in the womb or in a PVS, is of sacred and God-given worth such that killing (including euthanising, as a form of killing) is morally impermissible.

The notion of a sacred life lays behind Catholic teaching on the issue of euthanasia. A 1980 Catholic Declaration of Faith is clear and absolute in nature:

> ...no one is permitted to ask for this act of killing, either for himself or herself or for another person entrusted to his or her care, nor can he or she consent to it, either explicitly or implicitly, nor can any authority legitimately recommend or permit such an action. For it is a question of the violation of the divine law, an offence against the dignity of the human person, a crime against life, and an attack on humanity.[10]

The language is somewhat complex but the key points are given in our previous discussions in this chapter — life is sacred and so euthanasia, whether voluntarily requested or non-voluntarily encouraged for someone else, is morally impermissible. No legislator, guided by moral ideals, can ever morally recommend this type of killing, whether motivated by a mistaken sense of mercy or not.

9. Anti-Euthanasia: Argument Two

A related objection to euthanasia, premised on a commitment to Christianity, is the *objection from valuable suffering* (keep in mind that not all Christians, by any stretch, would defend an objection of this type). Let us return to the 1980 Catholic Declaration of Faith. The document states that:

---

8   1 Corinthians 3:16–18, https://www.biblegateway.com/passage/?search=1 Corinthians+3&version= NIV
9   J. Chaliha and E. Le Joly, *The Joy in Loving*, p. 174.
10 Sacred Congregation for the Doctrine of the Faith, 'Declaration on Euthanasia', http://www.vatican. va/roman_curia/congregations/cfaith/documents/rc_con_cfaith_doc_19800505_euthanasia_en.html

According to Christian teaching, however, suffering, especially suffering during the last moments of life, has a special place in God's saving plan; it is in fact a sharing in Christ's passion and a union with the redeeming sacrifice which He offered in obedience to the Father's will.[11]

Thus, even if someone requests euthanasia in order to avoid pain, that request should not be granted because it deprives a person of an element of God's plan for them; the experience of suffering at the end of life brings that person closer to sharing in the experience of Christ. This does not mean that Christians oppose palliative care (a type of care that does not attempt to extend life, so much as make an individual as comfortable as possible as they face the end of their life). However, it does explain why a life should be seen through to its natural end and why it might therefore be viewed as morally wrong to shorten it.

10. Anti-Euthanasia: Argument Three

The third anti-euthanasia argument to consider can be labelled the *slippery slope objection* (sometimes called the *Wedge argument*). This objection does not require any view regarding the Sanctity of Life or a deontological duty not to kill; indeed, the slippery slope objection is both teleological in nature and does not even require a denial that euthanasia might be desirable in certain instances when viewed in the abstract or in isolation.

The slippery slope objection is that *if* euthanasia were to become legal in some situations, then it would lead to euthanasia becoming legal and acceptable in situations where it is actually morally undesirable. To see the strength of such an objection, consider earlier pro-euthanasia arguments couched in terms of resource allocation and personal autonomy.

If euthanasia can be justified on teleological grounds when resources would be better deployed elsewhere, then what is to stop us justifying not merely voluntary and non-voluntary euthanasia, but involuntary euthanasia also? If euthanasia is justified on the basis of money and time being better spent on some patients rather than others, then why would permission be required from the patient or the patient's family?

If morality is determined by consequences, and consequences justify euthanasia, then we seem to be slipping down a dangerous slope to euthanising people without their consent. After all, if you are a teleologist (perhaps, an act utilitarian) you have already given up ideas concerning absolute rules against certain actions. It therefore may be objected that either life is sacred, or it is not, and if it is not then we may end up in a situation we find utterly morally indefensible even if we start from apparently moral motivations.

---

11   *Ibid.*

In addition, if personal autonomy is respected to the degree that someone can choose when to end their life, then what is to stop a seriously depressed person who is otherwise physically healthy from opting for voluntary euthanasia? Most people might view such enabling of suicide for patients with mental health needs as being very different from euthanasia for PVS patients or the terminally ill, but if personal autonomy justifies euthanasia then how can we justifiably draw a strong enough line so as to allow some people to choose death, but not others? Again, it may be objected that either personal autonomy matters or it does not. If we enable a person to have their life ended, then it is obvious they can never come to a different view on the value of their life at a later stage, as they might have had they still been alive. On this issue, it may be worthwhile revisiting the discussion from Chapter 1 regarding a person's preferences and whether they are only morally relevant if they stand up to some sort of psychological testing and counselling; the relevant idea is due to Richard Brandt.

In addition, opponents of euthanasia often suggest that if one group of people are euthanised, others may begin to feel pressure to take up that same option. If non-voluntary euthanasia is granted, and a legal, moral and cultural line in the sand is thereby crossed, may not elderly patients feel pressured to not be a burden to their families? May not the financially well-off elderly feel pressure to allow their children to inherit any accumulated wealth rather than see that wealth spent on their own care? Granting non-voluntary euthanasia in even a small number of cases may, over time, send us down a slippery slope to the non-morally defensible euthanising of many other types of patients who, as things stand, are quite content to remain alive since they have no reason to consider other options.

Of course, an easy response to any slippery slope objection is simply to deny that a change in one fact must lead to a suggested negative change elsewhere. Why think of negative consequences from a change in the law, when these consequences might not happen? Indeed, some slippery slope arguments are logical fallacies if they are premised on the idea that a possible negative outcome must, of necessity, follow from some change in policy. However, we should not "straw-man" the objection in this way (i.e. phrase it in such a weak way that it is easy to argue against). The slippery slope objection suggests that the negative outcomes might be probable, rather than be certain. Thus, a response should deal with the issue of probable negative consequences, rather than cheapening a plausibly reasonable objection through wilful misrepresentation of its structure. Researching the situation in Belgium, where the law regarding euthanasia is perhaps the most liberal in the world, should provide a good grounding to either support or oppose this line of thought, as would considering the application of Rule Utilitarianism.[12]

11. Anti-Euthanasia: Argument Four

A fourth anti-euthanasia objection is the *objection from modern treatment*. This objection brings together two distinct, but relevantly similar, lines of thought. Firstly, it might be suggested that to euthanise those who are terminally ill, or those in a PVS, is to kill people earlier than would otherwise happen and thereby to artificially eliminate their chances of living to experience a cure to their condition. At the very least, if not a cure, euthanised people are not around to benefit from any step-forward in treatment that might alleviate their suffering.

In addition, given the modern advances in palliative care it might also be argued that end of life care is now so advanced that euthanasia is not necessary in order to avoid suffering and so cannot be justified even on quality of life grounds. It might be thought plausible that a person with a severe and worsening disease who is not euthanised could have their condition and pain carefully managed by skilled healthcare professionals so as to greatly diminish any suffering.

In response to these types of objections, Singer grants that were euthanasia legalised then some deaths may occur for people who could have been treated had they been kept alive. However, he urges that:

> Against a very small number of unnecessary deaths that might occur if euthanasia is legalised we must place the very large amount of pain and distress that will be suffered if euthanasia is not legalised, by patients who really are terminally ill.[13]

On balance, Singer suggests, euthanasia would cause more pain to cease than pleasure missed by those who die early. Whether or not palliative care is able to reduce suffering to the extent suggested by the objection is something you may wish to consider and further research, as it would seem to be an empirical claim requiring contemporary evidence to further the discussion.

---

12   The following article highlights the use of the law in Belgium: 'Belgian Convicted Killer with "Incurable" Psychiatric Condition Granted Right to Die', https://www.theguardian.com/world/2014/sep/16/belgium-convict-granted-right-to-die

13   P. Singer, *Practical Ethics*, p. 197.

12. Allowing versus Doing

James Rachels (1941–2003) sums up the supposed moral importance of the distinction between allowing and doing in the euthanasia debate:

> *The distinction between active and passive euthanasia is thought to be crucial for medical ethics. The idea is that it is permissible, at least in some cases, to withhold treatment and allow a patient to die, but it is never permissible to take any direct action designed to kill the patient. This doctrine seems to be accepted by most doctors.*[14]

Thus, according to Rachels, most doctors at the time of his paper — and not much seems to have changed in the UK context since — would think it permissible to allow a patient to die (passive euthanasia, on our definitions) but think it impermissible to kill a patient even if they request it or if it is deemed to be in their interests (active euthanasia).

The plausibility of this distinction is supported by consideration of the Doctrine of Double Effect, as drawn from the normative Natural Law moral theory discussed in Chapter 4. Recall from the chapter on Natural Law ethics that one of the primary precepts for human beings is the preservation of life. No moral prescription, we might think, could speak more strongly and absolutely against euthanasia — especially given the Catholic background of Aquinas's Natural Law stance and the earlier reference to Catholic views in the context of the Sanctity of Life ethic. A secondary precept, derived from this primary precept, would certainly seem to deny the moral acceptability of artificial shortening of life. However, Natural Law theorists are able to to have a nuanced stance in the euthanasia debate.

A Natural Law theorist, via the Doctrine of Double Effect, can describe an action as moral even if it results in an outcome that might not be considered morally permissible in the abstract. If an act is directed by a desire to do moral good, yet has a foreseeable but unintended consequence of a bad effect, then this action may be moral so long as the bad effect was not aimed at, does not outweigh the good effect and is not directly the cause of the bad itself. If this brief comment is unclear, it is critical to look back to the relevant discussion of the Doctrine of Double Effect in the chapter on Natural Law.

Now, let us apply this doctrine directly to the context of euthanasia. A doctor may be aware that a patient has not long to live and is suffering immensely. The doctor may prescribe a multitude of painkillers to treat the pain, even though this will have the foreseeable but unintended effect of killing the patient as a result of the side-effects of the drugs. Indeed, a doctor may simply refrain

---

14   J. Rachels, 'Active and Passive Euthanasia', p. 511.

from offering painful treatment methods in order to avoid causing suffering, with the unintended but foreseeable consequence that the patient will die as a result of the non-intervention. These actions are not morally wrong, says the Natural Law theorist, because death is not intended directly but rather the morally good end of pain reduction is intended directly. Thus, the doctor who engages in active euthanasia by provision of a lethal cocktail of drugs in order to artificially kill a patient so that their suffering is reduced is morally wrong (for the good of "suffering reduction" is directly achieved by the bad of killing), while the doctor who withdraws treatment in order to relieve suffering, with the unintended but foreseeable outcome of death, acts morally justly (for the good of "suffering reduction" is achieved by not administering painful treatment, death is just a proportionately acceptable side-effect).

Both Rachels and Singer have little time for the distinction between allowing and doing, and the Doctrine of Double Effect, in this debate. Rachels says that:

> If a doctor lets a patient die, for humane reasons, he is in the same position as if he had given the patient a lethal injection for humane reasons...if the doctor's decision was the right (to not intervene on the patient's death) one, the method used is not itself important.[15]

Meanwhile, Singer comments that "We cannot avoid responsibility simply by directing our intention to one effect rather than another. If we foresee both effects, we must take responsibility for the foreseen effects of what we do".[16] Singer gives the example of a business seeking to save money in order to hire more workers. This outcome is good and motivates bosses to act to save money on their recycling bill, with the foreseeable but unintended consequence of polluting a local river. If we would not excuse the company for ignoring a foreseeable consequence, says Singer, then we do not really believe we escape responsibility for allowing death in the euthanasia context.

The application of the Doctrine of Double Effect, and Natural Law ethics in general, to the euthanasia debate should be considered carefully and in the light of the earlier chapter outlining the normative theory itself. Despite both Singer's and Rachel's attack, Natural Law and the Doctrine of Double Effect retain many proponents. If one views moral outcomes as based on more than consequences alone, then this approach may seem to have more merit than a preference utilitarian like Singer might grant it; this is for you to judge.

---

15   *Ibid.*.
16   P. Singer, *Practical Ethics*, p. 183.

SUMMARY

Euthanasia is an applied moral topic that has profound implications; successful moral arguments may lead to legislative changes that quite literally shorten or extend lifespans. There are a host of subtleties in the debate to which we can only pay lip-service — such as the acceptability of active euthanasia of depressed patients, the importance of pre-injury requests for treatment or for death; the best way of allocating medical resources; the powers of people over both their bodies and the bodies of incapacitated family members. Further issues are discussed in works such as that by J. David Velleman, and we suggest the references below as a guide to useful and enquiring texts.[17] However, we hope that you now feel confident to explain and evaluate the key arguments both in favour and against the various methods of euthanasia and the various contexts in which those methods may be employed.

COMMON STUDENT MISTAKES

- Making the slippery slope objection simpler than it is — it focuses on likelihood of future consequences, not certainty of future consequences.

- Dismissively suggesting that not being religious is enough to oppose Sanctity of Life claims out of hand. Life might have absolute value for non-religious reasons and this is an idea one should engage with.

- Dismissing the quality of life argument just because of a religious faith without proper engagement — the idea that a life should be prolonged even in the face of suffering needs suitable defence.

- Misrepresenting the Doctrine of Double Effect in application to euthanasia — keep in mind the more detailed knowledge gained from the chapter on Natural Law ethics.

- Thinking that pro-euthanasia views must be secular and that anti-euthanasia views must be religious. All options remain open.

---

17   J. D. Velleman, *Beyond Price: Essays on Birth and Death*, https://www.openbookpublishers.com/reader/349

ISSUES TO CONSIDER

1. What makes a life worth living? Is a life ever without value?

2. Should the Doctrine of Double Effect be ethically relevant? Is there a moral difference between allowing and doing?

3. What is assisted suicide? Is it different from Euthanasia?

4. If euthanasia is morally acceptable, should passive euthanasia ever be viewed as an acceptable method?

5. Can the slippery slope objection be blocked in this context? Answer with reference to the development of euthanasia laws in Belgium.

6. Is Rule Utilitarianism the only teleological theory that survives the slippery slope objection?

7. Is there something morally uncomfortable about the argument from resource allocation? If so, what?

8. If you were designing euthanasia laws, what would they look like?

9. Should a Sanctity of Life ethic have any role in twenty-first century medicine?

10. Is the morality of euthanasia determined by empirical factors such as levels of palliative care available?

11. Should a depressed patient ever be allowed euthanasia? Is personal autonomy something we must always respect? If not, when should it not be respected?

12. Could involuntary euthanasia (euthanasia against a person's wishes) ever be justified in any circumstance?

KEY TERMINOLOGY

Doctrine of double effect	Well-being
Palliative care	Sanctity of Life
Persistent Vegetative State	Straw-man

References

'Belgian Convicted Killer with "Incurable" Psychiatric Condition Granted Right to Die', *the Guardian* (16 September 2014), freely available at https://www.theguardian.com/world/2014/sep/16/belgium-convict-granted-right-to-die

Bible, New International Version, freely available at https://www.biblegateway.com/

Chaliha, Jaya, and Le Joly, *The Joy in Loving: A Guide to Daily Life with Mother Teresa* (London: Penguin, 1996).

Glover, Jonathan, *Causing Death and Saving Lives* (London: Penguin, 1990).

Madison-St. Clair Record, freely available at http://madisonrecord.com/stories/510564252-nursing-expert-testifies-that-plaintiff-s-bills-could-be-8-4-million

Hari, J., 'Peter Singer: Some People are More Equal than Others', freely available at http://www.independent.co.uk/news/people/profiles/peter-singer-some-people-are-more-equal-than-others-551696.html

Sacred Congregation for the Doctrine of the Faith, 'Declaration on Euthanasia', freely available at http://www.vatican.va/roman_curia/congregations/cfaith/documents/rc_con_cfaith_doc_19800505_euthanasia_en.html

Singer, Peter, *Practical Ethics* (Cambridge: Cambridge University Press, 2011), https://doi.org/10.1017/cbo9780511975950

Rachels, James, 'Active and Passive Euthanasia', *Biomedical Ethics and the Law*, 5 (1979): 511–16, https://doi.org/10.1007/978-1-4615-6561-1_33

Velleman, J. David, *Beyond Price: Essays on Birth and Death* (Cambridge, Open Book Publishers, 2015), https://doi.org/10.11647/OBP.0061; freely available at https://www.openbookpublishers.com/reader/349

CHAPTER 8

Business Ethics

There is no such thing as business ethics.

John Maxwell

A business that makes nothing but money is a poor kind of business.

Henry Ford

1. Introduction to Business Ethics

What is a business? Is Christian Aid a business? Is McDonalds? What about a university? This is a difficult and complicated question to answer but let us start from the claim that a *business is an organization that buys and sells goods or services for profit.*

If I buy some books from a shop, they are *goods* and the business makes a profit. If I pay the taxi driver to take me to the airport then that is a *service* and I increase the taxi company's profit.

Maybe then Christian Aid *is not* a business? Arguably there is no "customer" purchasing a good or a service, whereas McDonalds clearly *is* a business. But what about a university? Well that is a much harder and more controversial question, and one that we have posed below for you to consider. For any business, whatever its size, the key feature will be that it sells goods or services for profit.

Ethics arises because relationships exist. That is, if there is a relationship then there is a legitimate question of how *ought* we to behave in that relationship? In a business there are many different relationships and hence we can ask ethical questions regarding each of these relationships. Here are a few examples.

(a) A business has a relationship with its *shareholders* — the people who own a share of the company. However, if the shareholders want to reduce the wages of the workers so they can get a larger dividend, would they be doing something morally wrong? After all, they might arguably be said in some sense to "own" the business and can do what they want with it.

(b) A business has a relationship with its *customers* — the people who are buying the goods and services. For instance, if a business knowingly reduces the amount of health advice it provides on its labels in order to increase profits, has it done something morally wrong?

(c) A business has a relationship with its *employees*. If a business realises that it can increase productivity by scrapping paternity leave would it be morally wrong to do so? Conversely, if an employee is privy to some questionable practices and becomes a "whistle-blower" then has she done anything morally wrong?

(d) There are also ethical questions that arise regarding the business's relationship with *the environment*. If a business opens a new factory, giving a much needed boost to the local economy, but can only do so by building on a nature reserve, has it done something morally wrong?

(e) Also there are *others who are affected* by the business's activity. For example, if a mobile phone company constructs a new phone mast which causes a low hum to be heard by the local community, has the company done something morally wrong?

Of course, businesses have always made ethical decisions. The working conditions in factories before the 1847 Factory Act were certainly morally wrong, even if this was not recognised at the time.

This is in stark contrast to nowadays, when you find "value and ethic" statements in full view on the promotional material of any business. *Not* to be talking in terms of "values and ethics" is very bad business practice. The phrase that is often used in this context is a business's *"Corporate Social Responsibility"* (CSR). We can take CSR to mean: "[…] a business approach that contributes to sustainable development by delivering economic, social and environmental benefits for all stakeholders".[1] A great example of a company with a clear CSR is The Body Shop, who in 1988 became the founding member of the Ethical Trading Initiative.[2]

There is now a plethora of ethical rankings that tell the customer which businesses are best in terms of CSR, and which is the most ethical (e.g. Forbes, 'The World's Most Ethical Companies').[3]

Although it is now the norm for a business to have "ethics" statements, it is arguably *irrational* for companies *to be* ethical. Why might this be? Consider this basic argument.

1. A business's aim is to make a profit.

2. A business will make a profit if it can attract customers.

---

1 'FT.com/Lexicon', *Financial Time,* http://lexicon.ft.com/Term?term=corporate-social-responsibility--(CSR)

2 To see details of the Ethical Trading Initiative see http://www.ethicaltrade.org

3 See K. Strauss, 'The World's Most Ethical Companies 2016', http://www.forbes.com/sites/karsten strauss/2016/03/09/the-worlds-most-ethical-companies-2016

3. In the present context (at least in the West) a business will attract most customers if it *appears* to be ethical.

4. It will make *more* profit if it *appears* ethical rather than actually *being* ethical because it actually costs more to *be* ethical rather than simply *appearing* ethical.

Therefore, given (1)–(4) it seems more reasonable for a business simply to *appear* to be ethical, rather than actually being ethical.

Of course, there are many questions that arise from the above argument. For instance, we might think that the potential costs of being found out (i.e. appearing but *not* being ethical) far outweigh the costs of *actually* being ethical in the first place — hence (4) might be rejected. However, there remains a great attraction only to appear ethical and not go through a long, often expensive process to become ethical. It is of course then an open empirical question whether businesses *are* ethical or whether it is window dressing and simply a *cynical marketing device*.

In this chapter we are going to look at a few areas of business ethics and do so through the lens of the normative theories of Utilitarianism and Kantian deontology.

2. Employers and Employees

In 1992 Mike Ashley started the company Sports Direct; it grew rapidly to become the biggest sports retailer in the UK and one of the biggest in Europe. However, in 2016 the lid was lifted on what seemed to be draconian working practices for its employees and it was revealed that workers were not paid the minimum wage. One employee claimed that, "if we went to the toilet more than once every four hours we were called into the manager's office and questioned". "I lasted six days before I quit".[4] Employees were often searched when leaving the store after work — sometimes having to strip to their underwear. Employees were docked fifteen minutes' pay for being one minute late. "Sometimes on my zero-hours contract, I would end up working for ten days in a row, for ten hours a day. On other weeks I would get given only one three-hour shift the whole week. There was no routine".[5]

Did Sports Direct do something morally wrong? To make this a little more manageable, let us put aside the illegality of their behaviour. Let's assume that they did *nothing illegal* in their practice.

Given this we might think that they did not do anything morally wrong. After all, the employees were not press-ganged into working for the company. They were not chained to their desks nor denied access to exits. Employees were not prisoners or slaves but were rational human beings who chose to

---

4   D. Avis, 'Sports Direct: Former Employees Speak Out', http://www.bbc.co.uk/news/uk-36864345
5   *Ibid.*

work for this company. It is plausible that the employees simply failed to read the "small print" in their contracts. In this case why think that the business did anything wrong?

Remember that for an "act utilitarian" (see Chapter 1) an act is morally right if, and only if, it brings about more happiness than any other act, so maybe then Sports Direct *did not* do anything morally wrong.

In the case of Sports Direct, it might be that the *millions* of people who gained happiness from owning the cheap sports products outweighed the misery and unhappiness of approximately 27,000 employees. In which case it was morally acceptable for Sports Direct to treat its employees in the way that it did.

Moreover, the act utilitarian has no time for "rights" in general and an "employee's rights" in particular. However, we suspect most people would believe that what Sports Direct did *was morally wrong* and even if it were *legal*, people would judge that the company ought not to have acted in the way that it did.

That said perhaps we do not need to draw this conclusion *even if* we are act utilitarians. This is because Mill said it would be better to be a human dissatisfied than a pig satisfied. He thought that there were "higher" and "lower" pleasures. Only humans can experience higher pleasure, non-human animals cannot.

Mill argues that pleasure should not just be weighed on the qualitative "hedonic" calculus. If we introduce higher and lower pleasures, then we can respect the intuition that what Sports Direct did was morally wrong. Mill thought that higher and lower pleasures were *qualitatively* distinct. If this is true then we might think that the lower pleasures of, say, a million people having a new tennis racket or owning the latest trendy trainers, is outweighed by the higher pleasure of the three quarter of a million employees being treated fairly.

Furthermore, Consequentialist Theories also spell out the "utility" not in terms of happiness or pleasure but in other terms such as *welfare* and *preferences*. A preference or welfare consequentialist might then conclude that what Sports Direct did was morally wrong because its actions did not maximize welfare and/or preferences. Investigating this claim, though, would take us well beyond the scope of this chapter.

Moving away from *Act* Utilitarianism, we might think that the *rule* utilitarian would claim that the actions of Sports Direct *was* morally wrong because the rule "treat your employees fairly" is justifiable on utilitarian grounds. That is, people will *typically* be happier if this rule is followed than if it is not. Hence, a rule-utilitarian might conclude that what Sports Direct did was morally wrong as arguably Sports Direct did not treat its employees fairly.

What is important then is to realize that it is not as clear-cut as saying that a utilitarian *would* believe that a certain business practice is morally right or wrong. Rather it will depend on the specifics of the situation and how, according to the position, we should maximize pleasure, happiness, wellbeing, preferences etc.

So much for the utilitarians, what about the Kantians? (See Chapter 2.) Well, the Kantian talks in terms of duty and Categorical Imperatives; for the Kantian it is always morally wrong to treat someone as *solely* a means to an end.

On first look, we might think that this is precisely what Sports Direct did in treating its employees as a means to an end (profit). But it cannot be that simple. For if this were true then *all* businesses would be doing something morally wrong because all businesses use their employees to make a profit.

We need to think a bit harder about what Kant is saying. Kant is not saying that businesses cannot use people as a means to an end but that the key is whether the business is treating people *as rational and free*.

Using a taxi is not morally wrong even though we are using the taxi driver for our own end. This is because we pay the taxi driver and they are voluntarily entering into this means-end relationship. The same then could be said for the employees in a business. Sure, it is true that McDonalds, or Ford, or Body Shop are using their employees as a means to an end but this is acceptable because they pay their employees and their employees are entering the contract of work freely.

Perhaps though the Kantian would say that Sports Direct is *different* because it practised a form of *exploitation*. The people working for Sports Direct are very often from the poorest group of society. This means they do not have lots of jobs to pick from so it is not as if they could leave the job and quickly find another. Moreover, we might suppose that in leaving the job they might end up in a situation which is far worse, perhaps not being able to pay their rent, being on the street, having relationships break down.

In this case, we might wonder if the employees really are *freely* choosing to work for Sports Direct. If they are not, then Sports Direct *is* treating its employees as means-to-an-end even though it is paying them. In which case the Kantians would say that what was happening is morally wrong. We'll look at other features of the Kantian position when we consider other issues below.

3. Businesses and Customers

It is clear that businesses can directly affect how a customer thinks about goods or services, the world around them, and themselves. If they could not then they would not spend millions of pounds on advertising each year! But given this then they occupy a position of *trust*. With this trust comes a question regarding how much information a company should provide to the customer and in what form.

> In 2011 a court decision meant that banks had to compensate millions of people after they had been mis-sold Payment Protection Insurance (PPI) which was judged to be "ineffective and inefficient". It is beyond doubt that banks knew that PPI was a con, yet it was not in their interest to stop selling PPI because it was "a cash cow". In order to sell PPI banks tapped into the insecurity of customers by promising a "safety net". PPI promised to repay people's borrowings if their income fell due to illness or job loss.

We might think that here is a case where a business's actions towards the customer is morally wrong. But how might we explain this? Well, one obvious way of explaining it is via *trust*. As Doug Taylor, who works for "Which?", stated: "We've always known that people were being mis-sold PPI, but we were still amazed to discover the scale of it. It appears that salespeople are chasing their commissions, their bosses are chasing profits — *where's the sense of responsibility to the customer*?"[6]

But how far does this "responsibility" reach? It is of course not in a business's interest — that of making a profit — to give the customer a balanced and "honest" viewpoint. An advert for a computer that says: "this is very expensive; you are probably just buying the label. You do realize that the statistics say you'll use approximately 5% of its capacity, probably for games, a bit of word processing and surfing the web" will probably not get the company very far in terms of sales. So it seems unfair to compel businesses to be honest and balanced in *this* way.

But on the other hand a company cannot lie. This of course is why the "horsemeat" scandal and other "food fraud" cases have been so controversial.[7] It may be that people *would* choose to eat horsemeat but the trouble arises when they are deceived into eating it. These were cases where food companies deliberately lied, or deceived the customer for profit.

But what is lying? Well, it *is not* when someone fails to tell the truth but rather it involves *intentional deception*. But why ought companies refrain from lying?

Looking at Act Utilitarianism account it is quite hard to say why it would always be wrong to do so. Presumably, for the act utilitarian, it is not always morally wrong for a business to lie and to exploit the trust of the customer.

---

6   G. Wearden, 'How the PPI Scandal Unfolded', https://www.theguardian.com/business/2011/may/05/how-ppi-scandal-unfolded

7   'Horsemeat Scandal: Where Did the 29% Horse in your Tesco Burger Come From?', *the Guardian*, https://www.theguardian.com/uk-news/2013/oct/22/horsemeat-scandal-guardian-investigation-public-secrecy

If, by lying, a business produces more happiness than by not lying, then it is morally acceptable for the business to lie.

We might not think that we would get the same result for the rule utilitarian. A plausible rule might be "do not lie in a position of trust where there are reasonable grounds that you'll be found out". If this were justifiable through utilitarian grounds, then it would be unacceptable for businesses to lie to the customer. Yet, even on the rule utilitarian account it is true that it is *sometimes* morally acceptable for a business to lie.

This contrasts with the Kantian approach. If you recall, for the Kantian it is *always* morally wrong to lie. It is true in all instances that one ought not to lie. Kant uses the Categorical Imperative to show this. Let us reconsider the PPI case. It would be irrational for the head of a bank to want the maxim "lie to the customer if it means making a profit" to become a universal law. It is irrational because if this is a universal law then there would be *no trust in businesses at all* and therefore there could be no profit and no businesses. It is self-defeating and irrational. So it seems that on Kantian grounds the way that PPI was sold was morally wrong.

4. A Business and the Environment

As we discussed above it is common parlance amongst businesses to talk about *Corporate Social Responsibility*; in other words, a business works with the goal not just of profit but to be in step with the issues of society as a whole. Typically, though not exhaustively, this amounts to the business being ethically responsible towards the *environment*; this might include things such as not testing its cosmetics on animals or reducing the amount of non-recyclable plastic bags that the company uses.

But why should a business have any obligation to the environment? If a business is working within the law but using, say, environmentally unfriendly cement in the construction of its factories, why does this matter? Why should a business use a potentially more expensive product, thus reducing its profits, simply because it is more environmentally friendly?

It is true that the environment is one of the biggest concerns for businesses and is often an area where they are heavily criticized. This, like many of the other ethical issues, is only a relatively new phenomenon. In the past, in the name of profit, businesses could do what they wanted regarding the environment. There was a view that the world is such a massive place that a business polluting a pond, or mining on a green space did not really, in the grand scheme of things, matter. But the increase in globalization, the advancement of science, and the fact we live in connected communities has made people realize that businesses can, and do, affect the environment; climate change and the hole in the ozone layer are prime examples of this slow realization.

We can bring some of the issues into focus through an example:

> In 2000 heavy snow caused the collapse of a dam in Romania. The dam was holding back 100,000 cubic meters of cyanide-contaminated water. The water spilled over some farmland and then into the Someş river. Although no humans were killed the spill caused the death of a huge amount of aquatic life and the accident has been called the biggest environmental disaster in Europe since Chernobyl. The cyanide water was a by-product of the mining of gold by the Aurul mining company.

Did the company do something morally wrong? It might have done something illegal; perhaps it omitted to perform the appropriate load tests, or perhaps it forged safety documentation. But even if it did nothing illegal, did it do something morally wrong?

I suspect in the twenty-first century our answer will be "obviously yes!" But can we give any substance to this thought? What really is wrong? After all, we intentionally kill billions of fish and aquatic life for *food* every year.

What would we say if we are utilitarians? Well we cannot talk about environmental *rights*, for there are *no* rights and again we might find it hard to show why this was morally wrong if we are utilitarians. We might think that the gold produced might cause a lot of happiness, not least because it is used in jewellery, computers, electronics, dentistry, medicine etc. The fish, plants, and other aquatic life do not have a comparably high level of pleasure or happiness compared to humans so all things being equal it might *not* be morally wrong. Of course, as with the other cases this will depend on how we spell out the details of the case but Utilitarianism does not appear to be as clear-cut as we perhaps might have hoped.

For the Kantian, we only have moral obligations towards rational agents and thus there is no such thing as a business's moral obligation towards the environment, as the environment is not a rational *agent*. Now this does not mean that Kant believes a business can do whatever it wants towards the environment.

If a business treats the environment as a means to an end (profit) then they are *modelling* a certain type of behaviour and this behaviour could then lead to businesses treating humans as a means to an end, which is wrong. So although the exploitation of the environment is not morally wrong for the Kantian, it legitimises and hence increases the possibility of exploitation of *people*, which is.

5. Business and Globalization

The world is getting smaller and it is increasingly easy to contact and work with people across the world. Whereas in the past a UK business might set its sights on reaching a few cities in the UK, businesses now have greater international opportunities. This brings a whole host of new ethical issues but rather than apply our moral theories to these issues, we will leave this to the reader. The aim in this section is to start you thinking about some of the issues.

Nike, Gap, M&S, H&M, Walmart, Nestlé and many more companies have been exposed as using child labour. Although this may not be illegal in the country where the children were used, people think it is very wrong. But is it? Consider this quotation from a Cameroonian father who is also a farmer: "[child labour] is considered as part of the household chores children do to help their parents. I do not consider this child abuse because we are making money that is used to pay their school fees".[8]

We can understand then that a local rural economy may well be wholly dependent on the use of child labour and therefore a blanket ban on child labour would have a directly negative effect on the livelihoods of a large number of people. But how much then are "western ideals" simply idiosyncratic? Should there be a complete ban or is it the case that:

> A global ban [...] *shows disrespect for other cultures by imposing a* western mindset *as to the economic role of children. A more sensible policy would be to apply some basic rules of humane working conditions in conjunction with a targeted, evolving approach that duly considers the actual outcomes of implemented measures.*[9]

Or consider another issue. As we said, it was not until quite recently that there has been a move to make businesses more environmentally friendly. During the industrial revolution in the UK there was no such requirement. Now consider businesses in "developing" countries. They are often trying to start from scratch with very poor infrastructure and a poor understanding of the environmental impact of their work. In fact, the West imposing their environmental standards on businesses would effectively stop such businesses developing and may lead to their collapse. If a farmer in Kenya has not only got to produce crops, but has to do so in a more expensive "environmentally friendly" way then that famer might struggle to survive. What right then do

---

8   F. Wijen, 'Banning Child Labour Imposes Naive Western Ideals on Complex Problems', https://www.theguardian.com/sustainable-business/2015/aug/26/ban-child-labour-developing-countries-imposes-naive-western-ideals-complex-problems

9   *Ibid*. Here and hereafter the emphasis is ours unless otherwise stated.

businesses in the West have to impose these environmental standards on businesses in other less affluent countries?

There are many other examples of the ethical issues that come with the increase in globalization. In general, these arise when there is a clash of cultures. For example, some cultures operate by using bribes; what then should businesses do within that culture? What about when a Western business is located in a culture which treats women as second class citizens; how should the business treat their female employees and successfully operate? The general question then is how far can we impose — if at all — Western business ethics in non-Western contexts?

SUMMARY

The label "business ethics" is relatively new. The customer is now very sensitive to how "ethical" a business is and thus any signs of moral wrongdoing by a business will lead to a slump in profits. This leads to a general question whether there is any incentive to be — rather than simply appearing to be — ethical.

One question that we have not yet addressed is whether capitalism — the environment needed for businesses to exist — is itself immoral? Marx, and many others, certainly thought that a system that leads us to seek after more money and more material goods will crush and stunt *human flourishing*.

If our function as humans involves devoting time to being healthy, being with friends and family, developing hobbies and skills, educating ourselves etc., then the "for profit" mentality of capitalism could be seen as not allowing us to fulfil this role.

> The essence of capitalism is to turn nature into commodities and commodities into capital. The live green earth is transformed into dead gold bricks, with luxury items for the few and toxic slag heaps for the many. The glittering mansion overlooks a vast sprawl of shanty towns, wherein a desperate, demoralized humanity is kept in line with drugs, television, and armed force.[10]

Perhaps then the most ethical response to business is to refuse to play the capitalist game of business in the first place and to rethink what "business" might mean and how a "business" should act.

---

10   M. Parenti, *Against Empire*.

COMMON STUDENT MISTAKES

- Confusing the legal questions and the moral questions.
- Thinking that Kant says we can *never* use people as means.
- Assuming that equal opportunity means treating everyone the same.
- Assuming that some from a culture can speak on behalf of all that culture.

ISSUES TO CONSIDER

1. Do you think that a university is a business?

2. What do you think the difference is between a business and a company?

3. Find some examples of a business's ethics and/or values statement. What are they saying? What do you think of them?

4. Write an ethics/value statement for your school.

5. What do you think of the argument that it is irrational for a business to be ethical?

6. Find a few examples of adverts. Explain in your own words what they are telling the customer. Is this intentional deception? Is it lying?

7. Imagine that as an employee you are offered a bribe. How would the utilitarian tell us to act? What about the Kantian? Is it always wrong to take bribes in business?

8. Some workplace rules seem true in every culture — e.g. do not use violence. Others, perhaps concerning dress code, do not. How then are we going to decide between those values that should be part of ethical business practice and those that are merely idiosyncratic features of Western business practice?

9. Why should business care about the world they leave for future generations? After all, future generations do not exist.

10. How far do you think capitalism is immoral?

11. If you do think that capitalism is immoral then what alternative is there? Why is the proposed alternative more *morally* acceptable?

12. What do you think about the final quotation from Parenti? What do you think the utilitarian and the Kantian would say about this quotation?

KEY TERMINOLOGY

Goods	Corporate Social Responsibility
Services	Whistleblowing
Stakeholders	Capitalism

References

Avis, D., 'Sports Direct: Former Employees Speak Out', *BBC News* (22 July 2016), freely available at http://www.bbc.co.uk/news/uk-36864345

'FT.com/Lexicon', *Financial Time*, freely available at http://lexicon.ft.com/Term?term=corporate-social-responsibility--(CSR)

'Horsemeat Scandal: Where Did the 29% Horse in your Tesco Burger Come From?', freely available at https://www.theguardian.com/uk-news/2013/oct/22/horsemeat-scandal-guardian-investigation-public-secrecy

Parenti, Michael, *Against Empire* (Saint Francisco: City Lights Books, 1995).

Strauss, K., 'The World's Most Ethical Companies 2016', Forbes, freely available at http://www.forbes.com/sites/karstenstrauss/2016/03/09/the-worlds-most-ethical-companies-2016

Wearden, G., 'How the PPI Scandal Unfolded', *the Guardian* (5 May 2011), freely available at https://www.theguardian.com/business/2011/may/05/how-ppi-scandal-unfolded

Wijen, F., 'Banning Child Labour Imposes Naive Western Ideals on Complex Problems', *the Guardian* (26 August 2015), freely available at https://www.theguardian.com/sustainable-business/2015/aug/26/ban-child-labour-developing-countries-imposes-naive-western-ideals-complex-problems

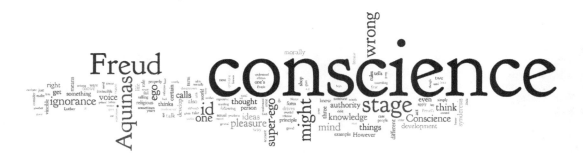

CHAPTER 9

Conscience

The bite of conscience, like the bite of a dog into stone, is a stupidity.

Friedrich Nietzsche

1. Introduction

Each of us has, at one time or another, talked about our conscience. We might have been "pricked by our conscience" or our conscience might have "butted in" when it was not wanted. We might be going on quite happily telling a lie to a friend, or might have accidentally walked out of a shop without paying for something and it is our conscience that makes us confess or stops us in our tracks spins us on our heels and takes us back into the shop.

People from different walks of life talk of the "conscience", from the religious believer, the politician, the celebrity, to every day folk; we might hear someone berate their conscience for nagging them to do something they do not want to. People might be labelled "conscientious objectors" because they feel their conscience is telling them to object to certain political actions, e.g. war. A protester might lament the erosion of their "freedom of conscience". And we can find concepts very similar to "conscience" in many non-Christian religious traditions both Eastern and Western throughout history and from around the globe.[1]

However, the nature of conscience is obscure and consequently the philosophical discussion of conscience is complex and has a long history. It draws on issues in philosophical psychology, philosophy of religion, epistemology, philosophy of mind, applied ethics, normative ethics and Metaethics.

In this chapter we'll give a general overview of two theories of conscience. One draws on Aquinas's account; the other Sigmund Freud's (1856–1939). Although Freud is not typically seen as a philosopher (he's a psychologist) his account will provide us with some insights which allows us to think philosophically about this thing we call "the conscience".

---

1   See P. Strohm, *Conscience*, p. 18, for a good overview of this.

2. The History of Conscience

In the twenty-first century conscience is not thought of as solely a religious idea. However talk of "conscience" was popularised, at least in "the West", due to its adoption by both Protestant and Catholic traditions. In this section we'll look how "conscience" is, and has been, used in order to draw out some general features.

"Conscience" played a role in one of the most famous speeches in the protestant reformation. **Martin Luther** (1483–1546), being charged with heresy and being forced to recant by Charles V, stands his grounds and says "Here I stand, I can do no other" and "I cannot nor will I retract anything, since it is never safe nor virtuous to go against conscience". Luther believed that his God-given conscience was not allowing him to recant, not even under the considerable pressure by the powerful people before him. Or consider a more recent example.

In the midst of political turmoil of the civil rights movement Martin Luther King Jr., who was under threat and constant pressure to change his views said:

> But, conscience asks the question, is it right? And there comes a time when we must take a position that is neither safe, nor politic, nor popular, but one must take it because it is right.[2]

Conscience is, then, powerful. It seems that it can move a person to put themselves in mortal danger, to "stand up and be counted", to act contrary to self-interest.

But it is not just saints and heroes that talk of conscience, conscience has been cited by the most repugnant and morally abhorrent people who have ever lived, racists, murderers, tyrants, dictators. For example as Bettina Stangneth's states in *Eichmann Before Jerusalem: The Unexamined Life of a Mass Murderer,*[3] a discussion of the inner life of one of the Nazi's most notorious officers: "Conscience was simply the 'morality of the Fatherland that dwells within' a person, which Eichmann also termed 'the voice of the blood'".

Conscience can be male or female or both or neither, it can be one voice or many, it can echo religious ideas, social ideas, racist ideas, lofty ideas or ideas found in the filth of human corruption. Conscience can develop at any particular age and dissipates at any age. It does not "speak", and it does "speak", and does not have a language of choice. All of these observations then leave a number of observations and questions.

2   M. L. King Jr., 'A Proper Sense of Priorities', http://www.aavw.org/special_features/speeches_speech_king04.html

3   S. Benhabib, 'Who's on Trial, Eichmann or Arendt?', http://opinionator.blogs.nytimes.com/2014/09/21/whos-on-trial-eichmann-or-anrendt

There seem to be (at least) three related functions that we think the conscience plays. First, *it tells us what we ought to do* as a *guide* for our lives. Second, it is a source of moral *knowledge*. That is, we might say "I *know* that stealing a pen is wrong because my conscience told me". Third it might be thought of as a *motivation*. That is, it might be the thing that actually gets us up out of our seat to act in certain ways, even when things are difficult or even life threatening.

Just to clarify, we can see the difference in the first two of these functions if we think of a tyrant who says for example: "my conscience tells me I have to kill all mentally ill people to help the country". Clearly this is a case where her conscience is telling her how she *ought to* behave. But, given that we think that killing the mentally ill is morally wrong, we do not want to say that in this case her conscience gives her *knowledge* of what is right and wrong. So it might be true that the conscience gives us guidance but not knowledge.

Equally the opposite seems true, that we might know what is right and wrong yet fail to be guided to do it. This predicament is what Shakespeare captured in this famous quotation: "conscience doth make cowards of us all" (Hamlet 3.1.78–82).

Consider another point. Conscience is *subjective* in that it is about one reflecting inwards on oneself, on how one might "feel" about certain things. It is not about looking *out* into the world, at a set of rules or laws. We experience the conscience differently than we would if a friend, priest, politician or Imam was telling us what to do. Of course, although conscience is "inward looking", that is not the same as saying that we just make up what the conscience allegedly tells us. For instance, we might think that what is right and wrong is dependent on God but also think that we come to know what is right and wrong through our conscience.

Finally it is worth noting that the term "conscience" was only formalized in its modern moral meaning in the mid eighteenth century (e.g. neither Plato nor Aristotle talk of conscience). However, note that just because a *term* is modern, or just because there is disagreement with how a term is used, that does not mean that the ideas themselves are new.

Consider the point that the terms "molecules" and "atoms" were recent inventions, and that in their development they might be used to talk about different things, and they engendered disagreement within the scientific community. This in itself does not lead us to the conclusion that there are no molecules and no atoms. So the lack of term "conscience", and disagreement about what "conscience" means does not mean that conscience is *merely* an "invention". With all these points in mind let's consider one of the key thinkers in relation to conscience, Aquinas.

3. Aquinas on Conscience

If you recall from Chapter 4, Aquinas developed a Natural Law theology. The basic idea is that through reason (what he calls *ratio*) we can come to recognize certain precepts that we ought to live by. Aquinas thinks that this reliance on thinking and reflection is revealed in the Bible:

> *They show that the requirements of the law are written on their hearts, their consciences also bearing witness, and their thoughts sometimes accusing them and at other times even defending them.*[4]

Notice then that for Paul — and Aquinas — the "conscience" *bears witness* sometimes accusing the person, sometimes defending them. For Aquinas *conscience is morally neutral*, it simply "bears witness", it is a "sign-post" and after all signposts do not opinions on things (see Aquinas, *Summa*, Part 1, Question 79, Article 13).

To be clear then Aquinas *did not take conscience to be a source of moral knowledge* but as a guide. This means that Aquinas, unlike Luther and post-reformation thinkers, took conscience to be *fallible*. For Aquinas we may be wrong in following our conscience as it can move us in the wrong direction/mislead us

For Aquinas the conscience is the act of applying the universal principles (the Eternal/Divine law) to actual real life situations.

Aquinas explicitly defines "conscience" as the "application of knowledge to activity" (*Summa Theologica*, I–II, I). So, if conscience for Aquinas is about the application of *knowledge* to activity, this raises the question how we get this knowledge? This is where another key technical term is introduced. The *synderesis*. Synderesis is not the same as conscience but is the innate ability of the mind — what he calls a *habit of the mind* — to apprehend the eternal/divine laws. The role of conscience is to apply the primary precepts discovered as the content of synderesis.

To get a better understanding of synderesis consider someone trying to work out the quickest way to get between two points. Through rational reflection they will see that it is the straight line. This "coming to recognize through reflection" is what Aquinas has in mind when he talks about synderesis. For Aquinas, unlike conscience, *synderesis is never mistaken*. Humans do wrong, thinks Aquinas, when *conscience* (and not synderesis) makes a mistake. This means that a *failure of conscience* needs to be clearly thought through on Aquinas's account.

---

4   T. Aquinas, *Romans*, 2:15.

For Aquinas, conscience errs because of *ignorance* about how to apply the eternal/divine laws, of which there are *two types*. Ignorance that *can be* overcome by using one's reason (*vincible ignorance*), and ignorance that *cannot be* overcome by using one's reason (*invincible ignorance*). Invincible ignorance is doing something wrong when one could not have known better; vincible ignorance is doing wrong when one *ought* to have known better. But how might this relate to conscience?

Imagine two people going into a gun shop. The first person has no criminal record, has never been in trouble with the police nor at school and they have no record of mental illness. He is, for all intents and purposes, a model citizen. This person buys a gun and goes on a killing rampage. The owner of the shop, by following her conscience, has not done something morally wrong because her *ignorance is invincible*; there was no indication that this would have been a likely outcome.

This contrasts to the person who is sold a gun even though he has a violent criminal record which would have shown up on a basic background check. In this case, the owner of the gun shop following her conscience has done something morally wrong because in this case her ignorance is vincible.

To conclude, Aquinas thinks all of us can know infallibly what is right and wrong through synderesis. However, even though we are infallible about this, we can, and do, make mistakes in applying this knowledge. It is our conscience (*conscientia)* which tells us how to apply this knowledge and moves us to act. It can go wrong through ignorance. Ignorance which could have been avoided (vincible) means our action is morally wrong. Mistakes deriving from ignorance we could not have avoided (invincible) means our action is *not* morally wrong.

In the next section, we will consider what Freud has to say about conscience, and explain how he reconceptualises it as a psychological and not theological concept, and in doing so argues we should not accept it as an inherently good notion.

4. Freud and the Conscience

Freud is best known as a psychologist and the architect of psychoanalysis. He is controversial and most philosophers and psychologists reject the ideas he presents. However, his ideas have been incredibly influential, and indeed his name has entered our everyday talk in the form of a "Freudian slip". Among Freud's many ideas his conceptualization of the structure of the mind is key to his views on conscience. He thinks the mind can be thought of as containing three parts: the *id*, the ego and the super-ego. *Freud's account of conscience is understood as the relation between these.*

For Freud the *id* is the collection of our primal drives, e.g. the basic desires for food, sex, drink and is the oldest part of the mind. The *id* cannot be properly formalized or understood and Freud likens it to chaos. It is instinctive, emotional and illogical. We cannot list all the drives that make up the *id* as they are inaccessible to us. Freud has a nice way of describing the *id*; he calls it: "…a cauldron full of seething excitations…". (SE, XXII.73). Although we can say very little about the content of the *id*, Freud did think that there was a general principle to help us understand the drives in the *id*, what he calls the "pleasure principle". This is the claim that what identifies and unifies the drives of the *id* is the avoidance of pain and pursuit of pleasure.

Now, as a very young child it may be OK to be driven by the pleasure principle; they crawl single-mindedly after the chocolate buttons to put in their mouth, they crave their mother's milk irrespective of anything else. However, as we develop we soon realize that we cannot simply act on the primal instincts of the *id* as we have to navigate ourselves in the social spaces we inhabit! We have to understand boundaries, sanctions and consequences. To successfully operate in the world, we need to consciously reflect and reason and ultimately, we have to delay instinctive behaviour and "weigh-up" the situation. Put bluntly someone whose *id* is unchecked would cease to be acceptable in society and find themselves physically, socially and emotionally isolated. It is what Freud calls the "ego" which plays this policing role.

But if we only have the *id* and the *ego* then it is unclear why we would not simply follow the pleasure principle. That is, although the ego rationally reflects, it needs something to weigh-up against the *id*. We need some *authority that monitors* what the ego is doing. This authority is what Freud calls the *super-ego*.

Early in our life our parents (as well as society, religious leaders etc.) tell us what we can and cannot do and chastise us for breaking rules, and as we grow older we internalize these things and "hear them" as a voice of authority. Imagine that your mum has always told you not to sit with your elbows on the table then you internalize this rule. So when you are much older and not living with your mum any longer the voice of your "super-ego" speaks with authority — "take your elbows off the table!" These are the very basics of Freud structure of the mind. Our ego balances the primal drives of the *id* with the voice of authority from the super-ego.

Where does the conscience come in? For Freud the *conscience is the form that the super-ego takes in addressing the ego*. When the internalized authority derived from parental (social/religious) rules and regulations controls the ego is it is understood as "the conscience". In our last example it is our "conscience" that tells us to remove our elbows from the table.

Notice then that our conscience often requires certain things from us which we fail to achieve and this gives rise to *guilt*. For Freud, the conscience can be thought of as synonymous with the "guilty conscience". Our ego is punished through guilt by the form of the super-ego we call conscience. Furthermore, Freud says that when the super-ego fails to deal properly with the *id* — when the pleasure principle is repressed — this forms what he calls *neurosis*.

You can also hopefully see the differences between Aquinas and Freud. First, the obvious point is that for Freud the conscience is *not* the voice of God. Second, unlike Aquinas, Freud thinks that the conscience could be bad, destructive and unhelpful. The conscience is the way the ego experiences the authority of the super-ego. But the super-ego is arrived at through the experiences we have. And, of course, we might have had really *bad* experiences growing up where parents are stifling, overly authoritarian, distant, cold, hard, violent, abusive etc. In these sorts of cases the conscience would be stifling, overly authoritarian, distant, etc. This means that although Freud does not think we can, or should, get rid of the conscience he does think we should treat it with a healthy dose of scepticism and hence not be kowtowed by the "guilt" that is our ego's punishment for falling short of the super-ego; conscience is the product of our often non-ideal upbringing rather than a divinely-inspired force for good.

5. Freud's Psychosexual Development Theory

Psychosexual Development Theory is a theory of sexual development from birth to death. Freud was the first thinker to look at the entire lifespan in terms of development. Freud thought that as we develop we move through different stages. At each stage our libido (sex drive) is focused towards different things. If we fail to move through a stage completely, or return to a stage, then problems arise and we might become fixated with the area associated with that stage. This can be a serious problem for our relationships and could be an underlying cause of mental illness.

The first stage is the oral stage from birth to about one and a half. This stage is where babies get pleasure through putting things in their mouth, pleasure in biting, chewing and sucking. For example, babies soon after they are born are breastfeeding and as the baby develops they navigate and explore the world through putting things in their mouth. Notice that during this phase babies are very dependent on others. According to Freud at this stage not only do we get information about the world, but we also fulfil the *id*. Babies who can bite, chew and such as much as they want are being guided by the *id*. Freud explains behaviours like smoking, chewing gum, overeating, with failure to move properly through this stage which prevented the successful development of the *id*.

The next stage, from about one and a half to three years, is the *anal stage*. Here pleasure is gained through *controlling going to the toilet*. This stage is about gaining control of one's body, and it starts with controlling the bladder and bowels (being potty trained). It is around this time that the ego develops. This control of their bodies is a source of pride and pleasure for children. Agents who fail to properly move through this stage are what are sometimes called "anally retentive". That is, someone who is overly controlling or out of control and messy, because — according to Freud — they do not want to let go of their waste, or do not care where or when they let go of their waste.

The next phase of development, from about three to six years, is *the phallic stage* in which a child discovers one's genitals, and importantly that they are different in men and women. This stage is where Freud thinks we develop the Oedipus and the Electra complex. A problematic phallic stage will cause problems with intimacy in later life.

The next stage, *the latency stage*, is from six years to the onset of puberty. This stage is not about pleasure in the body as the libido is "latent" or hidden — this is the stage where sexual desire is repressed and no new sexual desires emerge. At this stage girls play with girls in order to learn the role of a girl and boys play with boys in order to learn about the role of boys.. The child learns how to navigate the social world. A difficult latency stage leads to relational problems and understanding one's gender.

The libido then reappears in the final stage which lasts to our death and which Freud calls the *mature genital stage*. This is where the individual not only recognises the difference between men and women but also shows a desire to engage in a sexual relationship and, more generally, a pursuit of pleasure and happiness. People become sexually active, fall in love and get married. This is the stage where we acquire a fully developed conscience.

SUMMARY

The notion of "conscience" has appeared for thousands of years in different cultures, even though it has not always been called "conscience". Modern Christian orthodoxy popularised it and characterised it in relation to God's voice, and guidance. Aquinas thought that conscience is the way we understand how to apply what we know. In Aquinas's view, our conscience is fallible and might guide us wrongly. When our conscience "gets it wrong" we can be either culpable — through vincible ignorance — or not culpable — through invincible ignorance.

Freud is less convinced that conscience is a force for good, and he is certain that it has not got anything to do with God. For Freud conscience can be either a good *or* bad. We can think of our mind as having three parts, the *id*, ego and super-ego. The conscience for Freud is the form the super-ego takes when it is trying to keep the ego in line. It is internalized as the voice of authority. The super-ego is about following rules but those rules do not come from "on high", they derive from the upbringing we have had. So if we have had a repressive upbringing then the super-ego — the voice of conscience — will be repressive. How we develop these three features of the mind is through what Freud calls Psychosexual Development; if we do not develop correctly then we become fixated and repressive, form a neurosis and ultimately become mentally ill. Freud thought that this could be avoided by working through the Psychosexual Stages in the normal way, and can be treated through psychosexual counselling.

COMMON STUDENT MISTAKES

- Writing conscious when meaning conscience.
- Confuse synderesis and conscience.
- Confusing conscience as guidance with conscience as the source of knowledge.
- Believe Freud thinks the conscience is always bad.
- Thinking that for Aquinas conscience is way of knowing what is right and wrong.
- Thinking that because the *term* conscience is new, conscience itself is a modern invention.

ISSUES TO CONSIDER

1. Do you think you have a conscience? What does it tell you?

2. What is the difference between synderesis and conscience?

3. Do you think that everyone ultimately knows — if they reason correctly — what is right and wrong?

4. What is the difference between vincible and invincible? Is not most of the supposedly invincible knowledge, really vincible? We just need to try harder?

5. What are the possible different roles for the conscience?

6. Could the conscience be a morally bad thing?

7. Why does Freud think we need to be cautious about listening to our conscience?

8. How does Freud's account of conscience relate to his Psychosexual Development Theory?

9. What do you think about Freud's Psychosexual Development Theory?

10. Draw up a table of the key stages and accompanying characteristics of Freud's Psychosexual Development Theory.

11. Could it ever make sense to talk about animals/robots having a conscience? If not, why not?

12. Do you think conscience will still shape our lives in one thousand years?

KEY TERMINOLOGY

Pleasure principle	Vincible ignorance
Id	Invincible ignorance
Ego	Psychosexual Development Theory (oral, anal, phallic, latency and mature genital phases)
Super-ego	
Synderesis	

References

Aquinas, Thomas, *Summa Theologica*, freely available at http://www. newadvent.org/summa/

—, *Romans (Commentary on the Letter of Saint Paul to the Romans)*.

Benhabib, Seyla, 'Who's on Trial, Eichmann or Arendt?', *The New York Times* (21 September 2014), freely available at http://opinionator.blogs.nytimes. com/2014/09/21/whos-on-trial-eichmann-or-anrendt

Freud S. and Freud A., *Complete Psychological Works of Sigmund Freud* (New York: Random House, 2001).

Giubilini, Alberto, 'Conscience', *The Stanford Encyclopedia of Philosophy*, Winter 2016 ed., edited by Edward N. Zalta, freely available at https:// plato.stanford.edu/archives/win2016/entries/conscience/

King, Martin Luther, 'A Proper Sense of Priorities', 6 February 1968, Washington, D.C., freely available at http://www.aavw.org/special_ features/speeches_speech_king04.html

Strohm, Paul, *Conscience: A Very Short Introduction* (Oxford: Oxford University Press, 2011), vol. 273, https://doi.org/10.1093/ actrade/9780199569694.001.0001

CHAPTER 10

Sexual Ethics

Only when you [have sex] [...] are you most cleanly alive and most cleanly yourself. [...] Sex isn't just friction and shallow fun. Sex is also the revenge on death. Don't forget death. Don't ever forget it. Yes, sex too is limited in its power. [...] But tell me, what power is greater?[1]

There is no morality intrinsic to sex, although general moral rules apply to the treatment of others in sex acts as they apply to all human relationships.[2]

1. Philosophy of Sex Introduction

While we write this chapter, a court in the United Arab Emirates have detained a foreign couple in their twenties for having sex outside marriage and if found guilty they will both face a lengthy jail sentence.[3] Shortly after the 2017 General Synod vote in the UK on whether same sex couples could be "blessed" in church, the eminent theologian and academic Professor John Milbank tweeted: "There is no need to demand "celibacy" in gay relationships. That wrongly equates same sex physical affection with full (heterosexual) sex".[4] Now there might have been a subtle and sophisticated theological point here. Or there might not. Whatever the right response to Milbank is, what it makes clear, and what probably does not need pointing out, is that "sex" is, has been, and always will be an issue of great importance to people. Moreover, it makes clear that the very notion of "sex" is a philosophically interesting one. What, after all, is "sex"? What does it mean to talk about heterosexual sex as "full" sex in such a context? Was Monica Lewinsky correct to say that she did not have sex with Bill Clinton, the then president of the US, because it was "only" oral sex? What is the role of sexual pleasure in defining sex? What is consent? Is pornography wrong? What is sexual perversion? Of course, we can only deal here with a very small fraction of some of these issues (for an excellent survey

---

1   P. Roth, *The Dying Animal*, p. 69.
2   Alan H. Goldman, 'Plain Sex', p. 49.
3   'Couple "Detained in UAE for Sex Outside Marriage"', *BBC News*, http://www.bbc.co.uk/news/world-africa-39208946
4   https://twitter.com/johnmilbank3/status/831996919400513536

of articles see Sobel 2008) and our focus will be on some of the *ethical issues* to do with sex.

We start this chapter by discussing the very definition of "sex"; we then move onto discussing some of the things that different moral philosophers might say about sex. Hopefully you can see why this is the right order. For, we suggest, a lot of the ethical discussions about sex already presuppose what sex is, but that presupposition is controversial. Thus we need to be clear about the different ways to understand sex and this will enable us to explore more usefully the various moral issues associated with sex.

2. What Is It to "Have Sex"?

This question is not the same as what is "sexual orientation", or, what is one's sex — as opposed to one's gender. There might be some that would be bemused when faced with the question "what is it to have sex?" Typical (frustrated) philosophers! Is the answer not obvious? Sex is penis-in-vagina penetrative intercourse (*coitus*) — end of story. Well maybe…but consider some other questions. How essential is orgasm in the definition of sex? Imagine that two people engage in coitus but there is no orgasm: is this "having sex"? What about if one person has an orgasm where the other does not? Or imagine that people are involved in manual genital stimulation to orgasm, is this sex? What about people engaged in oral sex, can this count as "having sex"? What about rape? If someone is raped is it correct to say they have "had sex"? And things get even more confusing….

Given the definition of sex as coitus, then this obviously means that by definition homosexual sex is conceptually impossible. This might seem false and simply offensive. Sex as coitus also gives rise to some odd situations. Imagine a women asked her partner if he was a virgin and got the following response: "yes I am…I've only been involved in homosexual penis-in-anus penetrative intercourse". The women might be perplexed (to say the least). She might sensibly think he is deluded in calling himself a "virgin". Anal sex *is* sex, and consequently our initial definition of "sex" as *coitus* is incomplete.

Notice that things are also complicated by the fact that people who are involved in sexual activity sometimes themselves report uncertainty about whether they have actually had sex. We can imagine someone being asked: "did you have sex with her?" and receiving the answer: "well it depends…" It seems then that "having sex" is a more complex notion that we might have first thought. These points are worth keeping in mind when we talk about the ethical questions that are involved in "having sex". In particular, the reader should ask themselves if a particular account of "having sex" is being used and importantly what if that definition were changed.

3. Natural Law and Sex

If you recall when we discussed Natural Law Theory (NLT) in Chapter 4, something is good if that thing fulfils its function. A good knife is one that cuts well, a good guitar is one that plays well, etc. Therefore, in order to work out what "good" sex is we need to ask what sex is *for*. What is its function? In answering this question, we should then be able to work out what is morally acceptable sexual activity.

St. Aquinas and other Natural Law theorists would say that our sexual faculties have one true end — *procreation*. True, sex is pleasurable but it is pleasurable *in order* to fulfil this end. If this is correct then sexual activity is good if, and only if, it is consistent with procreation and bad in so far as it *frustrates* that end. It is important to understand that the outcome is independent of desires, wants, reasons, hopes, fears etc. and that for the Natural Law Theorist (NLT) it is simply an *objective fact* whether a sexual act is wrong or right, something which is not affected by culture, religion, etc. This means that for the NLT there are objective moral truths regarding how we ought, and ought not, to behave sexually.

We can say then that, for the traditional NLT, premarital sex, masturbation, bestiality, contraception, homosexual acts, pornography and adultery are all wrong. Premarital sex is wrong because children would be brought into the world outside the safe confines of marriage. Homosexual acts have no tendency towards procreation at all; contraception frustrates procreative ends; masturbation and pornography focus the sexual acts *inwards* towards oneself, frustrating procreative ends. However, it is vital to make a number of clarifications as people often misunderstand NLT.

The NLT is *not* claiming that *anything* that frustrates natural ends is wrong but rather only *human* acts. So, according to the NLT, the fact that, for instance, the Bonobo monkeys engage in "rape", "masturbation" and "homosexual" acts does not mean that they are doing something morally wrong.

Furthermore there is a difference between using something wrongly and *not using it at all*. We use a knife wrongly if we try to use it as a violin bow but not by leaving it in the knife drawer. So, not using sexual faculties (*celibacy*) *is morally acceptable* for the NLT.

However, on the face of it NLT does seem to have a lot of counter examples; there are lots of things that we agree *are not* wrong but *do* seem to frustrate natural ends. For example, imagine I regularly walk on my hands, or I am fed through a tube rather than using my perfectly good mouth, both these seem to be frustrating the natural ends of my hands and mouth, but surely such things are not *morally* wrong?

But, an NLT would agree because these sorts of examples are *not* cases of the faculty being used to "*frustrate*" the natural end of the hands or mouth. If on the other hand we wired someone's jaw shut so they could not eat through the mouth, or if someone *always* walked on their hands even though they had perfectly good legs, then this might be different.[5] But as it stands simply using a faculty for something other than what it is for is not the same as using that faculty to *frustrate* its end.

Furthermore, the claim is not that if you use a faculty *with the knowledge* that it will be frustrated then it is wrong; it is that if you *intend* to use it to be frustrated. So, for example, sex between a man and women when the woman is pregnant is not wrong for the NLT.

Also, the claim is not that if something is "unnatural" it is wrong. Deciding whether something is right or wrong is not the same as asking whether something is "man-made or not". If this was the case, wearing glasses and taking medication would be wrong and the NLT is not committed to this. So the use of sex toys, or various medications such as Viagra is not wrong even though they are unnatural.

We might think that linking sex to procreation in this way would take all the fun out of sex but this is not the case. Just as one can eat a dish in many different ways whilst always fulfilling the natural function of eating, one can be involved in different forms of sexual act, fantasy, etc. as long as it is part of the *long term function* of the sexual organs (so, for example, oral sex is not necessarily ruled out as long as it is, overall, part of a sex act that is intended for procreation).

As noted, the NLT does, though, rule out homosexual sex and all forms of contraception because having sex whilst using contraception is to use the sexual faculties whilst *intending to frustrate* their end.

The plausibility of this theory need not turn on how religious you are. We could give an *atheistic evolutionary biological* account that also talks about the "function" of our sexual faculties.

There are many things which we could ask regarding this overall NLT approach to the ethics of sex. However, the main question to ask turns on *why* we might think that just because something *is* the case; namely, it is the function of sexual faculties to reproduce, that this is how things *ought* to be.

---

5   These examples are cited by Edward Feser here: https://www.youtube.com/watch?v=rynlfg gqAcU&t=5773s

This "is/'ought" gap plagues many moral theories but seems particularly pressing here. Put simply, it does not seem problematic for someone using contraception to say: "true, I am intending to frustrate the natural function of my sexual faculties but *why* does that mean I *ought* not do it?"

Summary of Natural Law Theory's view on sex			
Sexual Act/Activity	Morally Acceptable	Morally Unacceptable	It Depends...
Celibacy	X		
Oral sex			X
Homosexual sex		X	
Contraception		X	
Premarital sex		X	
Adultery		X	
Masturbation		X	
Sex toys			X
Sadomasochism			X
Viagra	X		
Pornography		X	
Anal sex		X	
Prostitution		X	

4. Kant and Sex

Kant thinks that sex is morally permissible within the context of a heterosexual, lifelong, and monogamous marriage. Any sexual act outside these contexts — homosexuality, masturbation, adultery, premarital sex — is *morally wrong*. His reasons for thinking this are very complex, not least because his writing on the subject, like just about all of his writing, is incredibly dense, but broadly speaking, his views on sex are based on his Second Formulation of the Categorical Imperative (see Chapter 2): *act in such a way that you always treat humanity, whether in your own person or in the person of any other, never simply as a means, but always at the same time as an end.*

Kant, like St. Augustine (354–430) and sometimes Freud, is what Alan Soble (1947–) calls a sexual *pessimist* (Plato and many modern philosophers would be counted as sexual *optimists*). The broad feeling amongst the pessimists is that our sexual desires and impulses, and acting upon those impulses, are undignified. The sexual part of our nature is unbefitting to how humans should behave and threatens our proper moral life.

For Kant, sexual desire is the only impulse in us that takes the body of another human as the *object* of indulgence. Kant says regarding *sexual* appetite:

> *Far from there being any concern for the happiness of the loved one, the lover, in order to satisfy his [sexual] desire and still his [sexual] appetite, may even plunge the loved one into the depths of misery [...] [and after having sex] the person is cast aside as one casts away a lemon which has been sucked dry.*[6]

If you recall from Chapter 2, Kant believes that treating others as *whole persons* is key to being moral, but for him, this is precisely what is missing in sexual desires. That is, in sex we are treating others as *objects* and not treating them as whole persons and hence we are acting immorally. In the language of his second formulation of the Categorical Imperative: in having sex we are treating people *merely* as a means to an end. Consider this full expression of Kant's sexual pessimism:

> *Because sexuality is not an inclination which one human being has for another as such, but is an inclination for the sex of another, it is a principle of the* degradation of human nature, *in that it gives rise to the preference of one sex to the other, and to the dishonouring of that sex through the satisfaction of desire.*[7]

So if this is his general pessimistic view of sex how does that relate to a view on *ethics*? As it stands it looks like *any* sexual desire or act is going to be morally wrong, but if that is the case, then that means that for Kant the continued existence of the human race is evidence of immoral behaviour! That is surely wrong. Well, for Kant, the only reason it is not wrong is the role of marriage.

In the context of *marriage*, and only in marriage, Kant thinks that sex and sexual desire is more than simply treating another merely as a means to an end. But why?

First we must understand what Kant means by marriage:

> [Marriage] *is an agreement between two persons by which* they grant each other equal reciprocal rights, *each of them undertaking to surrender the whole of their person to the other with a complete right of disposal over it.*[8]

So we can avoid the charge of objectifying and using a sexual partner merely as a means to an end *because in sex within marriage you are treating each other as a whole person and thus there is reciprocity.* Sex within marriage is about the *whole person* and not simply the genitals, sexual desire and pleasure. How does this work? This is how Soble starts to approach this question:

> *But because the acquisition* [of another through sex] *in marriage is reciprocal, each person regains his or her personhood (and hence does not lose it, after all). When I "surrender" myself to you, and you thereby acquire me, but you also "surrender" yourself to me, and I thereby acquire*

---

6   I. Kant, *Lectures on Ethics*, cited in A. Soble, *The Philosophy of Sex: Contemporary Readings*, p. 200.
7   Cited in *ibid.*, p. 260.
8   *Ibid.*, p. 202.

you, which "you" includes the "me" that you have acquired, we each surrender but then reacquire ourselves.[9]

This reciprocity though is not present in non-marital sexual relationships. This is very hard to understand on many levels and we urge the reader not to get too caught up on this.

We wanted to show you that Kant is complex and that the answers are not simple. The greatest Kant scholars are still not sure how to understand his ideas on sex. The thing to remember though is that via the second formulation of the Categorical Imperative Kant thinks that sex outside heterosexual marriage is wrong. Within marriage it is acceptable.

5. Sex and Utilitarianism

As you will recall from Chapter 1 Utilitarianism does not rule out an act on the basis of it being *a particular act*. This means that if Utilitarianism is correct we cannot say that any particular sex act is *always* wrong. Premarital sex, or homosexual sex, or masturbation, or oral sex can be morally *acceptable*. The matter is decided by whether or not performing that act brings about more pleasure *overall* than not doing so. This leaves a few questions and qualifications that need to be made.

First, although sex will typically lead to pleasure that does not mean that Utilitarianism is committed to the claim that the act of having sex is always good. Utilitarianism *does* leave space for us to show that rape and paedophilia are morally wrong. For even though the rapist or paedophile might get pleasure from their act, it does not take much to see that the *overall* unhappiness, the mental and physical suffering of the victim, the distress of relatives and loved ones etc. is much greater because the act has taken place.

Second, just because sex is typically pleasurable it does not mean Utilitarianism is committed to the claim that we have a duty to have as much sex as possible. For there are things we can do that bring about more overall happiness. Or we might suppose that having sex all the time might have detrimental effects on relationships and one's mental and physical health.

Third, for Utilitarianism, heterosexual sex within a marriage might be morally *wrong* if there has been coercion or threats, or just a general unhappiness with perfunctory sex, where almost any other activity would bring about more happiness. (Notice then the contrast with the Kantian and the NLT accounts).

Fourth, adultery or having multiple sexual partners can be morally *acceptable*. We can imagine a case where, for example, the overall happiness is

---

9   *Ibid.*, p. 278.

increased if a married couple agree to have sex with other people to keep their own marriage fun and interesting. Or we might think that someone who is generally not interested in, or does not have time for, a long-term relationship is happier with mutually consenting multiple sexual partners (or prostitutes).

Fifth, Mill gives a different answer to Bentham to questions regarding what we ought to do when considering various sex acts because of his distinction between *higher and lower pleasures*. In general Mill did not value sex and he took the pleasures that arose from it to be fleeting and of lower value. This is because Mill thought that some pleasures are qualitatively distinct from others and thus outweigh other, lower, pleasures. Bentham however would not make this distinction (see Chapter 1 section 9).

So if we keep this distinction in mind we might be able to distinguish between *types* of sex acts. Perhaps some sex acts are lower and some higher than others? We'll leave the reader to think through some of the implications of this.

6. Sex and the Virtue Theory

Although virtue theorists do write about many applied ethical issues, they typically do not write about sex. Those that do (e.g. Elizabeth Anscombe (1919–2001), Peter Geach (1916–2013) and Roger Scruton (1944–)) often support a more conservative sexual ethic. However, there are a few (e.g. Raja Halwani (1967–)) who do not defend traditional accounts of sexual ethics and consequently, it is unhelpful to try and work out "the" virtue theory view on sexual conduct. So we will give the reader a framework to think through some issues that arise when you think about sexual ethics through the lens of virtue theory.

If you recall, virtue theory *is not* a theory devised to help us make decisions. We cannot ask a virtue theorist: "how should we *calculate* what to do in this or that situation"? When faced with this sort of question, the virtue theorist will answer that you should do whatever a virtuous *agent* would do. But what is it to be virtuous? Well, the general idea is that to be virtuous is to develop certain *dispositions or habits* so that we respond to things in the world in the right way, at the right time, with the right reasons, to the right extent.

To get a sense of this, recall the "Doctrine of the Golden Mean" from Aristotle (see Chapter 3 section 4). The idea here is that by acting *between excess and deficiency* regarding certain feelings we are acting rationally, that is, virtuously. If we keep doing this then we will develop a habit or disposition for this sort of action, and we will just get better at "seeing" what is required of us and responding in the right way in any particular situations. For instance, take "fear".

To have an excess of fear is to be *cowardly* whereas the lack of fear is to be *rash* or headstrong. To act rationally with regard to fear is to have the virtue of *courage*. The more we act courageously then the better we will be at having courage and thus will need less help from others in order to see what is courageous. We can repeat this for other virtues, e.g. the virtue of "generosity" would be the mean between stinginess and wastefulness.

When discussing sexual ethics a number of different virtues might be relevant. In terms of an Aristotelian approach the virtue that is relevant is *temperance* (the vice being *intemperance*). This virtue is to do with our *desires* or *appetites* — this includes the desire for food, drink, and importantly for us, sex. A rough modern interpretation of this virtue would be "moderation". The person who has the virtue of temperance will not either be a drunk or a glutton or be someone who is teetotal or who starves himself. In relation to sex, the agent who has the virtue of temperance will not simply be driven by unchecked sexual desires nor will he deny natural sexual desires completely but rather he will have sex at the right time, with the right people for the right reasons.

One way of seeing if our action is *intemperate* is if our actions conflict with our other goals and virtues. One example is health. Someone who is intemperate with regard to sex (e.g. promiscuous) would *potentially* become unhealthy — perhaps physically and emotionally. Or consider other things we might value such as friendship or education: in these too we can imagine how intemperance might make these ends hard to achieve — e.g. just consider how a friendship would be wrecked or made impossible with constant unwanted sexual advances. There are some other things that the virtue theorist might say about sex.

First, the virtue theorist would say that *rape is always wrong* because it violates the other person's *sexual* autonomy which is the choice of when and how to have sex and with whom. Second, *paedophilia is also always wrong for similar reasons*. Adultery *might* be wrong because an intemperate person would break the marriage vows *because of their sexual desire*.

So, like Utilitarianism, the answer to whether a virtue theorist would think a certain sexual activity is right or wrong will depend on whether a virtuous agent would do that act, and that would depend on whether the activity fitted within the Golden Mean.

SUMMARY

Philosophers since at least Plato have discussed sex as it raises a number of interesting philosophical questions. Sex is about relationships and interactions between people and consequently it seems to be a moral issue. Anyone that believes that sex is not a moral issue should ask themselves whether they think rape or paedophilia is morally wrong. However, when we move past such clear-cut cases, the issues become more subtle and complex.

We considered a number of philosophical theories which give very different views. The Natural Law Theorist uses the idea of function and goal to ground a "conservative" view of sex. The Kantian also uses the idea of autonomy and respect for a person to ground a conservative view of sex, with a splash of pessimism about the unbefitting nature of sexual desire thrown in for good measure. Utilitarianism and Virtue Theory are less pessimistic and, as with their views on the other issues we have looked at in this book, more open to see what arises in different situations.

The two questions we leave you with are these. Having read this chapter, what do you think sex is? And how should moral theory guide our sexual practice?

COMMON STUDENT MISTAKES

- Believing that Aquinas thinks that if sex doesn't lead to pregnancy it is wrong.
- Believing that for Aquinas sex has to be perfunctory and boring.
- Thinking that the Utilitarian must think we should be promiscuous.
- Not realizing that it isn't clear what "sex" means.
- Not realizing that how one defines "sex" will change how one answers moral questions.

ISSUES TO CONSIDER

1. Imagine you were visited by an alien. The alien says "I've heard lot about 'having sex'. What do you humans mean by this?" How would you respond?

2. Do you think that sex is a moral issue? If so, what sorts of questions should moral philosophers consider in this area?

3. Would the NLT think that using ear plugs or riding a bike were wrong? After all, they seem to frustrate the natural faculties of the ears and the legs.

4. Could you be an atheist and be a NLT?

5. In some countries same sex marriage is permissible. Do you think that in these countries Kant would say that homosexual sex is morally acceptable?

6. Why does Kant think having multiple wives or husbands is morally wrong?

7. Would you count Mill as a sexual optimist or pessimist?

8. For Utilitarianism could bestiality be morally acceptable?

9. What might Rule Utilitarianism (Chapter 1) say about some of these issues, e.g. whether adultery is morally right or wrong?

10. How might Mill's distinction between higher and lower pleasures be relevant in this context?

11. What virtues and vices might be associated with sex?

12. Use the Doctrine of the Golden Mean to think through the morality of a sexual activity.

KEY TERMINOLOGY

Sex	Autonomy
Natural Law Theory	Agency
Doctrine of the Golden Mean	Means and End

References

Aristotle, *The Nicomachean Ethics* (Oxford: Clarendon Press, 1908), freely available at http://sacred-texts.com/cla/ari/nico/index.htm

'Couple "Detained in UAE for Sex Outside Marriage"', *BBC News*, freely available at http://www.bbc.co.uk/news/world-africa-39208946

Goldman, A. H., 'Plain Sex', *Philosophy & Public Affairs*, 6.3 (1977): 267–87.

Halwani, R., *The Philosophy of Love, Sex and Marriage: An Introduction* (Oxford: Routledge, 2010), https://doi.org/10.4324/9780203856369

Mill, J. S., 'Utilitarianism', in *Utilitarianism and Other Essays*, ed. by Alan Ryan (London: Penguin Books, 2004).

Milbank, John [@johnmilbank3], 'There is no Need to Demand "Celibacy" in Gay Relationships. That Wrongly Equates Same Sex Physical Affection with Full (Heterosexual) Sex', https://twitter.com/johnmilbank3/status/831996919400513536

Bentham, Jeremy, 'An Introduction to the Principles of Morals and Legislation', in *Utilitarianism and Other Essays*, ed. by Alan Ryan (London: Penguin Books, 2004).

—, *An Introduction to the Principles of Morals and Legislation*, freely available at http://www.econlib.org/library/Bentham/bnthPML18.html

Roth, Philip, *The Dying Animal* (London: Random House, 2010).

Soble, Alan, *The Philosophy of Sex: Contemporary Readings* (Plymouth: Rowman & Littlefield, 2002).

—, *The Philosophy of Sex and Love: An Introduction* (Paragon House, 1998).

CHAPTER 11

Stealing

You shall not steal.[1]

1. Stealing: Introduction

The Bible reference above is *absolutist* in nature. It does not say that you should not steal so long as you have enough resources available to you, or that you should not steal if your neighbour has been good to you. Rather, it simply says that you should not steal full stop. Partly as a result of this particular commandment and the impact of Christianity upon social custom in many parts of the world, the message that stealing is a moral wrong is pervasive and fairly uncontroversial, at least *prima facie*. For example, if you hear that someone has been sent to prison for stealing, it would likely take something atypical for you to question whether or not the person deserved punishment for his or her crime. In this chapter, we apply the key normative theories of Kantian Ethics, Utilitarianism and Virtue Ethics to the issue of stealing.

2. Defining Stealing

Beginning a chapter on the ethics of stealing, it is important to make clear exactly what "stealing" amounts to. At first, this may seem like a fairly simple task; stealing is just the taking of another person's property without their consent. Indeed, if reality television programmes following British Traffic Police are anything to go by, this definition is of use not merely for philosophy classes, but for the real world also; theft of vehicles is often categorised as an example of TWOC — "taking without owners' consent".

Yet, it is not always clear that stealing comfortably fits this definition. For example, we might wonder if it is possible to steal an item even though the owner has given you consent to take it. The original definition would rule this out as a conceptual impossibility, but consider someone who, whilst inebriated (perhaps even drugged against their will), gives you permission

---

1   Exodus 20:15, https://www.biblegateway.com/passage/?search=Exodus+20

to take an item of value from their house. Even though you have their explicit permission, acting on this verbal instruction and stealing their television still might seem to be an act of theft.

As a second counterexample to the original definition, imagine that you are better at cards than someone else, although you hide this fact from them. If you play a game for real money, and beat them in hand after hand after hand, might it be suggested that you have stolen their money even though they freely entered into the game?

There are responses to these two examples, of course. We might deny that either is an act of stealing, or deny that proper consent was ever given — this seems particularly compelling in the first example. However, we can also cast doubt on the definition by focussing not on the issue of consent, but on the idea of property. For example, if a person is being paid by the hour, but spends an undue amount of time on social media or checking sports scores, have they stolen money or time from their employer? Or, as a second possible example, if I make up a joke that is then retold by someone else, have they stolen "property" without my consent? This is a genuinely important issue in the field of comedy, for example. Again, the original definition might be defensible as a mechanism for capturing such instances of stealing. However, if it is defensible, it is only because of a broad reading of the idea of property, taking the concept far beyond the physical.

Finally, consider the example of someone who fails to pay their legally due portion of tax to the government. Again, we might wonder if this person has "stolen" money just by refusing to hand over their financial property. If so, our reading of the original definition of stealing would again need to be rather broad.

All of this has hopefully opened your minds to the variety of acts that may or may not be labelled as stealing. We will proceed in this chapter with the rough understanding of stealing provided at the start of this section, but with a broad and liberal interpretation of both "property" and "consent".

3. Kantian Ethics on Stealing

In Chapter 2, we outlined the structure of Kantian Ethics, named after its creator Immanuel Kant. It would be best to engage with Chapter 2 before considering the application of Kantian thinking to the issue of stealing in this section. Background knowledge of this theory is therefore assumed in what follows.

To determine whether an act is morally permissible (acceptable) or not, we can utilise two formulations of the Kantian Categorical Imperative. According to the first formulation, if we consider the maxim behind an action (the general principle that supports the action in the mind of the person acting), then we should consider whether or not that maxim could be willed to become a universal law. According to the second formulation, we should consider whether or not the action involves treating another person merely as a means to an end, rather than an end in themselves.

To consider what guidance Kantian Ethics would provide regarding stealing, let us first take an example of stealing where the question of whether it seems possible that it might be morally acceptable can apparently be answered uncontroversially with a "no". Consider a person who steals a toy from a child when their parent's back is turned. The thief, in this case, seems to act on the maxim "take the property of others whenever you please". It seems that we could not will this maxim to become a universal law, because if everyone took the property of others whenever they pleased, then whole concept of property would break down. Thus, such a maxim could not be universalised without contradiction (much like the example of breaking promises). The reason for the breakdown of the concept of "property" in this case is clear if we think about the idea of "ownership". If anyone can take any object whenever they want, then no one can truly be said to own anything. For example, if I could (without moral condemnation) take the pen out of your hand on the basis of the universalised maxim as described above, then there is a clear sense in which you might have been holding the pen without ever owning the pen.

Indeed, not only does the act of theft as described fail against the first formulation of Kant's Categorical Imperative, it also fails against the second formulation. If you steal from the child, then you are quite clearly not treating the child (or the person caring for the child) as a free and rational agent with their own dignity; on the contrary you are using them merely as a means to your own end of securing property that you desire.

That Kantian Ethics speaks against the moral permissibility of stealing toys from children should be no surprise — any theory that did not speak against such actions would likely be in trouble. However, the structure of the Kantian response to this case is what really matters, for it is a structure that we can apply to other cases. Take an example of stealing that is plausibly moral defensible, perhaps involving stealing from a financially powerful and internationally influential supermarket chain in order to feed your hungry family. The Kantian view regarding this case will be informative as to the wider response of Kantian Ethics to stealing.

In this new example, the maxim behind the action might be thought to be "take the property of others only when it is necessary for survival" (putting this example into the most extreme and therefore plausibly morally defensible form that we can). Can this maxim be willed to be a universal law? Well, even as it stands, there are reasons for thinking that such a maxim could not be universalised. For one, food is always strictly necessary for our survival, along with water, medical treatment and, in the modern age, some financial resource. Indeed, even someone who burgles a house to steal a television might act on such a maxim if they plan on selling that television in order to pay a debt to a potentially violent individual. The breadth of such a universalised maxim thus brings us back to the issue that afflicted the previous maxim, and the concept of property may not survive universalisation of such a maxim.

Still, even in referring to the maxim in the more specific form of "take the property of others only when it is necessary for survival", it might be suggested that we are venturing away from the approach with which Kant would be happy. Alasdair MacIntyre (1929–) has suggested that when it comes to applying the test of universalisation the system can be manipulated by being overly specific with the maxim. He says:

> All I need to do is to characterise the proposed action in such a way that the maxim will permit me to do what I want while prohibiting others from doing what would nullify the action if universalised.[2]

Thus, on this view, I apparently could universalise the maxim "take bread from a financially powerful supermarket only when you or immediate family members are at the point of starvation". Indeed, less desirably, I seemingly could universalise the maxim "People with my fingerprint can steal from a shop whenever they feel hungry", since there would be nothing contradictory in this becoming a universal law; the concept of property would not break down if only I could steal things I desired. However, there is a question — as referred to in Chapter 2 when this formulation of the Categorical Imperative was explained in more detail — as to whether or not a maxim of this type could be understood as a universal law. This is because its application would clearly not be universal in the sense that it would apply only to me or, in the case of the first maxim of this paragraph, to a limited number of desperate people. This, therefore, forms the basis of a response that the Kantian can offer to the MacIntyre-style worry.

Indeed, the maxim universalised must also be the maxim acted upon, so, just because it might be the case that we could attempt to universalise a maxim of the form "take bread from a financially powerful supermarket only when you or your immediate family members are at the point of starvation" (as per the MacIntyre approach), this would not help someone who actually acts on the maxim "steal food when hungry", but tries to cover this maxim up with more dramatic language. Thus, even if the MacIntyre criticism has some bite to it, this will still cover only a very small number of instances of possible

---

2   A. MacIntyre, *A Short History of Ethics*, p. 126.

theft; moral assessment must be of actual maxims motivating behaviour, not reinterpreted maxims described as favourably as possible.

What is more complex in this example of stealing from the internationally owned and financially powerful supermarket is the question as to whether or not it involves the use of another person merely as a means to an end, thereby denying them their fundamental human dignity as a rational agent. In this case of stealing from a supermarket — an act sometimes referred to as a "victimless crime" — it is not immediately clear who might be being used merely as a means to an end. Is it the management of the supermarket? Is it the shareholders? Is it the shelf-stacking staff? Is it the security personnel on site? If stealing from a sole trader, this issue would not arise. However, it is far more complex in the modern context of large supermarkets. Working through specific instances of stealing, perhaps with real case studies, and seeing if those examples could escape falling foul of the second formulation of the Categorical Imperative, would be useful for you to consider for yourselves.

4. Act and Preference Utilitarianism on Stealing

Chapter 1 is the location of the full discussion of the broad normative moral theory of Utilitarianism. Utilitarian theories — Act, Rule, and Preference — are linked by their commitment to the view that it is consequence that determines the morality of actions, although the three theories have slightly different views on how this central claim should be interpreted in practice. Rule Utilitarianism and the ideas of John Stuart Mill will be discussed in section five of this chapter; for now our attention is focused upon the ideas of Jeremy Bentham and Peter Singer as defenders of Act Utilitarianism and Preference Utilitarianism respectively.

The *teleological*, consequentialist and relativistic nature of Utilitarianism may seem to make it more open to the idea that examples of stealing will sometimes be morally acceptable. This is because all that needs to be the case for an example of stealing to be morally right is for the good consequences to outweigh the bad consequences. Indeed, this very much seems to be the case in the example of a person stealing bread from a multinational supermarket chain in order to survive. Thus, the key issue for Act and Preference Utilitarianism when it comes to stealing is not "can stealing ever be justified" (this was the key question facing Kantian Ethics) but rather "does Utilitarianism justify stealing in too many cases".

Consider the following situations:

1. James has two children who are desperate for a particular Christmas present. If he steals the present, which he cannot afford to buy, from a

major international retailer then this action would very likely lead to far more pleasure for his children than pain for the company.

2. Matthew can illegally download a music album that he would greatly enjoy, saving himself money in doing so. Or, he can pay full price for the music and allow his money to line the pockets of an international pop star, her record label and a financially powerful music retailer. In this case, more pleasure would seem to be produced by an illegal download rather than a paid-for download.

3. A gang of thieves has the ability to steal 1p from every bank account in the world. The pain of losing 1p, even when multiplied an extremely large number of times, is minimal. However, the theft would make the thieves rich beyond their wildest dreams, filling their lives with extreme pleasure.

4. A football club requires a large donation in order to keep running its youth teams and providing pleasure for hundreds of children in the local area. Imogen, a fan of the club, breaks into the mansion of a millionaire and steals £10,000 worth of property to sell in order to raise the necessary funds to save the youth programme. If the goods stolen were of trivial importance to the millionaire, the balance of pleasure versus pain may favour the theft.

5. Bryony and Robert are going to miss a concert that they have been looking forward to for a very long time because their car has broken down. By chance, they notice an unlocked car parked on a driveway near them. If they steal the car, attend the concert, refill it with petrol and park it back on the driveway — all without the owner's knowledge — then their action appears to provide them with a great deal of pleasure and no pain at all to the actual owner of the car.

In all five cases as described (and we should not cheat and change the examples!) the Benthamite, hedonistic act utilitarian would seem to be forced to suggest that stealing would be morally right; indeed, not stealing may well be morally wrong in all of these cases because not stealing would fail to create the greatest pleasure for the greatest number. If we replace "pleasure" with "preference satisfaction" in the five cases, the situations do not seem to be different in any key respects, and so the preference utilitarian would seem to face the same issue.

In response, we should pay attention to Bentham's suggestion that act utilitarians would have "rules of thumb" that provide general guidance against stealing. We are better off being disposed not to steal, for example, because we cannot be sure of the consequences.

If James, for example, was caught then far more pain would result from his action than pleasure might have been generated if successful. Indeed, in the real world, thieves often have no idea what pain their victims suffer as stolen items can often have hidden sentimental value beyond any that a thief could recognise in the abstract (this seems most relevant to cases four and five). The thief who stole an iPad in Colorado Springs, for example, probably did not factor in the pain of an eight-year-old boy losing photos of himself with his recently deceased father.[3] Thus, even when we might think an individual act of stealing will produce the maximum amount of pleasure in a given situation, we should be wary of over-confidence in our analysis, and not downplay the painful consequences associated with that possible action.

As an objection, it can be asked whether or not such "rules of thumb" are enough to save the utilitarian from being overly promiscuous in terms of allowing morally justified stealing. There is good reason for thinking that Utilitarianism does not offer enough in respect of cautioning against stealing in general. Although stealing may be viewed as undesirable in some of the previous situations (and similar such cases) for the reason alluded to in the previous paragraph pertaining to rules of thumb, there are plenty of situations where the consequences obviously point to stealing if total pleasure or preference satisfaction is all that determines morality. We are sure that you can imagine many such situations yourselves where consequences are relatively easy to predict. There may be a difference between wanting to be less than absolutist about the wrongness of stealing, and being so liberal that stealing turns out to be morally required in a potentially enormous number of situations.

Act and preference utilitarians may make their final stand on this issue by suggesting that greater attention should be paid to the psychological costs associated with stealing. The pain of a victim will not be fully accounted for if we only think of immediate pains to do with finance and anger. In addition, we must recognise the psychological pain often resulting from the fear of having property stolen or a house burgled. This psychological distress may be so severe that it outweighs even large-scale pleasures resulting from the theft. In addition, it might be the case that engaging in an act of stealing in one potentially morally justifiable situation would make someone more prone to stealing in a second, or third or fourth situation where moral legitimacy is either more questionable or obviously not present.

Perhaps if one becomes comfortable with stealing and therefore less empathetic as a result, then the long-term costs of stealing — as they pertain

---

3   K. Leon, 'Family Seeks Stolen iPad with Photos of Deceased Father', http://fox21news.com/2014/10/03/family-seeks-stolen-ipad-with-photos-of-deceased-father/

to the character and future actions of the perpetrator — may be far higher than originally thought. This idea has much in common with Kant's indirect concern for animals, as discussed in Chapter 14.

Whatever your views on Act and Preference Utilitarianism as they impact the issue of stealing, it will be well worth your while coming up with your own examples and then applying the theories to those cases in order to make clear that you understand, and can defend, the scope of cases in which utilitarians would morally criticise or morally support stealing.

5. Rule Utilitarianism on Stealing

If you find yourself wishing to defend Utilitarianism, but are left uninspired by the extent to which Act Utilitarianism and Preference Utilitarianism can speak against instances of stealing, then Rule Utilitarianism may provide you with reason for optimism. As a reminder, the rule utilitarian suggests that moral action is action that would be recommended by the set of rules that, if followed, would promote the greatest good for the greatest number. On initial viewing, it might seem that a rule banning stealing would be a good candidate to be included in the set of rules that would produce the greatest good for the greatest number, especially given the potential psychological costs associated with stealing as described above.

Indeed, if we think more broadly about the "best set of rules", then it might seem likely that there would be a rule requiring adequate provision of food for those hungry or lacking resources, and a similar rule regarding provision of medical treatment and housing etc. Such provision would not be free, of course, but the best set of rules would very likely include provision for collecting adequate taxation, given that a pound spent on someone in distress is likely to facilitate greater future happiness than a pound spent by someone economically comfortable (though we encourage you to consider this idea in more depth, perhaps with your own examples).

Despite the previous ideas, it may be suggested that the best set of rules would allow for stealing "when necessary" and thus discriminate between "good" stealing and "bad" stealing in a way that satisfies the non-absolutist. How easy it would be to write such a rule that is consistent with promoting the greatest happiness for the greatest number, yet does not "get it wrong" with individual instances of stealing and their moral status, is something that you again should find it useful to consider. Here, it will be worth revisiting the distinction between Strong Rule Utilitarianism and Weak Ruse Utilitarianism as discussed in Chapter 1.

Finally, it is worth considering the impact of a style of "demandingness" objection as it pertains to applying Rule Utilitarianism in the context of stealing. Recall from Chapter 1, Mill's harm principle:

> The only purpose for which power can be rightfully exercised over any member of a civilized community, against his will, is to prevent harm to others. His own good, either physical or moral, is not a sufficient warrant.[4]

If the harm principle informs rules in the set that promotes the greatest happiness for the greatest number, then there would be no rule allowing people to take assets from private individuals in order to redistribute resources for the purpose of promoting happiness. A useful example to have in mind would be of jewels stored in a safety deposit box in perpetuity, when those jewels could be used in ways that would promote greater levels of happiness if stolen and sold. Such action — which seems to have the appearance of stealing from private individuals for the greater good in the style of Robin Hood — would not appear to sit neatly with Mill's own harm principle. At the very least, in would need a particularly interesting interpretation of the notion of preventing harm to others.

This entire issue in itself highlights the difficulty of actually fixing the rules by which the rule utilitarian wants us to judge specific actions in our minds, and this also raises another problem for the rule utilitarian in respect of the difficulty of practically applying the theory to stealing. It might be useful to return to cases 1–5 as outlined in section four and ask yourself what the rule utilitarian would suggest in those cases — does the answer of the rule utilitarian put them in a more or less attractive position than the answers of the act and preference utilitarians?

6. Virtue Ethics on Stealing

As a normative moral theory, Aristotelian Virtue Ethics was explored in Chapter 3 and, as with all of the theories discussed in this chapter, it is important to read everything here in the light of issues raised there.

The virtue ethicist is not interested in the moral status of individual actions, but rather is interested in the *character traits* and dispositions of the person performing those actions. Using reason to work out the virtuous Golden Mean in the different spheres of life, Aristotle suggested the following as virtuous and non-virtuous (vice) character traits.

---

4   J. S. Mill, *On Liberty*, http://www.econlib.org/library/Mill/mlLbty1.html

Feeling/Emotion	Vice of Deficiency	Virtuous Disposition (Golden Mean)	Vice of Excess
Anger	Lack of spirit	Patience	Irascibility
Shame	Shyness	Modesty	Shamefulness
Fear	Cowardice	Courage	Rashness
Indignation	Spitefulness	Righteousness	Envy
Situation			
Social conduct	Cantankerousness	Friendliness	Self-serving flattery
Conversation	Boorishness	Wittiness	Buffoonery
Giving money	Stinginess	Generosity	Profligacy

Thus, those who engage in the act of stealing on the basis of righteousness, courage and virtuous patience may be considered moral, whereas those who engage in the act of stealing on the basis of rashness, shamefulness and irascibility will not be considered moral. This reveals something interesting about the application of Virtue Ethics to stealing. According to Virtue Ethics, the very same act, performed by two different people, can be viewed differently from a moral perspective.

Take the act of stealing a loaf of bread from a supermarket, and then passing that loaf to a hungry and homeless woman on the street nearby. If a person commits this act out of self-serving flattery, then they act in accordance with a vice of excess. Yet, if someone else commits the very same act of stealing, but does so on the basis of righteousness and generosity, then they act in a virtuous way. This example is over-simplified, but the point is hopefully clear.

One of the bigger worries regarding Virtue Ethics is its lack of specific guidance, and this worry would seem to be at its most acute when it comes to seeking advice from Virtue Ethics over an applied ethical issue such as stealing. After all, how are we to determine if our stealing a loaf of bread would be based on righteous and generous character dispositions, or reflect rashness and self-serving flattery? How can we ascertain what the virtuous course of action would be in a specific situation?

One possibility is to look to the actions of virtuous people for guidance, but this raises the troubling issue of subjectivity. For example, if I view St. Augustine as virtuous, then I may view his complete aversion to stealing as representative of the Golden Mean. Bertrand Russell (1872–1970) says of Augustine that:

> It appears that, with some companions of his own age, he despoiled a neighbour's pear tree, although he was not hungry, and his parents had better pears at home. He continued throughout his life to consider this an act of almost incredible wickedness. It would not have been so bad if he

had been hungry, or had no other means of getting pears; but, as it was, the act was one of pure mischief, inspired by the love of wickedness for its own sake.[5]

Stealing for petty reasons looks to be the height of non-virtuous behaviour. However, if I view the fictional character Robin Hood as the paradigm of a virtuous person because of his willingness to steal from the rich in order to give to the poor, then I may have a different view as to which actions the virtuous character trait of generosity would give rise to. Or, more extremely, if I view a famous fictional pirate of the high seas as representing a virtuous individual, my views would once more be different; how do we decide which of these people are the right people to seek virtuous guidance from when it comes to stealing? Aristotle can refer to practical reason (*phronesis*) and human flourishing, but this may be a serious weakness.

In addition, we might wonder how to act when virtues themselves seem to clash, as well as when the advice of possible virtuous people also seems to clash. An act of stealing might seem to be both courageous and self-serving, or both brave and rash. Resolving how to act requires use of practical reason, but again this language might be thought unhelpful by the critic of Virtue Ethics as it is still being unhelpfully vague.

7. Metaethics and Stealing

AQA require you to understand how the various metaethical theories as discussed in Chapter 7 might be applied to the applied ethical issues on the specification, of which stealing is the first we have considered. Below, assuming some grasp of the theories from Chapter 7, we offer guidance as to how metaethical theories might relate to this issue. *Much of the guidance below is easily applicable to the other applied ethical issues also discussed in the remaining three chapters.*

Cognitivism and Realism

The combination of Cognitivism and Realism in this area would entail that moral claims about stealing are *truth-apt* propositions, expressing beliefs that will be made true by genuinely existing moral properties at least some of the time. For the utilitarian, moral claims regarding the ethical acceptability of individual actions will be made true by natural properties such as pleasure, happiness or preference satisfaction. For the intuitionist,

---

5   B. Russell, *History of Western Philosophy*, p. 364, https://archive.org/stream/westernphilosoph03
     5502mbp#page/n3/mode/2up

the non-natural property of goodness will make some of our moral claims regarding stealing true.

Cognitivism and Anti-Realism

The moral error theorist believes that our moral claims regarding the ethics of stealing are intended to be true, but can never achieve truth because no moral properties exist as truth-makers for those moral claims. Importantly, just because the moral error theorist cannot endorse the claim that "stealing can be morally wrong at least sometimes", this does not entail a love of stealing on their part. The moral error theorist may have a non-moral reason for opposing stealing on many occasions, or indeed supporting stealing on other occasions. Moral reasons are not the only reasons not to engage in stealing, as legal and social/personal reasons will also be a factor as they often speak against the wisdom of theft. Moral error theorists who care about the property rights of others, for example, may well strongly oppose stealing.

Non-Cognitivism and Anti-Realism

According to the simple non-cognitivist considered in this book, our moral utterances regarding stealing are not truth-apt because they are not expressions of belief; they are expressions of emotion or other non-truth-apt attitudes such as approval or disapproval. Thus, according to theories such as Emotivism and Prescriptivism, a phrase such as "stealing is wrong" expresses a negative emotional attitude towards stealing (Emotivism) or makes it clear that we do not want people to steal (Prescriptivism).

Whichever non-cognitivist theory you prefer, the non-cognitivist position is defined by the commitment to the idea that the moral utterances do not reveal something true about the world and do not even try to describe features of the world.

Therefore, we cannot criticise a thief as morally wrong when using this argument (something akin to the claim of the moral error theorist). However, if we adopt Prescriptivism, we might at least be able to criticise the thief for inconsistency if she speaks of the general wrongness of stealing whilst defending the rightness of stealing in her case. Despite this, one big worry for those interested in adopting a view like Emotivism or Prescriptivism is that it cheapens and eliminates the value of moral debate over the moral rightness of stealing, since we cannot defend our ethical claims as being genuinely true or false in the way that realist seeks to do and in the way that most people would wish to.

SUMMARY

Many will want to avoid an absolute moral view regarding the unacceptability of stealing, the kind of view that Kant might be thought to defend. Neither Utilitarianism nor Virtue Ethics offer an absolute prohibition against stealing, but each has their own problems. In terms of showing your understanding of these issues, applying normative theories to your own variety of cases is a tactic that may best enable you to write with confidence about the various nuanced issues afflicting each theory.

COMMON STUDENT MISTAKES

- Not applying the strengths and weaknesses of the various moral theories as discussed in theory-specific chapters.

- Having too narrow an understanding of stealing. It is advisable to discuss a range of cases (real and fictional).

- Assuming too much when explaining how a theory might be applied to an issue of stealing — give a full explanation, showing understanding, and using key terms.

ISSUES TO CONSIDER

1. Is keeping due tax from the government an example of stealing?

2. Can you create your own satisfactory definition of stealing?

3. How does the definition you arrived at in (2) fit with the idea of stealing ideas?

4. Does stealing once make you more likely to steal again?

5. Is it possible to measure the psychological pains associated with stealing?

6. Is an absolute prohibition against stealing defensible? Why or why not?

7. Do people you consider virtuous have any history of stealing?

8. Would the best set of rules for promoting the greatest good for the greatest number contain a rule absolutely prohibiting stealing?

9. Is it worth debating the ethics of stealing if you are an emotivist or a prescriptivist?

10. What would the error-theorist say about the morality of stealing?

KEY TERMINOLOGY

Categorical Imperative   Truth-apt

Universalisation

References

Bible, New International Version, freely available at https://www. biblegateway.com/

Leon, K., 'Family Seeks Stolen iPad with Photos of Deceased Father', *Fox21 News* (3 October 2014), freely available at http://fox21news. com/2014/10/03/family-seeks-stolen-ipad-with-photos-of-deceased-father/

MacIntyre, Alasdair, *A Short History of Ethics* (London: Routledge, 2002), https://doi.org/10.4324/9780203131121

Mill, J. S., *On Liberty* (London: Longman, Roberts, Green & Co., 1869), freely available at freely available at http://www.econlib.org/library/Mill/mlLbty1.html

Russell, Bertrand, *History of Western Philosophy* (Woking: Unwin Brothers, 1947), freely available at https://archive.org/stream/westernphilosoph035502mbp#page/n3/mode/2up

CHAPTER 12

Simulated Killing

Can you avoid knowledge? You cannot! Can you avoid technology? You cannot! Things are going to go ahead in spite of ethics, in spite of your personal beliefs, in spite of everything.[1]

Technology: the knack of so arranging the world that we don't have to experience it.[2]

1. Introduction

Ethics is about how we live in the world and how we interact with one another. Given that "simulated" killing is, well, "simulated", we might think that it falls outside ethical consideration. However, this chapter will challenge this claim. Simply granting that a scenario is not "real" does not mean that it should not be thought of as ethical. We think through how the various ethical theories we have looked at in this book might have something to say about simulated killing. The chapter relies on the work of Michael Lacewing (1971–) and Garry Young.[3]

Simulated killing can mean a number of things and at first it is perhaps easier to say what it is *not*. Obviously simulated killing is not actual killing, nor is it a description or representation of killing. So J. K. Rowling's description of the death of Voldemort will not count as simulated killing nor would Caravaggio's painting depicting John the Baptist's decapitation. However, acting in a film involving killing — *Schindler's List* for example, or acting Romeo killing Tybalt on stage, would. Furthermore, with the advent of computer games and virtual reality there are interesting, and arguably morally different, dimensions to simulated killing. Specifically, modern technology helps us all *be part of* the simulation.

Of course, one reaction to supposed ethical worries surrounding this topic might be simply — "grow up"! There are many horrific things — real things — going on in the world, poverty, torture, crippling debt. They are the

---

1   J. Delgado, quoted in John Horgan, 'The Forgotten Era of Brain Chips'.
2   M. Frisch. *Homo Faber: A Report.*
3   M. Lacewing, 'Simulated Killing', http://documents.routledge-interactive.s3.amazonaws.com/9781138793934/A22014/ethical_theories/Simulated killing.pdf. See in particular Garry Young's *Ethics in the Virtual World: The Morality and Psychology of Gaming.*

things that as ethicists we ought to be concerning ourselves with. In contrast these simulated things are just entertainment. After a killing scene in a film the actors will go home; the actors in Romeo and Juliet will dust themselves off and go out for a drink, and the pixels will be altered on the computer monitor and reformed due to electrical charges. No one is actually hurt!

However, to counter this more dismissive attitude, consider a few examples. The thing to keep in mind when reading them is whether this "who cares, it's not real!" attitude seems right? And if it is not, why?

1. A local high security prison has a large number of child killers. They often riot which causes massive destruction and suffering. However, the prison warden proposes a way of stopping the rioting. At little cost, each inmate can be given his or her own virtual reality headset that gives each prisoner the ability to engage virtually in his or her favourite child killing fantasy. Experiments have shown that the immersive nature of this seems to act like a safety valve and prisoners become quiet and helpful and are willing to get involved in educational and community programs. Should they be given the headsets?

2. It is common for armies to use very realistic computer gaming to train their soldiers. Imagine that soldiers are currently fighting in Syria and their Syrian training simulator — along with realistic Russian and US soldiers, realistic maps, civilian sites such as mosques etc. — is released for sale. Is there anything wrong with this?

3. As part of one level of the video game *Call of Duty — Modern Warfare 2* you are expected to participate in a mass shooting of civilians at a Moscow airport in order to pass yourself off as a Russian terrorist. If you play this level are you doing something morally wrong?

4. In June 2015 a video game called "Hatred" was released. The aim of the game is simple, to kill as many civilians as possible. The gamer controls the character through a town, shooting, burning, running over, blowing up, and executing random innocent people. (Equally controversial is *Super Columbine Massacre RPG!* Where players can play Eric Harris and Dylan Klebold and re-enact the Columbine High School Massacre). Is it morally wrong to play such games?

What is interesting is that we suspect that many of you reading this chapter would find some or all of (1)–(4) objectionable. Even, perhaps, morally objectionable.

In this chapter we will start by looking at different moral theories and how they might capture this intuition. We will then consider the type of cases, one's in which we are *observing the simulated killing*. We end by highlighting a famous philosophical problem that might relate to these issues, the *Paradox of Tragedy*.

2. Utilitarianism and Simulated Killing

For Utilitarianism no act, *qua* act, is right or wrong. So we cannot say that playing at killing others is wrong. What we have to focus on is how much happiness is created in particular examples of simulated killing.

In asking this question regarding the amount of happiness we might conclude that there is nothing wrong with (1)–(4). After all, the inmates, the players of *Call of Duty* or *Hatred* get enjoyment and there is a lot of happiness, no one is hurt, and there is no unhappiness. In fact, we can imagine that there might be more unhappiness if someone *stops* playing these games. Perhaps people who are stopped from playing their video games might turn to making life miserable for those around them or slump into depression. In fact, then, according to Utilitarianism it might be that playing a killer in a computer game is something that some people *morally ought to do*. In some situations, it might even be their duty to play such games.

This said, notice that the question is an empirical one (i.e. it is a question answered *a posteriori* rather than *a priori*). *If* playing the killer in simulated killing leads to more *unhappiness* than not doing so, then playing the killer is wrong. But *why* might such simulated killing bring about unhappiness?

Perhaps playing a killer makes people *more inclined to violent behaviour*? Perhaps it makes the player *less able to empathise* and trust, each of which might lead to the player being *more likely* to harm others (what McCormick calls "risk increasing acts"[4]). Or perhaps playing simulated killing desensitises the players to violence in ways which might be harmful to both themselves and other?

As Young (2014) reports the evidence relevant to these sorts of claims is mixed. In *some* cases, where a gamer perhaps already has a predisposition to violence, playing the killer will lead her to violence and harm. So the utilitarian would say it is morally wrong for this person to play such games. Whereas in other cases, where the player has a "normal" disposition, playing a killer in a video game may have no negative effects; in which case, it is not morally wrong.

So, for Utilitarianism *if* there is a clear link between risk-increasing acts and playing the killer in games *then* we might be able to say that such game playing is morally wrong. But the evidence does not support this claim. There is though, a further consideration to be made when thinking about playing the

---

4   M. McCormick, 'Is it Wrong to Play Violent Video Games?', p. 279.

killer. If you recall from Chapter 1 Bentham and Mill differ in their approaches to "happiness". Bentham famously claims:

> *Prejudice apart, the game of push-pin is of equal value with the arts and science of music and poetry. If the game of push-pin furnish more pleasure, it is more valuable than either...If poetry and music deserve to be preferred before a game of push-pin, it must be because they are calculated to gratify those individuals who are most difficult to be pleased.*[5]

Because "push pin is as good as poetry" Bentham would treat playing the killer in a video game in the same way as any other pleasure. However, you'll also recall that Mill thought that this was not quite right, and that push-pin (or, in our case, playing the killer in *Call of Duty/Hatred* etc.) is perhaps *not* of equal value as the pleasure we get from other activities such as poetry.

Maybe then when doing a utilitarian calculation regarding the pleasure involved in playing at killing we need to consider — not just the empirical questions highlighted above, but also whether such pleasure is higher or lower? We might reasonable conclude (though this is debatable) that it is a *lower* pleasure. Mill might argue that the inmate gaining pleasure from enacting virtue kill fantasies is not just of less quantity, but is of *less quality* than joining a drawing class or, say, visiting an Art Gallery.

Of course, introducing the distinction between higher and lower pleasure will not necessarily lead to the conclusion that playing the killer in video games is morally wrong. We might argue (can you?) that playing such games as *Call of Duty* can in fact lead to *higher pleasure*. Or we might agree that it is correct to think of such activities as a lower pleasure but *still* maintain that in some instances it would be right to play the killer in these games.

There are further things that Utilitarianism would have to take into account in each case. For instance, what is going to be important is not only the *type* of person playing the simulated killing — do they have a violent disposition? — but the *type* of killing that is simulated. Maybe the *way* that the killing is simulated: the age, race and gender of the person killed and the method of death are important. Perhaps, for example, a simulated killing which is highly sexualized is much more likely to bring about harm in the gamer. Or in contrast maybe the simulated killing of uniformed soldiers in a video game does not change people's outlook and behaviour. The simple point is that the utilitarian questions about "simulated killing" can only be answered if we first pin down the precise details of the situation.

Young is a good place to end this section:

> *We have a very good idea of the benefits of video games. Their economic impact is quantifiable as is the number of hours of entertainment they bring to gamers. GTA* [Grand Theft Auto] *alone sold*

---

5   J. Bentham, *An Introduction to the Principles of Morals and Legislation*, pp. 206–07, http://www.econlib. org/library/Bentham/bnthPML18.html

over 66 million games by 2008, evidence that at least this many people derive entertainment from game violence. Other heavily criticized violent games are likewise usually among the top sellers. There are also a number of educational benefits. The improvements in visual perception, hand-eye coordination, and other motor skills from gaming are also well documented. The difficulty only lies in deciding how much these benefits should weigh against any harm that games do, but this is a problem intrinsic to utilitarian theory and should not be counted against violent games.[6]

3. The Kantian and the Virtue Ethics Approach

We have placed these two theories together because in the end what they have to say about playing the killer in video games is going to be similar. Specifically, whether they think playing the killer is right or wrong is going to depend directly on the empirical data about how doing so will change the person playing the game.

Recall from Chapter 2 that Kant said that we have no moral duty towards animals because they are non-rational. But, he argues, that this does not mean we can treat animals cruelly. This is because if we did treat them cruelly we might become less able to act rationally and discharge our duties in areas where we do have a moral duty towards other. Put simply it makes us worse at being moral beings. An Aristotelian would say a similar thing. Namely, although it is not wrong to harm animals because of animals "rights", it is wrong because it does not help *us develop the right types of virtues*, e.g. sensitivity, empathy, compassion (see Chapter 14 for a discussion of this).

The point of this diversion into animal ethics is that the morality of playing the killer in video games will be dealt with in the same way. *If* playing the killer makes us less able to reason and hence discern our duty towards others, then Kant would say that we should avoid them. But, as stated above, this is an open question as the empirical evidence is inconclusive.

Shifting to virtue theory, *if* playing the killer makes us less virtuous — e.g. less courageous, empathetic, sensitive etc. — then the virtue theorist will claim this will make us less able to do the right thing at the right time to the right proportion. This means that playing the killer is to be avoided. So to the question "would the Aristotelian or Kantian think it is wrong to play the killer in video games?" the answer is: "Not directly, it just depends on the link between doing so and its *effects* on us *as moral agents*".

4. Films and Plays

Recall, we started this chapter by pointing out that simulated killing takes place in films and plays. Notice that this might include *watching* simulated

---

6   G. Young, *Ethics in the Virtual World: The Morality and Psychology of Gaming*, p. 131.

killing, or *acting* out the killing. *Playing* such characters is — we guess — of less direct relevance to our readers. Anyway, we suggest that we could treat playing the killer in films and plays in a similar way as we have in video games. Of course, there might be further complications when asking how playing a killer on stage or in a film differs psychologically from playing one in a video game. However, we suggest the issues are still fundamentally the same, it is just how we extract the empirical data — what sort of empirical questions we need to ask — which will be different. For example, perhaps physically holding a (fake) knife or gun makes us more — or less — likely to hold a real knife or gun. Or perhaps watching people being (virtually) shot and (virtually) bleeding makes us less — or more — sensitive to real blood and death. And perhaps this is fundamentally different to how playing a knife-wielding killer in a video game affects us. But again, this is an empirical and not a philosophical question. (It is interesting to note that because of the increase in the sophistication of virtual reality, the gap between playing video games and acting in films/plays might be closing.)

What then about simply *watching* simulated killing? Well, we do not need to rehearse again the general approaches discussed above. Does the utilitarian think that watching killing is wrong? Well it depends on the consequences. Does the Kantian or the Aristotelian? Well it depends on how it affects us as moral agents. And the answer to these questions is, again, an empirical matter.

We end with an ancient philosophical problem which has come to be known as the *Paradox of Tragedy*. Although it is not directly about ethics, it brings to the fore issues to do with authenticity and character which might have a direct link to other issues we have discussed.

5. The Paradox of Tragedy (or More Correctly the Paradox of "Negative Emotions")

Imagine that we go into a hotel room and we see bloody hand marks on the wall and in the shower. We feel disgusted, anxious and scared. We quickly turn around and get out of there as quickly as possible. Such emotions are unwelcome and make us uncomfortable. However, consider all the time and money spent on watching and making films which have upsetting scenarios. Watching films (of course it does not have to be a film — the same reasoning applies to plays or video games) generate in us disgust, anxiety and fear but we flock in our droves to such films. In fact, the more scary/disgusting/disturbing the film is, the more attractive it seem to audiences. Consider Hitchcock's groundbreaking *Psycho* for example. Here then is the "paradox". On the one hand negative emotions are not desired, whereas in other context they are.

Although it is not a genuine paradox it is certainly a tension — an odd thing that needs to be explained. We will not go into the possible explanations here. What is interesting to us is that this paradox seems to be particularly pertinent when we refer to simulated killing. Presumably we would find it particularly horrific if we witnessed real life killing, but if it is "simulated" perhaps these emotions — horror, fear, etc. are qualitatively different. Call them *fear*, *horror*, *disgust*.

This in turn might mean that we need to be less worried about the changes in our character that might come about through simulated killing because they are to do with *fear* not fear, *horror* not horror, *disgust* not disgust etc. Again, we do not need to go into the details of this. It is though just another dimension to simulated killing which may have moral significance and consequently deserve consideration.

SUMMARY

"Simulated killing" covers a number of different areas; it could involve playing the killer, or watching someone play the killer. In the first category it could be an actor on film or stage, or it could be someone playing a video game.

Initially we might think that because it is "simulated" this topic is outside ethics. But using Utilitarianism, Kantian and Virtue Ethical lenses we have shown that this is not the case. For Utilitarianism whether it is simulated or not is not important, the question is how much happiness each of these activities generates compared to doing something else. If it is more, then we ought to do them, if not, we ought not. For the Kantian and virtue ethicist the question is how being involved in simulated killing changes us as a person. If it makes us less able to be a moral agent — e.g. less rational or virtuous — then we ought not to be involved in simulated killing.

However, the main lesson from this chapter is this. Issues surrounding simulated killing are going to be addressed via *psychology*. Which is thus far inconclusive. So it seems the best we can say is that "yes simulated killing is a moral issue", but the decision of whether a particular activity is morally right or wrong will be advanced via experimentation.

COMMON STUDENT MISTAKES

- Thinking that the Utilitarian would say there is nothing wrong with simulated killing.

- Missing how important the psychological data is to the ethical question.

- Thinking that we can answer the Paradox of Tragedy by simply pointing out that sometimes we like bad things.

- Assuming that bad taste just means morally wrong.

ISSUES TO CONSIDER

1. Watch the 2015 film *Gamechangers* starring Daniel Radcliffe. This film looks at the court case between the creators of *Grand Theft Auto* and Jack Thompson. How do you think the film deals with the ethical issues? Do you think that a particular ethical theory comes out as more favourable?

2. What is "simulated killing"?

3. Reading (1)–(4) do you think that simulated killing generates a genuine moral issue?

4. How might you consider (a) the simulated killing of animals? Should it be treated any differently from the simulated killing of humans? (b) young children playing games that involve killing, e.g. a playground game of soldiers.

5. Should we treat "simulated killing" differently from other "simulated" actions, such as stealing or rape?

6. Do you think that the pleasure gained by the inmates in (1) is a "lower" pleasure?

7. What would the Kantian/virtue ethicist say about (1)?

8. Imagine a case in the future where one can buy ultra-life like AI robots. These robots can be "killed". They will "bleed", they have been programmed to beg for mercy, to whimper, etc. Once they have been "killed" they can be reset and "killed again". Should we treat this case differently? What happens if the robots are so lifelike that people no longer know the difference between them and real humans? Does that change things?

9. Governments have censored video games, such as *Call of Duty*, and *Hatred*. Are they right to do so? That is, even if we find them immoral, how might this relate to laws governing "simulated killing"?

10. What is the "Paradox of Tragedy"? Do you think it has any relevance when discussing the morality of simulated killing?

11. Use Google Scholar to find the most up-to-date research on the psychological effects of "simulated killing" (any version you want). What does the current psychological research tell us about the ethical issues raised in this chapter?

KEY TERMINOLOGY

Simulated killing

Paradox of Tragedy

Higher and lower pleasures

Risk-increasing Acts

References

Bentham, Jeremy, *An Introduction to the Principles of Morals and Legislation*, freely available at http://www.econlib.org/library/Bentham/bnthPML18.html

Frisch, Max, *Homo Faber: A Report* (Houghton Mifflin Harcourt, 1959).

Horgan, John, 'The Forgotten Era of Brain Chips', *Scientific American*, 293.4 (October 2005): 66–73, https://doi.org/10.1038/scientificamerican1005-66

Lacewing, Michael, 'Simulated Killing', freely available at http://documents.routledge-interactive.s3.amazonaws.com/9781138793934/A22014/ethical_theories/Simulated killing.pdf

McCormick, Matt, 'Is It Wrong to Play Violent Video Games?', *Ethics and Information Technology*, 3.4 (2001): 277–87, https://doi.org/10.1023/a:1013802119431

Young, Garry, *Ethics in the Virtual World: The Morality and Psychology of Gaming* (Abington: Routledge, 2014), https://doi.org/10.5860/choice.51-1780

CHAPTER 13

Telling Lies

I'm not upset that you lied to me; I'm upset that from now on I can't believe you.

Friedrich Nietzsche

1. Introduction

What is it to tell a lie? Is it always wrong to tell lies? Is it sometimes acceptable to lie, and if so, what are the conditions that make it OK? Humans have dealt with these types of questions, regarding lies and truth, ever since they began to interact with one another. Truth and trust are key to the working of our society, in fact people who are caught in a lie are sanctioned, blamed and punished. We have many examples of politicians being brought down by lies; Nixon and the ensuing Watergate is a good one (although see the final section regarding Politicians). Children are told "not to lie", religious leaders and religious texts condemn lying, relationship guidance talks about the importance of not lying to your partner etc. We will start to consider some of these questions and apply some of the thinking thus far discussed in the book to lying.

2. What Is It to Lie?

Let's consider some examples; when you read them you should ask yourself whether there is a lie involved.

1. A friend asks you where you went on holiday last year. You say "Cambridge", which they understand to be Cambridge, UK, but you really mean Cambridge, Massachusetts.

2. You are teaching chemistry to primary school children and you hold up a football and say "Atoms are just like this…"

3. You are having a really bad day: your partner has split up with you, you have lost your house keys, and your friend just shouted at you. You meet an acquaintance in the corridor; they say, "how are you?" You say, "fine thanks, and you?".

4. Your gran has saved up her pension, bought some wool, and knitted you a jumper. You hate it. She is visiting you and you put it on. She asks, smiling, "so, do you really like it?" You reply, "of course Gran, thanks so much for thinking about me".

5. You are taking a maths test and one question asks the solution to $\sin x^2 + \cos x^2$ You write "10" [the answer is "1"].

6. A recent divorcee keeps wearing his wedding ring.

7. You are smuggling Bibles into China. At the border, the guards ask you what you have in your truck. As it happens, you have hundreds of Bibles, so you say "oh, hundreds of Bibles". The guards think this is a joke and wave you through.

So what do you think? Are these cases of lying or not? Let's take them in turn.

(1) This does not fall into the category of lying as there was no intent on your part to mislead your friend.

(2) Is harder. Strictly speaking atoms are nothing like footballs; they are, for example, mostly space. And as Kirsten Walsh and Adrian Currie[1] state "the truth, the whole truth and nothing but the truth, is no teacher's maxim". This is because it is simply impossible to go into all the details of science or history, or chemistry etc. But does this mean that you are lying to the class? We think the answer is "yes" and in fact all teaching involves lying. Of course, whether this is right or wrong is something that we'll return to below.

(3) Arguably this would not be categorised as lying as the reply given is generally considered to be a standard answer to a standard question; the questioner would be expecting this reply in most circumstances.

(4) This does seem as if it is a clear case of lying. Having been asked a direct question by your gran, you look her in the eye and lie. Now whether this is wrong is something we consider below; it would seem that it is precisely for cases such as this that we have the phrase "little white lie".

(5) This does not seem to be a case of lying, rather just bad maths. It is certainly false but there is no lie involved.

(6) This could be a case of lying. If the social context is one in which we understand that wearing a wedding ring indicates that someone is married, then wearing a wedding ring when you are not married seems like a case of lying.

(7) This does not seem like a case of lying as you were completely honest in your reply to the guard. However, if there was an intention to deceive then this may not be the case. But as it stands (7) is not a case of lying.

---

1   K. Walsh and A. Currie, 'Caricatures, Myths, and White Lies', p. 424.

What then can we take from these quick examples?

Lying does not simply involve saying something false. That is what (5), the maths case, shows us.

Lying can involve things other than speaking; it can involve writing, signs and symbols; that is what (6) — the wedding ring — shows us.

In cases such as (3), even if we say something we know to be false, it is not necessarily thought to be a lie as the *intention* to deceive is missing.

That is why "yes I like the jumper Gran" in (4) is a lie. You intend that your Gran adopt the false belief that you do like the jumper.

Notice finally that in the Bible smuggling case if the person knew that by telling the truth — "yes there are Bibles in the truck" — then the guards would form the false belief that there were no Bibles in the truck, then this might count as lying. So for something to be a lie, what is important is the *intention to deceive* — but it need not be the case that what is being said is false.

Of course, all these claims are controversial but they at least give us some starting points for thinking about the moral question.

Finally, as an aside, it is a controversial and philosophically interesting question whether we can *lie to ourselves*. We do not discuss this here but "not lying to oneself" is a common phrase used by psychologists, self-help books, counsellors etc. It is then a genuinely interesting question which deserves consideration at some point — just not here.

We can now frame the moral question like this. When, if ever, is it morally acceptable to intend for someone to adopt a belief which you know to be false?

Let's consider this question through the lens of some of the theories already discussed in this book.

3. Utilitarianism

If you recall (Chapter 1) Consequentialism has two features. First is the definition of "*good*" (happiness, pleasure, well-being, preferences etc.) and *then* the consideration of right and wrong actions in relation to good. In particular, an action is right if, and only if, it brings about the greatest amount of happiness, pleasure, well-being, preference satisfaction etc.

The second feature is that everyone counts as equal in the calculations. That is, *your* good is as important as *my* good, which is as important as anyone else's good.

It follows from these two claims that *no action* is morally right or wrong irrespective of context. So we cannot say that lying is wrong because the action of lying will only be wrong if it brings about less good than not doing so. If I intend that you adopt a belief which I believe to be false but in so doing I generate more good than if I had not, then I have done something right.

Utilitarianism seems to be intuitive in some cases. Imagine, for example, a soldier captured and tortured but who still continues to lie and say that she does not know how to break the allies' codes, and in so doing she saves hundreds of thousands of lives. In this case people believe that she was right to have lied; given the horrific consequences of telling the truth she is morally required to lie. However, the intuitions work both ways and there are cases where we think that sometimes it is morally counterintuitive to be required to lie.

Consider a famous example from H. J. McCloskey known as *"McCloskey's Sheriff"*.[2]

> Imagine a scenario where there has been a serious crime in a town and the Sheriff is trying to prevent serious rioting. He knows that this rioting is likely to bring about destruction, injury and maybe even death. The problem is that he has no leads; he has not the slightest idea who committed the crime. However, he can prevent these riots by lying to the town and framing an innocent man. No one will miss the man and he is hated in the town. If he frames and jails this innocent man, convincing people to believe that it was this man that committed the crime, then the town will be placated and people will not riot. The consequentialist will judge in this case that it is morally required that the Sheriff lies even if this means that an innocent man is jailed. This then shows that the fact that the consequentialist says it is sometimes morally required to lie can lead to counterintuitive conclusions.

Let's consider a mundane case. If lying to your gran brings about the best consequences — i.e. she is happy, you are happy, and she continues to knit which makes her happy etc., then it is morally acceptable to lie. Notice, however, that the consequentialist would say that we *ought to* lie; not just that it is acceptable to lie but that we have a moral obligation to lie.

Of course, the utilitarian should try and think harder about the possible consequences and outcomes in order to try and prevent some new problems arising. Consider the sheriff example; it could be that the real criminal confesses resulting in worse consequences than if the truth had been told at the outset. Now, not only will there be riots but there will *also* be *no trust in the law enforcement*. So, in fact, *lying* would bring about *worse* consequences, which means it would be wrong to lie.

Or consider the gran example. If your brother tells his gran that you lied, then we can imagine that this might mean she would not be able ever to trust her grandchildren again, may give up knitting, and thus make her unhappier than if she had originally been told the truth about the jumper.

However, *because* no *action* is right or wrong *qua action* in Utilitarianism, it follows that the action of lying is neither wrong nor right. So to the question "does the utilitarian think that lying is wrong?" the answer is "it just depends".

---

2   McCloskey, 'A Non-Utilitarian Approach to Punishment'.

4. The Kantian and Lying

In contrast the Kantian (see Chapter 2) claims that actions are wrong or right, *qua* actions. So rather than first defining good and then defining the right and wrong actions they first define right and wrong. How they might do this will depend on what type of deontologist they are. The Kantians ground the rightness and wrongness on reason. In particular, we introduced one version of Kant's Categorical Imperative. We can show, using this, that Kant — and in fact all deontologists — think that the action of lying *is wrong in all cases*. Even if the consequence is saving a billion people, your own mother or an orphanage of children.

It is worth noting that in the other Kantian formula that we introduced, lying also comes out as wrong. Kant said that we should always treat others as an end in themselves, and never solely as a means to an end. We can see that this makes lying wrong. For if we lie to someone then we are *not treating them as an end in themselves* but are controlling what they can do by taking certain decisions out of their hands; we are basically saying we should be allowed to deceive them for our own ends. We are not treating them as rational agents and for the Kantian this is always morally wrong.

This might seem counterintuitive, and it is. However, it is perhaps less so if we revisit our definition of lying. Go back to the soldier case. Imagine she is being tortured for military codes. It seems that one way to stop the consequence that hundreds of thousands of people die would be simply to *say nothing*. And, given our definition, saying nothing would *not* be lying. So the Kantian may not be committed to the implausible conclusion that she has to reveal the secrets. Keeping silent is not the same as lying.

Furthermore, it is worth remembering that there are different ways of telling the truth! Saying to your gran: "I really appreciate all the work you've put in to my jumper, and my friend thinks it is an amazing jumper, but it really is not my style, I'm really sorry", seem less objectionable than "No, I do not like it".

So there are — maybe — ways of making Kant's theory less objectionable when considering lying by thinking harder about what it actually means to lie. Even so, it seems undeniable that there are *some* cases where we think it is morally acceptable to lie but for the Kantian there are no such cases.

Notice that it is not just the Kantian that would say this. Other deontological theories would as well. For example, the Divine Command Theory, the theory that says that actions are right or wrong depending on whether God commands or prohibits them. If God says lying is wrong — and at least in the main monotheistic religions He does — then it is, full stop. Or consider the Catholic theologian Aquinas.

5. Some Final Thoughts about the Political Context

As we write, Donald Trump has just been elected as US president. Whether you agree with his policies or not, what has been interesting is how the presidential campaign has been run; in particular, it has put under serious doubt our initial claim above, namely, that lying in public office is something to be avoided at all costs. However, Trump seems unaware and uninterested in truth — hence some people have suggested that he has ushered in a "post-truth" era.[3] This era seems to be created in part because of the propagation of false news stories on social media sites — so much so that Facebook and other social media groups have been working on ways to alert people to "fake news".

Thus, the questions we leave you with are whether you think that it makes sense to talk about lying in the political "post-truth" era. When Trump says "I won the popular vote because millions of people voted illegally" is this a lie? We do not mean is it true, because it is patently false. We mean do you think the concept of a lie has changed throughout time? Has the political landscape changed so dramatically that the concept of lie has no currency? Related, what is the moral status of lying? If politicians and constituents do not care about the truth, then does this affect the moral status of lying (at least in the political arena)? We do not attempt to answer these questions here but they show, as if we need reminding, that the moral status of lying is of vital importance at the local, national and international levels.

SUMMARY

Philosophers, in many issues, like to start by asking what we mean by the key term. Once we ask the question "what is it to lie?" it becomes quickly apparent that the issues are complex and unclear. To lie does not just mean to say something false, rather it has something to do with trying to get another person to believe what you claim to be true, when you in fact think it is false.

Different theories we have looked at so far in this book have different responses to the question "is it wrong to lie"? The utilitarian says "it depends". That is, if the consequences of lying are better than telling the truth then we are morally required to lie. The deontologist — the Kantian or Divine Command Theorist

---

3   See http://www.dailywire.com/news/4834/trumps-101-lies-hank-berrien for 101 of his lies.

for example — thinks that lying is always wrong. There are no situations at all when it would be morally acceptable to lie.

Both the consequentialist and the deontologist's responses seem to lead to counterintuitive claims. One possible way to respond to this is to revisit the definition of lying and claim that the counterintuitive responses to moral questions regarding lying arise because of a false or incomplete understanding of what it is to lie.

Finally, we might simply reject the requirement of capturing our intuitions at all. We might simply say, so much the worse for our intuitions! We finished this chapter with some general thoughts about truth and lying in the political arena.

COMMON STUDENT MISTAKES

- Thinking that Kant says that we should always tell the truth. Whereas in fact he says it is wrong to lie.

- Thinking that the utilitarian says that if a lie leads to pleasure then it is morally acceptable to lie.

- Mistaking being nasty with being immoral.

- Thinking that you require words to lie.

ISSUES TO CONSIDER

1. Read (1)–(7) at the start of this chapter. Do you think these are cases of lying or not? Give reasons for your answers.

2. Do you ever think it is morally acceptable to lie? When?

3. Could a robot lie?

4. In the local town there is a sign at the roundabout — "Happy birthday Keith, 40 today!" It has been there about a year. Is this lying?

5. Do you think it makes sense to talk about "lying to *oneself*"? If it does, how might this change our definition?

6. Reflecting on your answers so far would you agree with our definition of "lying"? Or do you think it needs modifying?

7. Give an example where the consequentialist would say we are morally required to lie.

8. How might the rule and the act utilitarian differ in their response to the question whether it is morally wrong to lie?

9. Give an example where the deontologist would say we ought not to lie.

10. If you had to go for either a deontological approach to lying or a consequentialist approach, which would it be?

11. Do you think that we are living in a "post-truth" era? If so, how does this change (if at all) how we think of lying?

KEY TERMINOLOGY

Lie	Duty
McCloskey's Sheriff	"Post-truth"
Rule-utilitarian	

References

McCloskey, H. J., 'A Non-Utilitarian Approach to Punishment', in *Philosophical Perspectives on Punishment*, ed. by Gertrude Ezorsky (Albany: State University of New York Press, 1972), 119–34.

Walsh, Kirsten and Adrian Currie, 'Caricatures, Myths, and White Lies', *Metaphilosophy*, 46.3 (2015): 414–35.

CHAPTER 14

Eating Animals

A man can live and be healthy without killing animals for food; therefore, if he eats meat, he participates in taking animal life merely for the sake of his appetite. And to act so is immoral.[1]

1. Eating Animals Introduction

The British, and many other nations, have something of an odd relationship with animals. I have, for example, just returned to begin typing up this chapter after adding extra straw for my chickens — chickens that I care for on a daily basis and chickens in whose well-being I am invested. This, however, followed on from my enjoyable consumption of a chicken dinner last night, a fact that would seem to suggest I am far less invested in the well-being of chickens more generally. This oddness in terms of the relationship between myself and my chickens is not, however, peculiar to me. Few people in the UK are vegetarians — the data has consistently suggested between 2% and 3% in recent years — yet many more would claim to identify as animal lovers.[2] In this chapter, the applied ethical issue of the moral acceptability of eating animals is considered; it remains to be seen what conclusions might be drawn to be either justify or condemn some aspects of our multi-faceted behaviour and attitude towards animals.

2. Justifying Meat Eating

It seems sensible to begin by considering on what grounds the eating of meat might be morally justified. To this end, two possible justifications are considered below.

Comparative Justification

It is hard to give a proper name to this oft-cited justification for the consumption of animal meat. When questioned as to why meat-eating is morally acceptable,

---

1   L. Tolstoy, *Writings on Civil Disobedience and Non-Violence.*
2   Data available at https://www.vegsoc.org/sslpage.aspx?pid=753

a fairly common reply relates to the comparison between humans as meat-eaters and other animals as meat-eaters. So, just as lions eat gazelles, bears eat salmon and foxes eat chickens (if they can get their paws on them), so humans eat pigs/cows/sheep etc. Given that it would be odd, even for the most ardent vegetarian, for us to morally criticise the lion, the bear or the fox, then it might seem to follow that there is a moral equivalence between the actions of these different species that extends to the actions of non-vegetarian human beings, such that we too should be free from moral criticism in our consumption of meat.

However, possible weaknesses in the above response should not be too challenging to identify. For one, we do not often base our moral judgments regarding the acceptability of certain actions on the behaviours of lions, bears and foxes etc. Indeed, the fact that lions sometimes eat human beings does not suggest to us that eating other humans may be morally acceptable. In addition, those who find eating some types of meat more acceptable than eating other types of meat (chicken as more acceptable than gorilla, for example) will find limited resource in this type of justification. If there is some merit in this blunt argument for meat-eating, it will very likely need to be brought out more precisely and sharply, perhaps within the context of a wider normative ethical theory.

Dominion-Based Justification

The second justification we will consider for meat-eating may have slightly more going for it, depending on your wider outlook on the world. According to the Bible, "[…] the Lord God formed a man from the dust of the ground and breathed into his nostrils the breath of life, and the man became a living being".[3] This verse is often interpreted as God providing man with a soul, and thus differentiating mankind from the rest of animal creation. In addition, after "the Flood", God says that "[everything] that lives and moves about will be food for you. Just as I gave you the green plants, I now give you everything".[4] It is therefore apparently quite clear that God has no objection to the eating of animals, although a number of Christians do opt for a vegetarian lifestyle for a variety of other factors (the fact that something is allowable does not make it necessarily desirable).

In the remainder of this chapter, however, we consider the ethical issues surrounding meat-eating from the perspective of Utilitarianism, Kantian

---

3   Genesis 2:7, New International Version, https://www.biblegateway.com/passage/?search=Genesis+
2%3A7&version=NIV

4   Genesis 9:3, New International Version, https://www.biblegateway.com/passage/?search=Genesis+
9:3&version=NIV

Ethics and Aristotelian Virtue Ethics; theories in which Biblical references are not central for deciding how to act. Thus, although a religious ethic focussing on Biblical teaching may seem to provide a clear answer on the justification of eating animals, students studying for the AQA exam must be familiar with the application of the three theories mentioned above in order to be well prepared for the exam. In the next section, we begin this process of applying the normative theories as previously outlined in Chapters 1, 2 and 3. The application of metaethical theories to this applied ethical topic can be understood from Chapter 6, and the discussion of Metaethics in an applied context in Chapter 11.

3. Act Utilitarianism

Utilitarianism, as explained in Chapter 1, comes in a variety of different forms — Act, Rule and Preference Utilitarianism as suggested by Jeremy Bentham, John Stuart Mill and Peter Singer respectively. It might seem that the views of Jeremy Bentham and other act utilitarians, when it comes to the acceptability of eating animals, would be fairly simple to ascertain. The act utilitarian of a Benthamite variety simply seeks to secure the greatest amount of pleasure for the greatest number of people. Although Bentham holds to the idea of equal consideration of interests — the pleasures of a queen should count no more than the pleasures of a peasant, irrespective of their social standing and societal power — this notion of equality might be thought of as applying to human beings only. If understood in this way, the view of the act utilitarian would be clear, as the pleasure of a human being when eating a beef burger would outweigh any morally relevant pain. After all, on this version of the equal consideration of interests, any pain that might be suffered by the cow would not have any moral weight in deciding how to maximise total pleasure.

However, Bentham did not adopt this anthropocentric (human-centred) approach to the principle of equal consideration. In one of his most famous passages, he states that:

> The day may come when the rest of the animal creation may acquire those rights which never could have been [withheld] from them but by the hand of tyranny. The French have already discovered that the blackness of the skin is no reason a human being should be abandoned without redress to the caprice of a tormentor. It may one day come to be recognised that the number of the legs, the villosity of the skin, or the termination of the [pelvic bone] are reasons equally insufficient for abandoning a sensitive being to the same fate [...]. The question is not, 'Can they reason?' nor, 'Can they talk?' but, 'Can they suffer?'[5]

---

5   J. Bentham, *An Introduction to the Principles of Morals and Legislation*, http://www.econlib.org/library/Bentham/bnthPML18.html

In this passage, Bentham makes it clear that animals cannot be excluded from the calculation of total pains and total pleasures associated with a particular act just because of their inability to talk or their deficient rational capacities in comparison to human beings. On the contrary, so long as an animal does experience some suffering or pain, then this suffering or pain must be factored into the calculation determining which act will produce the greatest pleasure for the greatest number; simply put, all suffering creatures — human or not — are part of the group of morally relevant beings.

This idea of equality of consideration for animals is justified by Bentham in the initial section of the passage, where a comparison to the ethical failing of racism is drawn. Bentham says that skin colour is deemed to be a morally irrelevant feature of an individual and affords no reason to ignore their pains or pleasures. So, just as denying moral relevance based on skin colour or race is arbitrary, and just as we in the contemporary world believe that denying moral relevance based on gender is arbitrary, denying moral relevance based on species alone is also arbitrary. If what matters is pain and pleasure, then the species that acts as host to that pain and pleasure would seem to be irrelevant.

Bentham's openness to weighing the pains and pleasures of animals in utilitarian decision-making has made him a heroic figure in animal rights and animal welfare movements. Whether you agree with Bentham or not, his views were certainly somewhat out of kilter with many of his philosophical contemporaries. For example, just a little over a century earlier, one of the most respected philosophers of all-time — René Descartes — was, according to some accounts, cutting open his wife's pet dog after nailing the poor creature to the wall in order to study its mechanistic movements. For Descartes, there was no moral issue in this type of action, since a soulless animal such as a dog could not feel pain and only mimicked the appearance of genuine pain. Bentham, had he known of Descartes actions, would have likely recoiled at the inability to recognise the morally relevant pains of the dog.

By putting the individual pieces of his theorising together, we can come to the view that Bentham would count the pains and pleasures of animals as morally relevant when considering the acceptability of eating animals, and he would seemingly count those pains and pleasures as just as valuable as the pains and pleasures of human beings given his commitment to a principle of equality when counting pains and pleasures. Thus, if the total pain (including pain suffered by animals) associated with acts of meat-eating were to outweigh the total pleasure associated with such acts, then Bentham and Benthamite philosophers would be forced to conclude that those instances of meat-eating were morally wrong.

Before moving on, it is worth noting that the language used in the paragraph above is important. Neither Bentham nor any other relativistic utilitarian would ever comment that eating animals is absolutely right or absolutely wrong. The ideas of relativism and absolutism are explored in more detail in Chapter 1, but for now it is worth reminding ourselves that the act utilitarian is interested only in working out how to bring about the good in each individual situation. Thus, meat-eating may be morally acceptable on this view if a research scientist, close to curing cancer, needs to eat a healthy dog in order to survive long enough to pass his research on. On the other hand, eating a turkey burger produced cheaply and with much suffering to the animal may not be justifiable because the pleasure associated with consumption is so minimal. These are, of course, "cardboard cut-out" cases, some distance from real-world ethical decision making in the context of Act Utilitarianism and eating animals. However, it will be of far greater benefit for you to consider the range of cases in which Act Utilitarianism may speak against eating animals, and the range of cases in which Act Utilitarianism will speak in favour of eating animals, in order for you to form either a robust critique or defence of the application of this theory in this applied context. Does Act Utilitarianism seem to provide the right sort of decision procedure, with the right sorts of conclusions?

4. Challenges to Bentham

One challenge to Bentham's act utilitarian view may be based upon the idea that the making of a moral distinction between animals and human beings is far from arbitrary and that there is a difference between such a *"speciesist"* (Peter Singer made this term famous) distinction and discriminatory thought-processes such as racism and sexism. Perhaps it is the case that the pleasures and pains of human beings are worth more, in virtue of our intellect or our capacity for higher-order thinking and experience.

However, we should be cautious when responding to Bentham in this way. Consider an elderly human being who is suffering from dementia, or a two-month-old baby, or a patient in a Persistent Vegetative State (as discussed in Chapter 7). All three of these individuals would seem to be lacking in rational capacity to fairly serious levels. To this end, in the portion of text removed from original Bentham quote, Bentham says that a "full-grown horse or dog is beyond comparison a more rational, as well as a more conversable animal, than an infant of a day or a week or even a month, old".[6] Thus, those who seek to draw a line in the sand in terms of rationality, a line that separates human beings from animals, a line that might justify eating those below the line but not those above the line, are faced with a seemingly insurmountable dilemma — either rationality is morally relevant and so some humans lack

---

6   *Ibid.*

moral standing, or rationality is not morally relevant and this attempt to separate humans from animals is a failure.

In order to overcome this problem, a *potentiality argument* may be put forward. Since babies of two months have the potential to become more rational than they currently are, and since this applies to dementia patients and PVS patients also if successful treatment could be discovered and administered, then the morally relevant line in the sand between humans and animals may be redrawn on the basis that all humans have potentially higher rational skills that any non-human animal has.

However, Singer has a clever response to this potentiality suggestion, which is clear if we consider the powers of Prince Charles. Whilst he is a *potential king*, Prince Charles is currently only a prince. This means that, at the moment, he has only the rights of a prince, not a king. He will not earn kingly rights until he actually becomes a king. Analogously, although a two-month-old is potentially more rational than a dog or a horse, they should not acquire any extra moral consideration until that potential is actualised. Therefore, any attempt to morally separate animals and humans on grounds of rationality or intellect is again seemingly confronted by the dilemma as stated in the previous paragraph.

5. Utilitarian Reasons for Eating Animals

The previous two sections should make clear that for utilitarians such as Bentham and Singer, there will be times when it is morally wrong to eat animals; when the pain associated with eating animals outweighs any corresponding pleasure. It is worth noting, however, that Singer is very clear that eating animals can be entirely morally justifiable, and not just in extremely unlikely situations. It is true that Singer is scornful of the moral acceptability of eating factory-farmed foods, as the following quote suggests:

> *These arguments* [relating to the moral relevance of pains afflicting animals] *apply to animals who have been reared in factory farms — which means that we should not eat chicken, pork or veal, unless we know that the meat we are eating was not produced by factory farm methods.*[7]

Singer also objects to the consumption of eggs that are not sourced from free-range chickens; the same would presumably apply to the eating of the chicken itself. However, this type of objection to the eating of particular animals, in particular conditions, does point us towards the situations in which meat-eating may be morally acceptable to a preference utilitarian such as Singer.

---

7   P. Singer, 'Equality for Animals?', p. 174.

If chickens, for example, are allowed to roam freely, before being painlessly killed (something that seems entirely possible, even if this is not what is always achieved in reality), then the balance of preference satisfaction may swing in favour of the hungry family seeking a healthy diet and away from the continued existence of the chicken itself — chickens, as those who deal with them will know, are unlikely to have the mental capacity to have long running future preferences that will go unfulfilled if their lives are cut short.

Indeed, even Bentham himself supported the idea of eating animals, despite all that was suggested earlier. Animals farmed and killed, thought Bentham, may suffer far less pain than animals left to die in the harsh reality of the unmanaged wilderness. Well-managed and quickly administered slaughter may lead to less pain than starvation, disease or violent death after the attack of a predator.

In an ever changing world, where the practices associated with animal slaughter vary from company to company and culture to culture, the utilitarian cannot provide a clear-cut answer on the general acceptability of eating animals. Singer sums this up when he says that:

> [...] *the important question is not whether animal flesh could be produced without suffering, but whether the flesh we are considering buying was produced without suffering. Unless we can be confident that it was, the principle of equal consideration of interests implies that it was wrong to sacrifice important interests of the animal in order to satisfy less important interests of our own; consequently we should boycott the end result of this process.*[8]

The various criticisms applied to Utilitarianism in Chapter 1 — objections based on demandingness, or based on issues of calculation of pleasures or preferences, for example — are not irrelevant in this chapter. However, for the sake of avoiding repetition, you should consider the application of these criticisms yourself when coming to your view regarding the potential success of utilitarian (act and preference) responses to eating animals.

Given the previous comments, it may be suggested that the lack of discussion of Mill and Rule Utilitarianism, as well as a discussion of higher and lower pleasures, is a critical omission from this chapter. In a sense, we agree. However, once the issues regarding the application of Utilitarianism to the act of eating animals have been set out as above, then applying rule-utilitarian-style thinking should be a far easier task. For now, the following issues are suggested for consideration.

1. Is meat-eating a higher or lower pleasure? Does it make a difference if lamb is consumed in a greasy-spoon café, or if it is prepared by a

---

8   *Ibid.*, p. 175.

world-renowned chef? Should the moral acceptability of eating an animal turn on the way in which an animal is prepared for consumption?

2. Are animals worth less than humans because they cannot access higher pleasures?

3. Would an outright ban on factory farming be a rule that, if universalised, would lead to the greatest good for the greatest number? What other rules might be advocated by a rule utilitarian in this applied ethical setting?

Answering these questions, in the light of the discussion in both this chapter and Chapter 1, should provide a solid grasp of utilitarian thinking in this area.

6. Kantian Ethics and Eating Animals

According to Immanuel Kant, a human being is "[…] a being altogether different in rank and dignity from things, such as irrational animals, with which one may deal and dispose at one's discretion".[9] Of course, the idea that humans have no responsibility to animals, and therefore may seemingly consume them at will, is open to the same objections as outlined in section 4. However, putting those concerns to one side, it may then seem as though Kant has given us a usefully clear statement of his ethical thinking as it may be applied in this context.

Kant is clear that we have no Direct Duties towards animals because the eating of animals does not fall foul of the two formulations of the Categorical Imperative as explored in Chapter 2. The eating of animals can become a universal law, as there is no issue with either conceiving this action as being universalised or willing the universalising of this action. In addition, eating animals does not itself entail the treating of another person merely as a means to an end (and Kant is clear that animals exist themselves only as a mean to an end[10]). Of course, we may treat a person merely as a means to an end in seeking to secure food, but there is nothing necessary about this taking place when animals are consumed. Thus, eating animals will generally be permissible and will only be impermissible when we act wrongly towards a fellow human being in securing our food — the animal itself is not relevant to the assessment of our duty.

Yet, for all of the above, Kant does encourage us to treat animals with care and concern rather than with no consideration at all, despite our lack of a direct duty to care for them. Kant says of a person that "[if] he is not to stifle

9   I. Kant, *Lectures on Anthropology*.
10   I. Kant, 'We Have no Duties to Animals', p. 395.

his human feelings, he must practice kindness towards animals, for he who is cruel to animals becomes hard also in his dealings with men".[11] Those who are needlessly cruel to animals, who kill wantonly or who treat animals with scant regard for their suffering, become familiar with this approach to life and will be, as a result, less likely to act in accordance with duty in their dealings with other human beings. Our duty to animals, says Kant, is therefore indirect rather than direct — it exists only in so far as it pays out in our dealings with our fellow humans.

In terms of applying this line of thought to eating animals, Kant would have no objection so long as we were not cruel or unkind in our approach. Perhaps it is the case that the eating of factory-farmed foods could be considered an act, or an endorsement of, cruelty. In any case, it seems that, rather ironically, Singer and Kant end up in much the same position when it comes to advice regarding how to act in the sphere of eating animals.

It is worthwhile noting, finally, that contemporary Kantians such as Christine Korsgaard (1952–) have objected to Kant's own disregarding of the notion of Direct Duties towards animals. Korsgaard does not accept that it is permissible or acceptable to treat a pain-experiencing creature merely as a means to an end, since "[…] it is a pain to be in pain. And that is not a trivial fact".[12] It therefore may be an open question whether Kantians should allow for Direct Duties to animals, even if Kant himself did not.

7. Virtue Ethics and Eating Animals

Being an agent-centred moral theory, it would be a misunderstanding of Virtue Ethics to expect absolute moral answers on the ethical acceptability of eating animals. Rather than attempting to make ethical judgments on the morality of specific instances of eating animals, Virtue Ethics instead opts to discuss the dispositions and character traits associated with virtuous people, who then may provide guidance when it comes to whether or not the virtuous person would eat no animals at all, just some animals, or all animals on offer.

From the explanation of Virtue Ethics offered in Chapter 3, we should draw the following important lesson from the outset. It is not possible that vegetarianism could be a virtue in and of itself, since vegetarianism is a way of life rather than a character trait or a disposition. Rather, if we are to follow virtue-ethical thinking, we should ask in what circumstances and at what times would a disposition to refrain from eating meat be virtuous, and when such a disposition might be labelled as a vice of excess or deficiency.

---

11 *Ibid.*
12 C. Korsgaard, *The Sources of Normativity*, p. 154.

Rosalind Hursthouse draws interesting comparisons between the arguments of Singer in this area and the approach of the virtue ethicist.[13] Hursthouse suggests that Singer, in arguing against cruelty to animals from his preference utilitarian perspective, provides evidence in favour of the view that the eating of animals will often reflect a vice-like character trait rather than a virtuous character trait. Given that many of us are aware, when we purchase our meat, that the animal in question may have led a rather unpleasant existence, our willingness to ignore this information hardly coheres neatly with exercising the virtuous mean of compassion in the sphere of life of shopping or making dietary decisions; wilful ignorance may be viewed as vice of deficiency.

The example above of shopping in the value aisle for our food puts the issue of eating animals into a particular setting, perhaps the choice of cheap chicken for dinner rather than a more expensive and less attractive vegetarian alternative. However, it is not difficult to conceive of a situation in which meat-eating might be considered to be the result of a virtuous characteristic, such as the eating of an animal in order to promote the health of your children when other options are unavailable (perhaps through economic factors). In this setting, a stubborn commitment to vegetarianism over and above a clear-headed recognition of the needs of your children may represent an action based on a vice of excess. (Roger Scruton is one virtue ethicist who speaks of the virtue of meat-eating; his ideas are worth exploring for a slightly different virtue-ethical response to this issue).[14]

Of course, rather than the specific study of virtuous responses in two outlined cases, it would be useful to have more general guidance. Again, focussing on promoting compassionate rather than cruel decision-making when it comes to choosing whether or not to eat animals, Hursthouse says:

> […] *we need a substantial change in our outlook to get any further — in virtue ethicists' terms, a clearly seen and effective recognition of the fact that human beings, and thereby human lives, are not only interwoven with each other but with the rest of nature. Then, and only then, will we apply virtue ethics correctly to what we are doing.*[15]

Aristotle was more concerned with the application of the virtues as they pertained to human conduct, but human flourishing is supposed to be a whole-life process and it is therefore not without motivation to focus on our dispositions towards animals as Hursthouse does. Whether this guidance is an accurate interpretation

---

13   R. Hursthouse, 'Applying Virtue Ethics to Our Treatment of the Other Animals', http://www.hackettpublishing.com/pdfs/Hursthouse_Essay.pdf

14   R. Scruton, 'Eat Animals! It's for Their Own Good', http://articles.latimes.com/1991-07-25/local/me-54_1_animal-rights

15   R. Hursthouse, 'Applying Virtue Ethics to Our Treatment of the Other Animals', p. 154, http://www.hackettpublishing.com/pdfs/Hursthouse_Essay.pdf

of Aristotelian ideas, or whether it is an independently advantageous extension of Aristotelian ideas, is something that is worth reflecting on in the context of the virtues as actually outlined by Aristotle, and provided in Chapter 3. A key question to answer is whether or not Hursthouse's reasoning is in line with core Aristotelian thinking, or has she created a rival version of Virtue Ethics?

Of the criticisms that might be applied to Virtue Ethics, the objection from unclear guidance may seem highly troubling, even in spite of the ideas above. Considering the following three issues may help you to clarify your thoughts as to the practical usefulness of Virtue Ethics for deciding how to act in this setting.

1. Who are the virtuous role models from whom we can learn when it comes to eating animals? TV chefs, who speak of "doing justice to the animal" when cooking it? Vegetarian campaigners? Peter Singer?

2. TV presenters such as Bear Grylls and Ed Stafford are often dropped into inhospitable locations for our entertainment, and can only survive by killing animals for food. Does their killing reflect a virtue, or a vice?

3. Angela is a vegetarian who is eating with a friend at a highly expensive restaurant. Angela's friend has paid for dinner, and has chosen the courses to eat. One dish involves the eating of carefully prepared duck. Would it be virtuous for Angela to eat the duck, or to stand by her beliefs even in an extreme situation? (It is worth researching Singer's idea of the "Paris Exemption" to develop your answer.)

If you can answer these questions, you should feel more confident in terms of your ability to apply virtue ethical thinking to the issue of eating animals.

8. Cora Diamond

To conclude this chapter, we will briefly reflect on the ideas of Cora Diamond, who offers a perspective on the ethical acceptability of eating animals that stands apart from the normative ethical theory-based views hitherto discussed (AQA also recommend reading Diamond's article).[16] Much of the focus in this chapter has been on the question of whether animals are morally relevant, or whether they have rights to the same degree as humans when it comes to considering the ethical acceptability of consuming them. Diamond objects to this approach entirely and does not seek to criticise the morality of eating animals via talk of moral rights; she has a different kind of criticism altogether.

---

16   C. Diamond, 'Eating Meat and Eating People', http://www.laurentillinghast.com/DiamondEatingMeat.pdf

For Diamond, the notion of "moral rights" for animals is irrelevant when it comes to explaining the moral acceptability of eating animals, because we make decisions in other spheres of life that eating certain entities is unacceptable without any associated talk of rights. Specifically, Diamond suggests that our aversion to eating the human dead is not based on the moral right of the dead body not to be eaten, but because we feel uncomfortable at the very mention of the possibility of consuming human dead bodies, or amputated human limbs. This uncomfortableness is explained not by talk of rights, but by the idea that "a person is not something to eat". This is a thought that comes about because of the nature of our interactions with human beings and human body parts in our lives.[17]

Extending this line of thinking to the issue of eating animals, Diamond takes issue with the following line of argument:

> If
> You would not eat human beings
> and
> You would not eat your pets
> then
> You should not eat other animals (at least higher primates, perhaps) because there is no meaningful difference between such animals and things that you would not eat.

For Diamond, such an argument is extremely unpersuasive. This is because it misses, in its cold and logical form, the fact that pets, like dead human bodies and amputated human limbs, are also not things to be eaten. As Diamond says, pets are given names, we let them into our houses and we interact with them in ways that we do not with wild animals. Wild animals may be things to eat, just as a chicken on display in a supermarket is something for me to eat whereas my own chickens in the garden are not.

This approach may be appealing to a non-cognitivist, anti-realist interpretation of moral thought and moral talk (these theories are explained in Chapter 6). We might wonder if the cries of the campaigner regarding the moral status of certain animals as "things not to eat" are designed to pick up on genuinely existing moral properties in the world as the cognitivist or realist would like, or whether these calls reflect a non-cognitivist, perhaps an emotivist-style, attitude.

However, Diamond herself holds a vegetarian position that she thinks can be advanced, not by cold and logical arguments as previously identified, and not by talk of moral rights, but by reshaping our relationship with animals to add to the list of things not to be eaten. To this end, Diamond offers a Jane

---

17 *Ibid.*, p. 468.

Legge poem, *Learning to be a Dutiful Carnivore*, as an exemplar of tactics that may be far more effective for securing movements towards vegetarianism:

> Dogs and cats and goats and cows,
> Ducks and chickens, sheep and sows
> Woven into tales for tots,
> Pictured on their walls and pots.
> Time for dinner! Come and eat
> All your lovely, juicy meat.
> One day ham from Percy Porker
> (In the comics he's a corker),
> Then the breast from Mrs Cluck
> Or the wing from Donald Duck.
> Liver next from Clara Cow
> (No, it doesn't hurt her now).
> Yes, that leg's from Peter Rabbit
> Chew it well; make that a habit.
> Eat the creatures killed for sale,
> But never pull the pussy's tail.
> Eat the flesh from "filthy hogs"
> But never be unkind to dogs.
> Grow up into double-think
> Kiss the hamster; skin the mink.
> Never think of slaughter, dear,
> That's why animals are here.
> They only come on earth to die,
> So eat your meat, and don't ask why.[18]

This poem, says Diamond, does not preach a form of behaviour, but instead challenges assumed beliefs regarding which animals are acceptable sources of food and which are not. If we view animals as fellow creatures rather than as objects for consumption, then we may change our relationship with them such that killing and eating them will seem as out of bounds as consuming a dead human being. Cannibalism is not always viewed as being morally wrong, of course, as difficult situations will change our perspective; most of the time, however, we recoil at this possible act without the need for formal utilitarian or Kantian justifications.

Diamond's paper is worth your careful attention, and she responds to a challenge that her line of argument opposing unethical treatment of animals might create unfortunate analogies with ways in which we should oppose sexism and racism. In cases of sexism and racism, we might hope that moral rights justify fair and equal treatment, rather than the mere fact that we might happen to see people as fellow creatures (a fact that appears to depend on us,

---

18   *Ibid.*, pp. 472–73.

and not the person who should have the moral right). We might suggest that our recoiling at racial discrimination follows from the moral right a person has, not that our recoiling is what makes such discrimination morally wrong. Whether you find Diamond's approach compelling or not matters more, in all likelihood, than whether you agree with her conclusions; if her method is sound, then does this show a weakness in the approaches of the normative theories based on reference to rights or duties?

SUMMARY

Few moral theorists will claim that eating animals is absolutely and completely acceptable in all circumstances and at all times. Even Kant recoiled at the idea of cruelty to animals in spite of his expressed denial that humans possess any duty towards animals. This fact suggests that conclusions regarding the ethical acceptability of eating animals may often be determined by empirical and real-world data regarding the preferences, pains or pleasures of animals and the impact of the processes of rearing and then slaughtering animals for human consumption. The real-world situation is constantly in flux, but this chapter should provide you with the moral framework into which real-world research can be plugged, in order to explain the different key theories, as well as coming to your own viewpoint.

COMMON STUDENT MISTAKES

- Over-simplifying Kant's position on animals — no Direct Duties does not mean no duties at all towards animals.

- Completely avoiding metaethical issues that may be relevant to criticising moral positions — such as the Open Question Argument against a naturalistic utilitarian who associates goodness with pleasure (see Chapter 6).

- Claiming that the issue of eating animals must turn on the issue of equal consideration of interests and the rights of animals, without considering the argument of Diamond.

- Failing to give due consideration to Emotivism and/or Prescriptivism as non-cognitive ways of interpreting this debate.

- Falling into the total vegetarianism versus total meat-eating narrative without drawing deeper distinctions as to when meat-eating might be acceptable and when it might not be.

ISSUES TO CONSIDER

Some questions are provided at the ends of sections 5 and 7.

1. Moral statements regarding the acceptability of eating animals are often emotional. Does this mean the emotivist explanation is the best explanation?

2. Do all animals deserve equal consideration of interests? Do only some animals? Which ones?

3. Should we expect clear moral answers when it comes to the acceptability of eating animals?

4. Does moral disagreement in this applied ethical area lend support to Anti-Realism?

5. How much of this moral issue turns on empirical data regarding the treatment of animals before slaughter?

6. Should you apply your favoured normative moral theory in order to find the correct conclusion in this ethical area, or should you check your favoured normative moral theory to see if it gets it right in this ethical area?

KEY TERMINOLOGY

Speciesism	Direct Duties
Equal consideration of interests	Indirect Duties

References

Bentham, Jeremy, *An Introduction to the Principles of Morals and Legislation*, freely available at http://www.econlib.org/library/Bentham/bnthPML18.html

Bible, New International Version, freely available at https://www.biblegateway.com/

Diamond, Cora, 'Eating Meat and Eating People', *Philosophy*, 53.206 (1978): 465–79, https://doi.org/10.1017/s0031819100026334; freely available at http://www.laurentillinghast.com/DiamondEatingMeat.pdf

Hursthouse, Rosalind, 'Applying Virtue Ethics to Our Treatment of the Other Animals', in *The Practice of Virtue: Classic and Contemporary Readings in Virtue Ethics*, ed. by Jennifer Welchman (Indianapolis: Hackett Publishing, 2006), pp. 136–55, freely available at http://www.hackettpublishing.com/pdfs/Hursthouse_Essay.pdf

Kant, Immanuel, 'We Have No Duties to Animals', in *Ethical Theory*, ed. by Russ Shafer-Landau (Oxford: Blackwell Publishing, 2007), pp. 395–96.

—, *Lectures on Anthropology*, ed. by Allen Wood and Robert Loudon (Cambridge: Cambridge University Press, 2012).

Korsgaard, Christine, *The Sources of Normativity* (Cambridge: Cambridge University Press, 1996), https://doi.org/10.1017/cbo9780511554476

Scruton, Roger, 'Eat Animals! It's for Their Own Good', *Los Angeles Times* (25 July 1991), freely available at http://articles.latimes.com/1991-07-25/local/me-54_1_animal-rights

Singer, Peter, 'Equality for Animals?', in *Ethics, Humans and Other Animals: An Introduction with Readings*, ed. by Rosalind Hursthouse (London: Routledge, 2000), pp. 169–79.

Tolstoy, Leo, *Writings on Civil Disobedience and Non-Violence* (Philadelphia: New Society Publishers, 1988).

Glossary

Absolutist: A normative moral theory is absolutist, rather than relativistic, when it suggests that an action is wrong (or right) in all circumstances, without exception. For example, murder might be thought to be absolutely wrong, irrespective of any circumstances.

Act-centred: A normative moral theory that associates moral rightness/ wrongness with actions (e.g. Utilitarianism).

Active euthanasia: If a person is actively euthanised it means that their death was caused by external intervention rather than natural causes, most likely through a lethal injection or the voluntary swallowing of a deadly cocktail of drugs.

Act Utilitarianism: See Consequentialism.

Agápē: Greek word meaning "love". Refers to the love *of God* for humans and humans *for God*. The "highest" form of love. *Agápē*, as discussed by Fletcher, is an *attitude* and not a feeling, one which does not expect anything in return and does not give any special considerations to anyone.

Agápē calculus: Introduced by Fletcher. The claim that we ought to always act so as to bring about the most *love* for the most people.

Agent-centred: A normative moral theory that associates moral rightness/ wrongness with people (e.g. Virtue Ethics).

Agent-Neutrality: The view that moral decisions should be made without special weighting being given to personal feelings.

Anal stage: The second stage of Freud's Psychosexual Development Theory roughly from one and a half to three years old. Pleasure is gained through *controlling going to the toilet*. This stage is about gaining control of one's body, and it starts with controlling the bladder and bowels (being potty trained).

Antinomianism: The term introduced by Fletcher which says that morally an agent can do whatever he or she wants in a situation.

Anti-Realism: Simply the denial of Realism. Anti-realists deny the existence of any mind-independent, objective, moral properties.

Apparent good: Introduced by Aquinas when discussing his Natural Law Theory. An apparent good is when a secondary precept is out of line with the Natural Law so we are not morally required to follow it.

A priori: Knowledge gained through reason alone, without needing to test/experience the world.

A posteriori: Knowledge gained as a result of experience of the world.

Attitudinal Hedonism: The theory of well-being which holds that what makes a life go well is entirely determined by the amount of pleasure a person experiences where pleasure is understood as an *attitudinal state* (i.e. *taking pleasure in* something) rather than a sensation. Fred Feldman is a defender of this view.

Belief: A psychological state. If you believe something, then you take that something to be true.

Biting-the-bullet: The argumentative strategy of simply accepting an apparently awkward conclusion as a non-fatal implication of a theory.

"Boo/hurrah" theory: See Emotivism.

Categorical Imperative: Kant's supreme principle of morality. Using this we can work out how we ought to behave. It is a command (imperative) which should be followed irrespective of the consequences (categorical).

Categorical Imperative 1: Universalization: "...act only according to that maxim through which you can at the same time will that it become a universal law".[1]

Categorical Imperative 2: Means and ends: "So act that you use humanity, in your own person as well as in the person of any other, always at the same time as an end, never merely as a means".[2]

Categorical Imperative 3: Kingdom of ends: "...every rational being must so act as if he were through his maxim always a lawmaking member in the universal kingdom of ends".[3]

Cognitivism, Psychological: Not to be confused with Realism. It suggests that when we make moral claims of the form "murder is wrong" or "helping others is right" we are giving voice to our beliefs, rather than our non-belief states such as emotions.

---

1   I. Kant, *Moral Law,* p. 15.
2   *Ibid.,* p. 66.
3   *Ibid.,* p. 21.

Cognitivism, Semantic: Not to be confused with Realism. It suggests that when we make moral claims of the form "murder is wrong" or "helping others is right" our claims can be true or false (what philosophers call truth-apt).

Conscience (Aquinas): For Aquinas conscience is morally neutral, it simply "bears witness", and it is a "sign-post" to what is right and wrong. It is *not* a source of moral knowledge. This means that for Aquinas conscience is *fallible*. He calls it the "application of knowledge to activity".

Conscience (Freud): For Freud the conscience is the form that the super-ego takes in addressing the ego. This understanding of "conscience" can be thought of as synonymous with the "guilty conscience".

Consequentialism: A normative moral theory that states that the moral value of an action is determined wholly by the consequences of that action (e.g. Act Utilitarianism).

Demandingness objection: A challenge to Utilitarianism. If it is not the case that pleasure needs to be merely promoted but actually *maximised at all opportunities*, then an extremely high bar is set.

Deontological: A normative moral theory that focuses on *duty* rather than outcomes.

Direct Duties: Used in discussion of Kantian ethics. Direct Duties are those duties arrived at via a formulation of the Categorical Imperative.

Dispositions: In respect of Virtue Ethics, dispositions are tendencies in our psychology. For example, I may have the disposition to be angry if someone steals from me, or the disposition to be forgiving if someone steals from me.

Divine Command Theory: The metaethical view that what is right/wrong is what is commanded/forbidden by God.

Divine Law: Introduced by Aquinas as part of his Natural Law Theory. The Divine Law is discovered through *revelation*. Divine laws are those that God has, in His grace, seen fit to give us and are those "mysteries", those rules given by God which we find in scripture; for example, the ten commandments.

Doctrine of Double Effect (DDE): Introduced by Aquinas in *Summa Theologica*. If an act fulfils four conditions then it is morally acceptable. If not, then it is not. The first is that the act must be a good one; the second is that the act must come about before the consequences; the third is that the intention must be good; the fourth, it must be for serious reasons.

Ego: On of the three parts of the mind according to Freud. The "ego" polices the *id* to allow a person's social interaction in the world.

Electra omplex: In Jungian psychoanalysis, the name given to the unconscious desire experienced by girls to have a sexual relationship with their fathers, and consequently being in competition with their mothers.

Emotivism: A metaethical theory. A form of Psychological Non-Cognitivism that holds that moral judgements are expressions of the speaker's emotions rather than a description of anything. This is not to be confused with subjectivism or relativism (sometimes referred to as the "boo/hurrah" theory).

Empirical: A method for gaining knowledge that requires sense-experience and interaction with the world as studied by science.

Epistemology: The philosophical study of knowledge. Questions might include, "What is knowledge?"; "Can we know something *a priori*"? "What can we know?"

Eternal Law: Introduced by Aquinas when discussing his Natural Law Theory. God's rational purpose and plan for *all things*. The Eternal Law is part of God's *mind* it has always, and will always, exist. The Eternal Law is *not* simply something that God decided at some point to write.

Eudaimonia: The Aristotelian idea of "the good life"; best translated as "flourishing".

Euthanasia: The act of seeking to provide a good death for a person who otherwise might be faced with a much more unpleasant death (see also voluntary/non-voluntary and passive/active euthanasia).

Euthyphro dilemma: A challenge to Divine Command Theory (DCT). Introduced by Plato in his dialogue *Euthyphro*, it suggests there are two questions you can ask about DCT, but each answer that can be given is problematic. The questions: (i) is something good *because* God commands it. Or (ii) does God command it *because it is* Good.

Felicific Calculus: See Hedonic Calculus.

Guilt: Freud uses this term to refer to the feeling that arises when our conscience requires certain things from us which we fail to achieve.

Golden Mean: In Virtue Ethics, the morally virtuous middle way between the vices of excess and deficiency.

Good will: The Kantian idea of our specific will which is good through its willing *alone* rather than what it effects or accomplishes.

Harm principle: John Stuart Mill's principle that: "The only purpose for which power can be rightfully exercised over any member of a civilized community, against his will, is to prevent harm to others. His own good, either physical or moral, is not a sufficient warrant".[4]

Hedonic Calculus: Jeremy Bentham's way of calculating the pleasure/pain associated with a possible future action.

Hedonism: A theory of well-being which hold that improves a person's life is entirely determined by the amount of pleasure that person experiences; no other factors are relevant at all.

Higher and lower pleasures: Distinction made by Mill between the quality of pleasure. Higher pleasures are those pleasures of the intellect brought about via activities like poetry, reading or attending the theatre. Lower pleasures are animalistic and base; pleasures associated with drinking beer, having sex or lazing on a sun-lounger.

Humean Theory of Motivation: The view that motivation only arises when a belief combines with an appropriately related desire — where desire takes the lead role. Further it is the view that beliefs and desires are distinct mental states such that a belief cannot entail a desire.

Hume's fork: Hume divided knowledge into two camps — knowledge gained from relations of ideas and knowledge gained from matters of fact.

Hypothetical Imperative: A command that applies to someone only because of the desires/wants of the agent, e.g. you ought to go for a run *if* you *want* to get fit.

Id: One of the three parts of the mind according to Freud. *Id* is the collection of our primal drives, e.g. the basic desires for food, sex, drink and is the oldest part of the mind. The *id* cannot be properly formalized or understood and Freud likens it to chaos.

Indirect Duties: Discussed in relation to Kantian ethics. A duty we owe to X (for example, animals, the environment) is in fact a duty we owe to humans. E.g. we have an indirect duty towards animals because if we treat animals badly then we will not uphold our duties towards humans.

---

4   J. S. Mill, *On Liberty*, http://www.econlib.org/library/Mill/mlLbty1.html

Intrinsic: Something is intrinsically good if it is essentially or necessarily good, just in and of itself; it does not rely on anything else for it to be good.

Intuitionism: A view in moral Epistemology that holds that there is at least one moral belief, and possibly many, that are self-evidently justifiable. This does not rule out other ways of justifying moral claims, nor does it mean that intuitionists believe judges to be infallible.

Invincible ignorance: From Aquinas. Ignorance that cannot be overcome through the use of reason. Doing something wrong when they *could not* have known better.

"Is/ought" gap: The supposed problem of deriving an "ought" (prescriptive) claim from a (descriptive) claim.

Latency stage: The fourth stage in Freud's Theory of Psychosexual Development, roughly from six to the onset of puberty. At this stage sexual desire is repressed. There are no new sexual desires formed. Girls plays with girls in order to learn the role of a girl and boys play with boys in order to learn about the role of boys.

Legalism: Term used by Fletcher to refer to a system of ethics such that someone in that system "blindly" observes moral rules without being sensitive to the situation.

Maxim: A general principle or rule upon which we act.

Mature genital stage: Fifth and final stage of Freud's Theory of Psychosexual Development.

Moral Error Theory: Combination of Semantic Non-Cognitivism, Anti-Realism and the Truth-maker Theory of Truth. The conclusion is that *all* moral claims that we make are *systematically and uniformly false*.

Natural Law: Introduced by Aquinas when discussing his Natural Law Theory. When humans act in accordance with their purpose/function of reason then they act according to the Natural Law (see primary precepts and secondary precepts).

Naturalism, Realism: The view that moral properties exist and are as natural as those properties discussed and examined in the sciences.

Naturalistic Fallacy: According to G. E. Moore, the idea that moral properties can be reduced to natural properties. Moore believes that one commits the naturalistic fallacy by claiming that goodness = pleasure/happiness/preference satisfaction.

Nihilism: Associated with theories that try to eliminate values. For example, Moral Error Theory can be labelled nihilistic because it denies the existence of any moral values in the world.

Non-belief state: A psychological state that is not related to taking something to be true. It is typically thought to be a non-descriptive or non-representational state. For example, an emotional state such as joy, or anger.

Non-Cognitivism, Psychological: When we make moral claims of the form "murder is wrong" or "helping others is right" we are not giving voice to our beliefs, we are rather expressing our non-belief states such as emotions.

Non-Cognitivism, Semantic: When we make moral claims of the form "murder is wrong" or "helping others is right" our claims are *neither* true nor false. They are not truth-apt.

Non-Naturalism: The view that if moral properties exist they could not show up on the scientific picture of what exists.

Non-voluntary euthanasia: Non-voluntary euthanasia occurs when a decision regarding premature and merciful death is made for one person by another person, because the person to be euthanised is unable to make a decision for themselves.

Normative: A normative moral theory is a theory designed to provide guidance for how to behave/live.

Neurosis: Term used by Freud to refer to when the super-ego fails to deal correctly with the *id*. In particular, when the pleasure principle is repressed.

Objective List Theory: A theory of well-being which hold that what makes a life go well is determined by a list of items (e.g. loving relationships, meaningful knowledge, autonomy).

Oedipus complex: In psychoanalysis, the name given to the unconscious desire of a child to have a sexual relationship with a parent of the opposite sex; most likely this is expressed as a boy's sexual attraction to his mother.

Open Question Argument: Put forward by G. E. Moore. It attacks naturalist realist positions in Metaethics. It holds that *if* moral *properties* (e.g. goodness) are natural properties (e.g. pleasure) then moral terms (e.g. "goodness") must be synonymous with natural terms (e.g. "pleasure"). However, it is always an open question — the answer is not obvious to us — to ask whether a moral term means the same as a natural term. This means that moral terms are *not* synonymous with natural terms. This means that moral properties cannot be identical with natural properties.

Oral stage: First stage in Freud's Theory of Psychosexual Development, from birth to about one and a half. This stage is where babies get pleasure through putting things in their mouth, pleasure in biting, chewing and sucking.

Palliative care: "If you have an illness that can't be cured, palliative care makes you as comfortable as possible, by managing your pain and other distressing symptoms. It also involves psychological, social and spiritual support for you and your family or carers. This is called a holistic approach, because it deals with you as a "whole" person".[5]

Paradox of Tragedy: Also known as the paradox of negative emotions. Not a genuine paradox. The oddity that in real life negative emotions are not desired whereas in other contexts, such as horror films, roller-coasters, dramas they *are* desired.

Passive euthanasia: Passive euthanasia occurs when a person is allowed to die due to the deliberate withdrawal of treatment that might keep them alive.

Persistent Vegetative State (PVS): A state of being in which a person is biologically alive, but shows no sign of psychological interaction with the world. The state is labelled persistent when it is unlikely this condition will alter through any treatment.

Phallic stage: Freud's third stage in his Theory of Psychosexual Development; roughly from three to six years. It is about discovering one's genitals, and importantly that they are different in men and women. This stage is where Freud thinks we develop the Oedipus, and the Electra complex. A problem moving through this stage will cause problems with intimacy in later life.

Phronesis: From Aristotelian ethics referring to "practical wisdom". Arguably the most important virtuous disposition or character trait.

Pleasure Principle: Idea put forward by Freud. This is the claim that what identifies and unifies the drives of the *id* is the avoidance of pain and pursuit of pleasure.

Preference Utilitarianism: A non-hedonistic version of Utilitarianism. The greatest good for the greatest number *cannot* be reduced to pleasure in either raw or higher forms. Instead, what makes a life go better for a person is entirely determined by the *satisfaction of their preferences* (e.g. defended by Peter Singer).

---

5   NHS definition, http://www.nhs.uk/Planners/end-of-life-care/Pages/what-it-involves-and-when-it-starts.aspx

Prescriptivism: A metaethical theory claiming that our moral utterances express more than just emotional approval and disapproval. Instead, our moral utterances express a subjective prescription for others to act in accordance with our moral judgments (e.g. Hare).

Prima Facie: "On first impression/look" or "At first glance/appearance".

Primary Precepts: Introduced as part of Aquinas's Natural Law Theory. They are overarching *general rules*. They are *absolute* and binding on all rational agents. His examples are: protect and preserve human life; reproduce and educate one's offspring; know and worship God; live in a society.

Principle of Charity: An argumentative strategy of granting one's opponent to be rational and giving the strongest interpretation of their argument.

Principle of Utility: The principle that an action is moral if and only if it leads to the greatest good for the greatest number. Associated with **Utilitarianism**.

Problem of Parity: A challenge to **Utilitarianism**. Utilitarianism does *not* allow you to give *extra moral weight* to the life of a loved one (see **Agent-Neutrality**).

Queer: The idea of J. L. Mackie, associated with Moral Error Theory. Something is queer if it is utterly unlike any other existing property/entity.

Ratio: Aquinas's term for the reason that helps discover the Natural Laws.

Realism: The view that moral properties exists independently of human beings and can be located in the world.

Relativistic: A normative moral theory is relativistic, rather than absolutist, when it allows that an action can be moral in one situation but immoral in another situation. For example, the morality of stealing might be thought to be relative to the situation in which stealing takes place.

Real Good: Introduced by Aquinas when discussing his Natural Law Theory. A real good is when a **secondary precept** is accordance with the **Natural Law** and consequently we are morally required to follow it.

Rule-Utilitarianism: The view that should create a set of rules that, if followed, would produce the greatest amount of total happiness (e.g. defended by John Stuart Mill). See also, **Strong** and **Weak Rule Utilitarianism**.

Sanctity of Life: The idea that life holds absolute value, very likely justified by the idea that life is God-given.

Secondary Precepts: Introduced by Aquinas when discussing the Natural Law Theory. Secondary precepts are *not generated by our reason* but rather they are imposed by governments, groups, clubs, societies etc. Examples, might include: do not drive above 70mph on a motorway; do not kidnap people; always wear a helmet when riding a bike; do not hack into someone's bank account.

Semantic: Semantic concerns are concerns about words and their meanings; it relates to a focus on language and meaning.

Speciesism: Term introduced by Peter Singer. The claim that treating non-human animals differently from humans based purely on the arbitrary fact that they are from one species rather than another is morally wrong. Singer takes it to be morally equivalent to treating another person differently based on a difference in gender (sexism) or in race (racism).

Straw-man: A straw-man argument is an argument phrased deliberately in its weakest form, so that it is easy to defeat. Straw-men arguments allow a person to avoid arguing with a difficult objection on "level ground".

Strong Rule Utilitarianism: Guidance from the set of rules that, if followed, would promote the greatest amount of total happiness must *always* be followed.

Super-ego: One of the three parts of the mind according to Freud. The super-ego is the voice of authority issuing prohibitions, inhibitions and moral constraints.

Synderesis: Term introduced by Aquinas. Synderesis is *not* the same as conscience but is the innate ability of the mind (a *habit of the mind*) to apprehend the eternal/Divine laws.

Teleological: A teleological normative theory is one concerned with consequences (e.g. Utilitarianism).

Teleologist: Someone who holds that every object has a final cause/goal/end/purpose.

Telos: For Aristotle, *telos* is the purpose of something.

Theory of Psychosexual Development: Developed by Freud. A theory of sexual development from birth to death: includes the oral, anal, phallic, latency and mature genital stage.

Thought-experiment: A hypothetical situation — often fantastical — used to highlight and challenge the intuitions we have on various topic. E.g. Judith Thomson's "the transplant surgeon" (see Chapter 1).

Truth-apt: If a claim is truth-apt then it is *capable* of being true or false. N.B. the claim may never be true but it could still be capable of being true or false. This above explanation of the meaning of the phrase "truth-apt" is itself truth-apt, for example.

Truth-maker Theory of Truth: A claim is true *if and only if* some feature of the world, such as properties, makes it true.

Tyranny of the Majority: A challenge to Utilitarianism. It seems that Utilitarianism is open to cases where the majority are morally required to exploit the minority for the greater good of maximising total pleasure.

Utility: A term used by utilitarians to refer to the pleasure/pain/preference satisfaction associated with of a particular action.

Utilitarianism: See Consequentialism.

Verification principle: The principle that states that if a sentence is not analytic or potentially empirically verifiable then it is *meaningless*.

V-rules: Introduced by Rosalind Hursthouse. She suggests that Virtue Ethics provides guidance in the form of "v-rules". These are guiding rules of the form "do what is honest" or "avoid what is envious".

Vincible ignorance: From Aquinas. Ignorance that can be overcome through the use of reason. Doing something wrong when one *ought to* have known better.

Virtue: A morally correct character disposition or trait, as opposed to a character disposition or trait that represents a moral vice.

Voluntary euthanasia: Voluntary euthanasia occurs when a person chooses someone to terminate their life in order to avoid future suffering.

Weak Rule Utilitarianism: Guidance from the set of rules that, if followed, would promote the greatest amount of total happiness *can be ignored in circumstances where more happiness would be produced by breaking the rule.*

Well-being: The measure of how well a life is going, for the person whose life it is.